ACCOUNTABILITY AND REVIEW IN THE COUNTER-TERRORIST STATE

KU-642-269

Jessie Blackbourn
Fiona de Londras
Lydia Morgan

BRISTOL
UNIVERSITY
PRESS

First published in Great Britain in 2020 by

Bristol University Press
University of Bristol
1-9 Old Park Hill
Bristol
BS2 8BB
UK
t: +44 (0)117 954 5940
www.bristoluniversitypress.co.uk

North America office:
Bristol University Press
c/o The University of Chicago Press
1427 East 60th Street
Chicago, IL 60637, USA
t: +1 773 702 7700
f: +1 773-702-9756
sales@press.uchicago.edu
www.press.uchicago.edu

© Bristol University Press 2020

British Library Cataloguing in Publication Data
A catalogue record for this book is available from the British Library

Library of Congress Cataloging-in-Publication Data
A catalog record for this book has been requested

ISBN 978-1-5292-0624-1 paperback
ISBN 978-1-5292-0623-4 hardcover
ISBN 978-1-5292-0626-5 ePub
ISBN 978-1-5292-0625-8 ePdf

The rights of Jessie Blackbourn, Fiona de Londras and Lydia Morgan to be identified as
authors of this work has been asserted by them in accordance with the Copyright, Designs
and Patents Act 1988.

All rights reserved: no part of this publication may be reproduced, stored in a retrieval system,
or transmitted in any form or by any means, electronic, mechanical, photocopying, recording,
or otherwise without the prior permission of Bristol University Press.

The statements and opinions contained within this publication are solely those of the authors
and not of the University of Bristol or Bristol University Press. The University of Bristol and
Bristol University Press disclaim responsibility for any injury to persons or property resulting
from any material published in this publication.

Bristol University Press works to counter discrimination on grounds of gender, race,
disability, age and sexuality.

Cover design by Chris Wilson, blu inc.
Front cover image: Getty Images 918027804
Printed and bound in Great Britain by CMP, Poole
Bristol University Press uses environmentally responsible print partners

Contents

List of Acronyms

9/11	11 September 2001
CPR	Civil Procedure Rules
CPS	Crown Prosecution Service
ECHR	European Convention on Human Rights
FOSIS	Federation of Student Islamic Societies
HEFCE	Higher Education Funding Council for England
IOPC	Independent Office for Police Conduct
IPCO	Investigatory Powers Commissioner's Office
IRA	Irish Republican Army
ISC	Intelligence and Security Commission of Parliament
JCHR	Joint Committee on Human Rights
MCB	Muslim Council of Britain
NATO	North Atlantic Treaty Organization
Ofsted	Office for Standards in Education, Children's Services and Skills
PIRA	Provisional Irish Republican Army
RUC	Royal Ulster Constabulary
TEO	Temporary Exclusion Orders
TPIM	Terrorism Prevention and Investigation Measures
TRG	TPIM Review Group

Acknowledgements

The Joseph Rowntree Charitable Trust funded the research that underpins this work, and we are grateful for this support. Our advisory board, comprising Yasmine Ahmed, Lord Alex Carlile, Baroness Helena Kennedy and Professor Javaid Rehman, offered assistance at various points and we are very grateful for their involvement.

The outcome of the research reflects our views alone, and not those of the Trust, its members and staff, or the members of the advisory board.

At various points we received supplementary funding from Birmingham Law School and Oxford Law Faculty; we are grateful to both. We are thankful to Caitlin Philpott, Anneloes Hoff and Alvin Hoi-Chun Hung for research assistance. Thanks to Katie Hayward at the Centre for Socio-Legal Studies, University of Oxford and Louise Gordon at Wolfson College, Oxford who assisted with the logistics for the stakeholder workshop we conducted there in September 2018.

Parts of this work were presented at the Law and Society Association conference in Toronto, and at research seminars at Birmingham, Northumbria, and the University of New South Wales. We received excellent feedback at these sessions and are grateful to those who participated. We are grateful to the anonymous reviewers at Bristol University Press and to the editorial team led by Rebecca Tomlinson for their support for and work on the book. Thanks also to Nairn, Sinead and Sebastian for their support during the research and book writing process.

Most importantly we are grateful to all those who agreed to speak with us for this project in formal interviews, or in our workshop and/or informal conversations. Their perspectives and experiences helped us to shape and refine our research questions and, most importantly, to gain a greater insight into counter-terrorism review in the United Kingdom.

Introduction: Accountability in the Counter-Terrorist State

> Our response to counter-terrorism is built on an approach that unites the public and private sectors, communities, citizens and overseas partners around the single purpose to leave no safe space for terrorists to recruit or act ... so that our people can go about their lives freely and with confidence.[1]

This opening paragraph of *CONTEST: The United Kingdom's Strategy for Countering Terrorism* demonstrates that counter-terrorism is everywhere in the contemporary UK. It has become a quotidian part of the law, institutions, activities and preoccupations of the state. Counter-terrorism is no longer temporary or exceptional. It is permanent and everyday, even though its effects and intrusions continue to be justified by the rhetoric of necessity, exceptionalism and extraordinariness. Within this counter-terrorist state, questions arise about how to give effect to the fundamental constitutional and democratic commitment to accountability. The answer, we argue, lies at least to some degree in an assemblage of actors, institutions and activities that we call 'counter-terrorism review'.

Conceptualising counter-terrorism review

Throughout this work, we use the term 'counter-terrorism review' to describe the assemblage of actors, processes and actions related to accountability for the counter-terrorist state.[2] Our use of this term is intended to move us past a narrow construction of counter-terrorism review as comprising only juridical processes of review.[3] While judicial consideration of counter-terrorism law is part of counter-terrorism review, it is not sufficient to capture the broad range of activities to which the term could be applied. As Dawn Oliver tells us, 'access to the courts alone cannot protect us from bad government'.[4] While courts play a critical role in assessing lawfulness, this is not and should not be the only standard by which we might hold the state to account in counter-terrorism.[5] In other words, while judicial review tells us *something* about counter-terrorism, that is largely limited to questions of law. Nor is political review sufficient: review through parliamentary committees or parliamentary debate is part of counter-terrorism review, but it is not all of it. We use the term 'counter-terrorism review' to include *and go beyond* these two forums (courts and politics) and their various review functions, even though the workings and relative merits of both are dominant in the literature of counter-terrorism 'oversight'.[6]

A focus on courts and politics and, indeed, on 'oversight' alone is too narrow to capture the wider range of activities that are observable when we look at *who is asking questions about counter-terrorism, what questions they are asking, and what the implications of these enquiries are.* In addition to formal politics and courts, we are concerned with the operation and implications of bespoke counter-terrorism review bodies and actors (such as the Independent Reviewer of Terrorism Legislation), of complaints bodies (such as the Independent Office for Police Conduct), of general regulators whose regulatees may have a role in making or implementing counter-terrorism (such as the Office for Students) and of civil society. All of these entities are engaged to different degrees in activities concerned with figuring out what is happening in the broad field of 'counter-terrorism'.

We understand counter-terrorism review as involving the evaluation and assessment of counter-terrorist activities, laws and policies according to a range of standards, some of which are legal, and others of which are political, social or economic. We are interested in the three elements of evaluation identified by Deirdre Duffy: considering the merits of the matter under review, engaging with 'reality' and having capacity for action.[7] Building on this, we understand counter-terrorism review as legal, political and policy processes that consider the application and impacts of counter-terrorism law and policy in theory as well as in practice, with a view to assessing its merits and contributing towards its improvement.

Of course, as the materials we present in this book will attest, these are complex and challenging activities in the counter-terrorism context. The proposition that evaluating counter-terrorism law or policy involves considering its merits or worth[8] might seem reasonably uncontroversial.[9] However, the basis against which the evaluation takes place may well differ across reviews. Processes of judicial review will ask questions relating to legality, for example, while a political review might ask about adherence to democratic values or efficiency. Operational reviews might use different standards again (such as effectiveness), and regulatory reviews might concern themselves with compliance and implementation rather than impact. Civil society might be concerned primarily with societal acceptance or unintended consequences for belonging and cohesion. And any of them might use a mixture of these standards. As will become clear throughout this book, the notion that counter-terrorism review consists, among other things, of considering the merits of the law, policy or operation under consideration does not mean that every form of review applies or needs to apply the same standard or standards.

Although different parts of counter-terrorism review may apply different standards, to be evaluative review should be rooted in reality (or 'evidence based') so that counter-terrorism's actual, rather than theoretical, application and impact can be ascertained.[10] Of course, data are not neutral, and neither is expertise in respect of such data, statistics or information.[11] The quantitative material that is engaged with reflects multiple layers of decisions: decisions about what and when to count (and not to count), and about what information to consider. In other words, a 'mere' commitment to engage with *some* evidence does not necessarily mean that a review will have a comprehensive evidence base. What evidence is considered, how (if at all) qualitative evidence is engaged with and to whom reviewers speak and listen are all relevant when thinking about whether a review mechanism is engaging in 'reality' in a meaningful way. That is not to suggest that every form of counter-terrorism review needs to engage with every form of data, experience and expertise. Indeed, secrecy, information asymmetry and difficulty in establishing causal links between particular laws and the prevention of, or rapid response to terrorist activities pose real challenges for evaluative review in the counter-terrorism context. However, the ability to engage with a variety of evidence (including 'secret' materials) across the assemblage may ameliorate the use of review as a 'box-checking' exercise,[12] which is vital if review is going to deliver meaningful accountability.[13]

Finally, theories of evaluation suggest that review ought to be capable of bringing about action. It ought to have the capacity to prompt change and contribute to the improvement of what is being evaluated.[14] We approach this with some caution. The concept of 'improvement' is challenging in the counter-terrorism sphere. It is not always possible to identify a causal connection between a law and policy and the reduction or escalation in level(s) of risk.[15] Furthermore, because the broader values at stake in counter-terrorism – rights, a peaceful, tolerant and stable polity, societal cohesion,[16] and so on – are complex and contested, the ways in which they are impacted by counter-terrorism are difficult to measure. Importantly, stakeholders might not agree on what constitutes 'improvement'.[17] An NGO that believes that counter-terrorist financing restrictions unduly restrict their ability to react to humanitarian crises in certain parts of the world might see the reduction, or even elimination, of these rules as an 'improvement'. Financial institutions engaged in managing risk in relation to them, on the other hand, might consider that more stringent processes that in fact constitute over-compliance with the legal rules would be an improvement, as such an approach would minimise their risk of legal liability for accidental non-compliance. Finally, we must be conscious that counter-terrorism review need not result in some kind of discernible 'change' for it to have demonstrated a capacity for action. It may affirm that current law and policy is sufficient and need not be added to, slowing down the further development and extension of the counter-terrorist state. Where 'no change' follows a counter-terrorism review it does not mean that this review did not have the capacity for action, but rather that the action it resulted in is difficult to discern, and perhaps only capable of speculative identification. Similarly, resulting change may take considerable time to emerge and so need be identified at different temporal distances.

Taken together, these three characteristics suggest that counter-terrorism review should be retrospective; it should consider what has happened, its impacts and effects, rather than being predictive or anticipatory. But review cannot be understood in a linear fashion. Forward-looking processes, such as pre-legislative scrutiny, might involve an element of retrospective counter-terrorism review, considering the impacts and operation of existing law, or analogous provisions from other statutes, for example, even though that is not its primary purpose. Similarly, some structures of informal and networked activity within the larger edifice of counter-terrorism law and policy may mean that a non-formal, advance engagement might take place before any formal prospective *or* retrospective process begins. A government department might float a proposal with the chair of a relevant parliamentary committee before making a formal proposal and, in informing its response to a 'speculative' proposal of that kind, the committee or its chair may reflect on the operation of existing policies or laws. Or a regulatory body might engage in a consultation on proposed changes, and, as part of that, receive evidence on the operation of the law or policy as it currently exists, which it then considers in deciding whether and how to proceed with the proposed new approach.

Counter-terrorism and the challenge of accountability

Oversight, scrutiny and transparency of our counter-terrorism work is world-leading, and includes the reports we publish, the involvement of independent judges who review government agencies' use of intrusive powers and government applications for TEOs [Temporary Exclusion Orders] and TPIMs [Terrorism Prevention and Investigation Measures], an independent reviewer of terrorism legislation, and accountability to Parliament. We will continue to engage extensively with the public, civil society, academia and Parliament, and through community outreach. We aim to listen and respond to improve our approach to keeping the public safe.[18]

What the government describes under the heading of 'governance and oversight', we consider under the richer, accountability-related concept of 'counter-terrorism review'. While governance and oversight are important in themselves, they conjure up conceptions of an efficient, well-managed state with expectations of value for money, orderly organisation of resources and institutions, and effective pursuit of objectives. But accountability is about more than 'mere' good governance. It is about values, rights and legitimacy. Moreover, accountability is a potential casualty in the pursuit of counter-terrorism. Our interest in this book is in whether counter-terrorism review can help redress that by optimising accountability in the counter-terrorist state.

As we argue in Chapter 1, the UK is a counter-terrorist state: a state in which counter-terrorism law, policy discourse and operations are mainstreamed across the domains of law and government in forms that are conceptualised and designed as being 'permanent' in at least some cases. This contrasts sharply with the paradigmatic understanding of counter-terrorism law, policy and action as that which is done *in response to* an extraordinary threat or risk and *in order to* restore normalcy, at which stage these laws, policies and measures would be suspended or cease to operate, at least to their fullest extent.[19] Now, counter-terrorism has become a permanent part of state activity,[20] with implications for the ways in which the state structures its counter-terrorism work. Increasingly this work is undertaken through permanent legislation, institutions, regulatory requirements of institutions and sectors not traditionally associated with counter-terrorism, and heavily resourced policing and intelligence operations. In spite of the apparent 'normalisation' of counter-terrorism that this suggests, these measures carry significant implications for the power of the state to infringe on individual liberty and human rights. It seems that, even while normalised, counter-terrorism continues to be seen as a field in which the risks of failure are so grave as to justify and necessitate intrusive and repressive measures.

One of our core claims is that this shift to a counter-terrorist state has important implications for how we enact the liberal democratic commitment to accountability.[21] As a general matter, accountability relies upon values that stem in part from the Enlightenment principle of publicity, which rejected the paternalistic view of politics according to which 'government necessarily relies on noble lies – myths and deceptions designed to secure loyalty and love of country'.[22] The core of accountability is the democratic argument that citizens need to know what work the government does in order to confirm its legitimacy;[23] any other approach suggests that the 'public is incompetent to judge fairly the proceedings of a political assembly'.[24] Accountability, then, is akin to answerability and liability,[25] where government is conducted according to fixed and published rules, on the basis of information and procedures that are publicly accessible.[26] As Normanton puts it '[a]ccountability is ... the test of obedience and judgement, the moment of truth'.[27]

It is already well accepted that approaches to and mechanisms of accountability may need to adjust to the changing shapes and nature of the state if that state is to retain its legitimacy.[28] The counter-terrorist state operates through a mixture of directly applicable powers (using criminal law, administrative measures and police powers, for example), indirect coercion (through counter-extremism, for instance) and regulatory power (by imposing duties to disrupt terrorist financing on financial institutions, for example). This combination of traditional power, indirect coercion and regulation diffuses counter-terrorism across state and non-state actors, making it difficult to ensure accountability. This difficulty arises not only from the multi-level nature of the counter-terrorist state but also because conventional accountability mechanisms have tended to defer to the executive in respect of 'security',[29] and seem to struggle to accommodate claims of secrecy within a commitment to accountability in the counter-terrorism context.[30]

Bovens writes that accountability can be understood in a broad, normative sense, as a virtue, and in a narrow, descriptive sense, as a mechanism.[31] As a virtue, it is the commitment to being accountable to some forum in the sense of accepting the requirement to *give account* of and for one's actions to ensure government work is done with caution, delicacy, economy and modesty.[32] The normative sense of accountability goes beyond simply apprehending the possibility of giving account and feeds into a set of judgements about what is the *right way* to go about the activities in question.[33] While we may be reliant on the collective motivations of political actors for virtue- or duty-based accountability to be ensured, formal politico-legal structures have developed multiple mechanisms intended to secure accountability.[34] To this end, states now have organisational structures that identify the appropriate forum,[35] require actors to account, and impose some consequence for action.[36] Taking the state as the overall accountable entity, the organisational structure contains multiple accountability mechanisms: judicial review, judicial and non-judicial inquiries, parliamentary committees, oversight committees, ombudsmen, regulators, reviewers, parliamentary debate and questions, administrative law principles such as collective cabinet and individual ministerial responsibility,[37] and 'bureaucracy'. Most of these can also be discerned across the counter-terrorism review assemblage.

Regardless of the forum or mechanism in question, four elements for accountability are usually identified: a responsible actor, who gives an account, to a forum of some kind, where the giving of the account carries some consequences. In the 'traditional' or pre-regulatory state we could identify with relatively little difficulty who the account giver should be (the responsible minister and government of the day), to whom account should be given (some other element of the state) and what the consequences might be (anything from electoral punishment to removal from office or imprisonment for unlawful activity).[38] In that configuration of the state, accountability lines were fairly plain, and – at least in theory – provided the polity with assurance that accountability as a mechanism would likely interact effectively with accountability as a virtue. In the new, counter-terrorist state these organisational structures and their operation are more difficult to grasp. As a result, questions arise about whether the constitutional labour that accountability does for liberal democratic legitimacy is being undertaken.

The research

If the UK is now a counter-terrorist state, and if accountability is precarious within that state, might counter-terrorism review serve an accountability-enhancing function? Our hypothesis was that it might, although it was not clear whether it does.

From the outset, we supposed that the abstract picture of counter-terrorism review might differ from how it is conducted in practice. To test this assumption, we undertook a paper-based mapping exercise, conducted 24 semi-structured 'elite' interviews and held an invitation-only workshop with key stakeholders.

Having received the relevant ethical approval,[39] we first undertook a desk-based review aimed at assessing how we should define counter-terrorism. We combined our pre-existing knowledge with the Government's conceptualisation of counter-terrorism, drawn from the main Government counter-terrorism policy and strategies, in particular CONTEST.[40] Working from this document, the subsequent annual reports,[41] and relevant commentary from the Joint Committee on Human Rights and the Home Affairs Committee,[42] we identified the main institutions, objectives, strategies and key activities or fields of UK counter-terrorism. This exercise allowed us to grasp the scale and depth of counter-terrorism in the UK, which we outline in Chapter 1, and to identify the many institutions and actors that could be involved in counter-terrorism review. This also underpinned our decision to include Prevent – a counter-extremism policy – within the category of counter-terrorism, as that is clearly the policy field in which the Government develops and executes it.

We then undertook a mapping exercise, identifying the actors and institutions involved in counter-terrorism review; compiling the relevant legislation, policy and case law; and assessing the different ways review could be initiated or triggered. We cross-referenced the resulting map of review mechanisms with the understanding of counter-terrorism we had already developed, starting with specific counter-terrorism powers and identifying the potential reviews to which they may be subjected. The results of this mapping exercise helped to identify the reviews of Prevent and TPIMs that we present in Chapter 2, as well as to identify whom it would be useful for us to interview. The interviews were conducted to ascertain whether the practice of counter-terrorism review conformed to or troubled what our desk-research had revealed. The workshop allowed us to test our early analysis with a group of knowledgeable participants.

We chose this combination of methods to generate an extensive picture of the current state of counter-terrorism review. Speaking to the actors who undertake and engage with the various bodies and mechanisms we had identified helped us to understand how counter-terrorism is reviewed in practice and what values are pursued, as well as to test our hypotheses about the structure, interaction and quality of review in practice. In undertaking our interviews we were conscious of Kvale and Brinkmann's claim that an interview's purpose is to obtain descriptions so that we can interpret the described phenomena.[43] In short, interviewing counter-terrorism review actors grounded our research in the reality of what appears to be a complex but as yet little understood web of accountability. Combining desk-research and interview analysis provided access to conceptions of how review functions, what its purpose is and what values are associated with it that would be difficult, if not impossible, to ascertain using positivist and doctrinal methods alone.[44] Such an approach is particularly beneficial in counter-terrorism, where security classifications, concerns and redactions impact on what information is available in the public domain, including in published reports. By accessing the social understanding of counter-terrorism review,[45] we gained insight into the meaning of review and its relationship with accountability from the actors who undertake and engage with it. In short, interviewing counter-terrorism review actors grounded our research in the reality of what appears to be a complex, and, at times particular, form of accountability in the counter-terrorist state.

We aimed to speak to persons we describe as 'elite', by which we mean the professionals and civil society representatives with an in-depth knowledge of counter-terrorism review gained from working within or close to the procedures and mechanisms of counter-terrorism review we had identified. We spoke to actors who represented or worked within the independent, parliamentary, arms-length, regulatory and civil society bodies that undertake counter-terrorism review of some kind. With respect to political actors, we were careful to invite persons from across the range of political viewpoints and leadership levels to participate. We also approached Special Advocates who work in closed material procedures; representatives from the Investigatory Powers Tribunal, the Investigatory Powers Commissioner's Office, and the Independent Office for Police Conduct; and representatives from a range of civil society organisations. Hoping to secure 10–12 interviews, we invited almost 100 people to interview, and subsequently spoke to 24 of them.

Taken as a group, our interviewees were drawn from across the counter-terrorism review actors and mechanisms. They included two former Home Secretaries, two former Independent Reviewers of Terrorism Legislation, several Special Advocates, a number of high-level parliamentary actors (such as Select Committee staff), persons working in regulatory and complaints mechanisms, persons leading on the implementation of Prevent in educational settings, civil servants, lawyers and representatives from a range of civil society organisations. It is difficult to be sure that we had a diverse range of political viewpoints as we did not ask interviewees to identify their political leanings, but we do know that despite our best efforts the political actors we interviewed only represented one of the main political parties.

With the participants' permission, all but one interview was recorded and transcribed. For the interview that was not recorded, detailed notes were taken and the interviewee approved the resulting 'script'. During all interviews, the interviewer took notes to record our initial responses and understandings of the interviewee's views.[46] Before transcription, each interviewee was assigned a participant 'P' number, which we use to refer to them throughout the book.

When designing our interviews, we were conscious that choosing interview questions is part art, part science.[47] We were largely concerned with the nomothetic, the general understanding, but had to explore idiographic, or particular, understandings of counter-terrorism review to access it.[48] With a view to employing an adapted grounded theory analysis, we chose a semi-structured approach to capture a range of opinions and allow 'more leeway for following up on whatever angles are deemed important by the interviewee'.[49] We identified a base list of relevant questions (included as the Appendix to this book), which could be elaborated on depending on an interviewee's knowledge and responses, giving us the flexibility to follow the main research questions while pursuing the 'ideas and issues immediately that emerge during the interview'.[50] We matched the questions to our initial research queries but ensured that they were open enough to enable the participant to elaborate on the elements they thought significant, developing a set of questions that had a good balance between descriptive and evaluative open questions, and questions that sought to understand the processes and procedures of review. This ensured that there was a balance between probing and challenging participants' claims, while ensuring that we were open to and guided by their interpretation. Without this second aspect, it would have been difficult for us to move from the idiographic to the nomothetic.

We followed an adapted 'grounded theory' approach to the analysis, seeing the data as iterative, allowing the analysis to arise from the data itself, and then 'moving back and forth between data gathering and analysis'.[51] Such methods 'consist of systematic, yet flexible guidelines for collecting and analysing qualitative data to construct theories "grounded" in the data themselves. The guidelines offer a set of general principles and heuristic devices rather than formulaic rules.'[52] For us, the 'data' are the interviews and desk-research combined, from which we hoped to identify what the interviewees themselves thought about counter-terrorism review rather than imposing our own views.[53]

The analysis proceeded in three steps. First, the research team read the interview transcripts alongside the contemporaneous field notes in an inductive manner, making general conclusions from specific observations.[54] Then the interviews were read two further times and more notes were made. Second, by combining these notes with NVivo analysis, themes began to emerge, which we then drafted as memos and took back to the main data deductively to check whether the specific interpretation fit with the themes and their explanation.[55] Having coded the data in this manner, a number of themes emerged. We tested these against our initial aims and refined them. Third, we convened an invitation-only workshop with stakeholders from across the counter-terrorism review assemblage to present our preliminary findings and test whether these ideas cohered with their understanding of counter-terrorism review and its relationship with accountability. Workshop participants included practitioners, reviewers, industry and civil society actors, and academics involved in counter-terrorism and counter-terrorism review in the UK, some of whom had also been interviewed for the project.[56] It was conducted under the Chatham House Rule. We integrated the discussion and suggestions from the workshop with our existing analysis to ensure our research findings were robust and practicable.

These three elements form the foundation of our understanding about counter-terrorism review as a means of achieving accountability in the counter-terrorist state.

Limitations of the research

As with all qualitative research, the research design, our execution of the design and the resulting findings have limitations. In terms of research design, we acknowledge that a pilot study may have been helpful to develop more sophisticated concepts that could then be further tested.[57] However, this approach was effectively prohibited by the context and objectives of the research itself. Gaining access to elite participants, such as senior political and operational figures, is often a one-time-only event. We also accept that an approach that seeks to treat data as iterative and the associated analysis as emergent carries its own dangers.[58] In such a study it is inevitable that the researcher's preconceptions will play a role in guiding the research. While the grounded theory approach accepts this as a challenge, it seeks to overcome it by constantly comparing and checking the ideas that develop against the data. We also mitigated this second methodological limitation through the team's collaborative approach (working both independently and collectively with the interview transcripts) and by presenting the preliminary findings at the workshop.

The findings are constrained by only capturing 'elite' views and not having access to broader perceptions, the difficulty we found in accessing and detailing regionalised aspects of counter-terrorism review and, finally, the prominence of the Independent Reviewer of Terrorism Legislation in the findings.

Focusing on 'elite' views, as noted above, was a conscious choice that enabled us to make sense of matters that remain opaque at a distance. However, it left little space to consider broader public perceptions on the importance, function and impact of counter-terrorism review. We allowed for this constraint in two ways. First, we looked to the growing literature on the public perception of counter-terrorism both in the UK and internationally to contribute to our account of the counter-terrorist state.[59] Second, we used this literature in conjunction with our interviewees' views, many of whom have access to and document public perception of counter-terrorism and counter-terrorism review, to corroborate our findings.

Counter-terrorism and counter-terrorism review are whole-of-state activities, but often undertaken by different authorities across the constituent parts of the UK. We expected to be able to draw out differences between the counter-terrorism review that takes place in England, Wales and Scotland and that in Northern Ireland, but this turned out not to be the case. The Independent Reviewer of the Justice and Security (Northern Ireland) Act 2007 is not a public-facing office in the same way as the Independent Reviewer of Terrorism Legislation, so we found it difficult to make contact and secure an interview. While some of our interviewees mentioned this office, little detail emerged about its reports, its activities or the distinctions in interpretation about the purpose of review.[60] Similarly, although some materials on regionalism arose from our desk-research and interviews, these were slender and usually illustrated the overall complexity of counter-terrorism review rather than as a standalone element. We believe this means there is still research to be undertaken on the different regional interpretations and interactions of counter-terrorism review beyond this book.

Finally, we note that the Independent Reviewer of Terrorism Legislation is prominent throughout the book, particularly in comparison with other mechanisms within the assemblage. However, not only did nearly all of our interviewees reference the Independent Reviewer (sometimes extensively), but Government and Parliament seems to rely heavily on the Independent Reviewer's work, and there is a marked openness and publicity to the activities and reports of the Independent Reviewer (once they are published by the Government). As a result, the prominence of the Independent Reviewer in this book reflects the data that we hold on counter-terrorism review in the UK.

The structure of the argument

As we have already outlined, our starting proposition is that giving effect to accountability as a constitutional expectation of legitimate government is challenging in the counter-terrorist state, but that counter-terrorism review may operate as a 'web of accountability' that assists us in meeting that challenge. We progress that argument throughout the four main chapters of this book.

In Chapter 1, we develop our argument that the UK should now be understood as a counter-terrorist state. That is, a state in which counter-terrorism law, policy, discourse and operations are mainstreamed across the domains of law and government in forms that are conceptualised and designed as 'permanent' in at least some cases; in which non-state actors are responsibilised for counter-terrorism; and in which all persons are the subjects of counter-terrorism, although not necessarily equally attended to by state and non-state counter-terrorism power. While the counter-terrorist state might be understood as an iteration of what other scholars deem the security state,[61] the secret state,[62] or the 'neo-democratic turn',[63] we are committed to articulating and demonstrating the specific condition of the counter-terrorist state. Counter-terrorism is paradigmatically considered to be temporary, emergency related and oriented towards the 'restoration' of normalcy. As a result, both law and politics have tended to accede to exceptionalist narratives of necessity and demands for trust, and have allowed for states to act more repressively and less accountably than would ordinarily be acceptable. However, if counter-terrorism *is* now normal, it is important to recognise that, not least to consider critically whether political and legal behaviours and expectations have shifted accordingly to re-establish both the virtue and the practice of accountability in the counter-terrorist state. To ascertain whether counter-terrorism review acts as a web of accountability, we move on to consider its operation in practice, keeping in mind accountability as our analytical benchmark.

In Chapter 2 we look at the reviews themselves. Focusing on two case studies – Prevent and TPIMs – we analyse the relevant legislation, parliamentary debates, litigation, review outputs, regulatory practice and civil society reports to explore whether, when, how and against which evaluative standards counter-terrorism review operates in the UK. We show that in some cases what could operate as counter-terrorism review in fact operates only as reporting, information provision or compliance monitoring (if not enforcement). Where evaluative review does take place, it is often focused on operational and legal questions, rather than questions of unforeseen and societal impacts, although less so where civil society undertakes the review.

Having considered specific reviews in Chapter 2, in Chapter 3 we report the findings from our interviews on how actors within the counter-terrorism review assemblage perceive review, undertake review and operate in relation to one another. Our analysis reveals that while counter-terrorism review can operate reasonably well to evaluate counter-terrorism, much of that is dependent on goods that only the Government can disperse (such as access to security-cleared information, or perceived political credibility) or which Government largely controls (such as the allocation of parliamentary time), and on an informal division of labour within the assemblage, although that too can be disrupted or hampered by the imposition of intra-assemblage hierarchy and status by Government action.

All of this shows that while counter-terrorism review has substantial accountability potential, and many actors within the assemblage work hard to make good on that potential, structural factors beyond the control of the counter-terrorism review assemblage have an enduring, limiting impact on their capacity for success. Drawing on both the literature and the interview analysis, we identify these factors in Chapter 4 as being the persistence of state secrecy, the abundance of Executive control over review and the conditions of review, the limitations of Parliament as the ultimate accountability forum and the absence of trust within the counter-terrorist state.

Why focus on counter-terrorism review?

As will become clear, this is a book about the review of counter-terrorism, and not about counter-terrorism itself. We engage with the substance of counter-terrorism law, policy, programmes and strategy in the UK only to the extent necessary to contextualise and analyse counter-terrorism review. This does not mean that we endorse or oppose the counter-terrorist state and the ways in which it is instantiated in the UK. Rather, it reflects our belief that counter-terrorism review is an assemblage that requires naming and standalone consideration of this kind. This is, in part, a reflection of what Susan Marks calls the power of naming. It enables us to bring together what may at first seem a disparate set of activities to establish for our analysis an 'agenda for conceptual reflection, empirical study' and, we hope, 'institutional redesign that gives shape and focus to an immense range of large and small questions' about evaluation, review and decision-making in the counter-terrorist state.[64] In doing so against an analytical framework that draws on the concept of accountability, we hope to undertake what Charles Taylor calls an 'act of retrieval',[65] articulating a 'higher' principle that may lie behind the practice of counter-terrorism review and then analysing and critiquing the practice from that perspective.

In focusing on review in this way, we hope that we have avoided the dangers of allowing the 'cultural life' of review to overtake the fundamental questions of rights, security and securitisation that of course bubble underneath the surface.[66] We know that '[a]s monopoly holders of the means of legitimate physical and symbolic violence, modern states possess a built-in, paradoxical tendency to undermine the very liberties and security they are constructed to protect'.[67] We are also keenly aware that, rather than optimising accountability, counter-terrorism review may in fact operate as a tool of governmentality and *as part of* the counter-terrorist state.[68]

In that mode, review might legitimate the laws, policies, logics and programmes that it pursues, ultimately reinforcing rather than challenging 'very real imbalances of representation and socio-political agency' within the counter-terrorist state.[69] Indeed, the existence of a hegemonic consensus on counter-terrorism that we detect across Westminster-based politics (see Chapter 1) certainly raises the possibility that counter-terrorism review does play this role.

As we argue in the Conclusion, avoiding this requires a dispositional shift away from exceptionalism, securitisation, rights-scepticism and risk aversion on the part of the actors that shape, pursue and execute the counter-terrorist state. Counter-terrorism review may be capable of increasing accountability, but it depends first on a meaningful commitment to accountability on the part of the counter-terrorist state and its primary protagonists.

Notes

[1] HM Government, *CONTEST: The United Kingdom's Strategy for Countering Terrorism* (Cm 9608, 2018) para 1.

[2] We use the term 'assemblage' to describe counter-terrorism review in the UK. In doing so, we use it to describe the 'holding together' of actors and processes of review and their co-production of a common sense of counter-terrorism review, *but* not to suggest they constitute a 'system'. For an analysis of the concept of 'assemblage' drawing on its philosophical and artistic provenance see, for example, John Phillips, 'Agencement/Assemblage' (2006) 23(2–3) Theory, Culture & Society 108.

[3] On which see Fergal F. Davis and Fiona de Londras, 'Counter-Terrorism Judicial Review: Beyond Dichotomies' in Fergal F. Davis and Fiona de Londras (eds), *Critical Debates on Counter-Terrorism Judicial Review* (Cambridge University Press 2014).

[4] Dawn Oliver, 'Accountability and the Foundations of British Democracy – the Public Interest and Public Service Principles' in Nicholas Bamforth and Peter Leyland (eds), *Accountability in the Contemporary Constitution* (Oxford University Press 2013) 289.

[5] See Mark Elliot, 'Ombudsmen, Tribunals, Inquiries: Re-fashioning Accountability Beyond the Courts' in Bamforth and Leyland 233, 234; Fiona de Londras, 'Accounting for Rights in EU Counter-Terrorism: Towards Effective Review' (2016) 22(2) Columbia Journal of European Law 237.

6   See for example the contributions to Davis and de Londras (n 3).

7   Deirdre Niamh Duffy, *Evaluation and Governing in the 21st Century: Disciplinary Measures, Transformative Possibilities* (Palgrave Macmillan 2017). Duffy uses the term 'being actionable' which we have replaced here with 'having capacity for action', albeit that both capture the same range of capacities.

8   Although it is a complex area, we note here that merit and worth are not the same thing in evaluation science. As Lincoln and Guba put it, '[m]erit ... is context-free, but worth can be determined only in relation to an actual context': Yvonna S. Lincoln and Egon G. Guba, 'The Distinction between Merit and Worth in Evaluation' (1980) 2(4) Educational Evaluation and Policy Analysis 6; Thomas D. Cook and William R. Shadish Jr., 'Program Evaluation: The Worldly Science' (1986) 37(1) Annual Review of Psychology 193; Michael Scriven, 'The Logic of Evaluation' (Ontario Society for the Study of Argumentation Conference, Windsor, June 2007).

9   Many of our interviewees mentioned assessing the justification of a counter-terrorist power as well as its effectiveness or efficiency when we asked them what counter-terrorism review might be understood as (P5; P6; P13; P17; P21). This was evident too in the verbs and 'actions' that interviewees used when discussing or defining counter-terrorism review: assessing (P1), testing (P3), evaluating (P5; P17; P20), making governments perform better (P6), critiquing (P6), examining (P13), monitoring (P20), encouraging changes and improvements (P6; P22; P23), addressing gaps (P10), refining policy (P21), scrutinising (P15; P22) and striking the right balance between security actions and rights protection (P7; P8).

10 Lincoln and Guba (n 8).

11 For a broad analysis see, for example, Lorenzo Fioramonti, *How Numbers Rule the World: The Use and Abuse of Statistics in Global Politics* (Zed Books 2014).

12 On meaningful accountability see Mark Bovens and Thomas Schillemans, 'Meaningful Accountability' in Mark Bovens, Robert E. Goodin, and Thomas Schillemans (eds), *The Oxford Handbook of Public Accountability* (Oxford University Press 2014).

13 Ibid 675–7.

14 Carol H. Weiss, *Evaluation Research: Methods for Assessing Program Effectiveness* (Prentice Hall International 1972).

15 For a broader analysis of the challenges of evaluating the effectiveness of counter-terrorism see Beatrice de Graaf, *Evaluating Counterterrorism Performance: A Comparative Study* (Routledge 2011).

16 If counter-terrorism is underpinned by a repressive set of laws and policies that undermine social cohesion, contribute to a sense of grievance, or undermine feelings of 'belonging', it may actually undermine security seen in the longer term: See generally Martha Crenshaw, *Explaining Terrorism: Causes, Processes, and Consequences* (Routledge 2011).

17 Paul Cairney, *The Politics of Evidence-Based Policy Making* (Springer 2016); Alex Stevens 'Telling Policy Stories: An Ethnographic Study of the Use of Evidence in Policy-making in the UK' (2011) 40(2) Journal of Social Policy 237.

18 HM Government (n 1) para 333.

19 We acknowledge that of course the return to 'normalcy' was rarely if ever complete; instead the concept of 'normalcy' was itself adjusted by reference to the period of 'exceptionalism', baseline rights protections were generally recalibrated downwards, some institutions (such as extraordinary courts) continued to operate and were sometimes extended, and remnants of the 'extraordinary' regime often

remained within the 'ordinary' law. For a sample of the extensive literature on this see, for example, Jessie Blackbourn, *Anti-Terrorism Law and Normalising Northern Ireland* (Routledge 2015); Alan Greene, *Permanent States of Emergency and the Rule of Law: Constitutions in an Age of Crisis* (Hart Publishing 2018); Oren Gross, '"Once More unto the Breach": The Systematic Failure of Applying the European Convention on Human Rights to Entrenched Emergencies' (1998) 23 Yale Journal of International Law 437; Ian Zuckerman, 'One Law for War and Peace? Judicial Review and Emergency Powers between the Norm and the Exception' (2006) 13(4) Constellations 522.

[20] Indeed, even some human rights institutions now claim that counter-terrorism and emergency measures need not be 'temporary' in order for their proportionality to be established. See, for example, *A. and others v the United Kingdom* [2009] ECHR 301.

[21] See for example Laura K. Donohue, *The Cost of Counterterrorism: Power, Politics and Liberty* (Cambridge University Press 2008).

[22] David Luban, 'The Publicity Principle' in Robert E. Goodin (ed), *The Theory of Institutional Design* (Cambridge University Press 1996) 154.

[23] See for example John Rawls, *Political Liberalism – Expanded Edition* (Columbia University Press 2005) 13; Ian Shapiro, *The Moral Foundations of Politics* (Yale University Press 2012) 200; Robert A. Dahl, *Polyarchy: Participation and Opposition* (Yale University Press 1971).

[24] Carl J. Friedrich, 'Nature and Function of Secrecy and Propaganda' in Susan Maret and Jan Goldman (eds), *Government Secrecy: Classic and Contemporary Readings* (Libraries Unlimited 2009) 85.

[25] Andreas Schedler, 'Conceptualising Accountability' in Andreas Schedler, Larry Jay Diamond and Marc F. Plattner, *The Self Restraining State: Power and Accountability in New Democracies* (Lynne Rienner Publishers 1999) 14.

[26] Christopher Hood, 'Transparency in Historical Perspective' in Christopher Hood and David Heald (eds), *Transparency: The Key to Better Governance? (Proceedings of the British Academy)* (Oxford University Press 2006) 2; and Christopher Hood, 'Transparency' in Paul Barry Clarke and Joe Foweraker (eds), *Encyclopedia of Democratic Thought* (Routledge 2001) 863–68.

[27] E. Leslie Normanton, 'Public Accountability and Audit: a Reconnaissance' in Bruce L.R. Smith and Douglas Hague (eds) *The Dilemma of Accountability in Modern Government: Independence Versus Control* (Macmillan 1971).

[28] See, for example Julia Black, 'Constructing and Contesting Legitimacy and Accountability in Polycentric Regulatory Regimes' (2008) 2(2) Regulation and Governance 137; Colin Scott, 'Accountability in the Regulatory State' (2000) 27(1) Journal of Law and Society 38; Robert D. Behn, *Rethinking Democratic Accountability* (Brookings Institution Press 2001); Deirdre Curtin and Linda Senden, 'Public Accountability of Transnational Private Regulation: Chimera or Reality?' (2011) 38(1) Journal of Law and Society 163; Cass R. Sunstein, *After the Rights Revolution: Reconceiving the Regulatory State* (Harvard University Press 1990); Giandomenico Majone, 'From the Positive to the Regulatory State: Causes and Consequences of Changes in the Mode of Governance' (1997) 17(2) Journal of Public Policy 139; Matthew Flinders, *The Politics of Accountability in the Modern State* (Routledge 2001); Mark Bovens, *The Quest for Responsibility: Accountability and Citizenship in Complex Organisations* (Cambridge University Press 1998); R.A.W. Rhodes, 'The Hollowing Out of the State: The Changing Nature of the Public Service in Britain' (1994) 65(2) Political Quarterly 138.

[29] On the tendencies towards deference of both the judiciary and 'politics', for example, see the survey provided in Fiona de Londras and Fergal F. Davis, 'Controlling the Executive in Times of Terrorism: Competing Perspectives on Effective Oversight Mechanisms' (2010) 30(1) Oxford Journal of Legal Studies 19.

[30] Secrecy and transparency in counter-terrorism review occur in several ways: on the procedural impact of secrecy in UK counter-terrorism trials, see Martin Chamberlain, 'Special Advocates and Amici Curiae in National Security Proceedings in the United Kingdom' (2018) 68(3) University of Toronto Law Journal 496; on state secrecy in general see Lydia Morgan, '(Re)Conceptualising State Secrecy' (2018) 69(1) Northern Ireland Legal Quarterly 59; on intelligence, national security work and accountability, see Hugh Bochel, Andrew Defty and Jane Kirkpatrick, *Watching the Watchers: Parliament and the Intelligence Services* (Palgrave Macmillan 2014) and Hans Born, Loch K. Johnson and Ian Leigh, *Who's Watching the Spies: Establishing Intelligence Service Accountability* (Potomac Books 2005) chapters 5 and 12.

[31] Mark Bovens, 'Two Concepts of Accountability: Accountability as a Virtue and as a Mechanism' (2010) 33 West European Politics 946.

[32] Andrew Barry, Thomas Osborne, and Nikolas Rose, *Foucault and Political Reason. Liberalism, Neo-liberalism and Rationalities of Government* (University of Chicago Press 1996) 8.

[33] Here can be observed some conceptual slippage between accountability and good governance of which Bovens is rightly cautious: Mark Bovens, 'Analysing and Assessing Accountability: A Conceptual Framework' (2007) 13(4) European Law Journal 447, 449–50.

[34] Andreas Schedler, 'Conceptualising Accountability' in Schedler, Diamond and Plattner (n 25) 14.

[35] These mechanisms are not solely legal or solely political but, rather, extend across a wide variety of possible approaches. See Flinders (n 28), and accounts in Bamforth and Leyland (n 4).

[36] In this narrow, descriptive sense 'accountability is a relationship between an actor and a forum, in which the actor has an obligation to explain and justify his or her conduct, the forum can pose questions and pass judgement, and the actor may face consequences.' See Bovens (n 33) 450.

[37] Vile wrote that the doctrine of ministerial responsibility to Parliament is 'the crux of the English system of government': M.J.C. Vile, *Constitutionalism and the Separation of Powers* (Oxford University Press 1967) 231. However, there is some dispute as to whether this remains the case. See generally Patrick Weller, 'Cabinet Government' in Brian Galligan and Scott Brenton (eds) *Constitutional Conventions in Westminster Systems: Controversies, Changes and Challenges* (Cambridge University Press 2015) 72–90; William Moyes, Julian Wood and Michael Clemence, *Nothing to Do with Me? Modernising Ministerial Accountability for Decentralised Public Services* (Institute for Government 2011); Philip Giddings (ed), *Parliamentary Accountability: A Study of Parliament and Executive Agencies* (Palgrave Macmillan UK 1995). In contrast, Tomkins suggests a shift to judicial accountability for ministerial action: Adam Tomkins 'The Guardianship of the Public Interest: a British Tale of Contestable Administrative Law' (2016) 24(2) George Mason Law Review 417.

[38] The concept of the regulatory state is borrowed from Colin Scott, 'Accountability in the Regulatory State' (2000) 27(1) Journal of Law and Society 38. See also Tony Prosser, *Law and the Regulators* (Clarendon Press 1997); Michael Moran, 'The Rise of the Regulatory State in Britain' (2001) 54(1) Parliamentary Affairs 19.

[39] University of Birmingham Research Ethical Approval ERN_17-0490 and ERN_17-0490A

[40] HM Government, *Countering International Terrorism: The United Kingdom's Strategy* (Cm 6888, 2006); HM Government (n 1).

[41] Home Office, *CONTEST: The United Kingdom's Strategy for Countering Terrorism: Annual Report for 2015* (Cm 9310, 2016); Home Office, *CONTEST: The United Kingdom's Strategy for Countering Terrorism: Annual Report for 2014* (Cm 9048, 2015); Home Office, *CONTEST: The United Kingdom's Strategy for Countering Terrorism: Annual Report for 2013* (Cm 8848, 2014); Home Office, *CONTEST: The United Kingdom's Strategy for Countering Terrorism: Annual Report for 2012* (Cm 8583, 2013).

[42] For example we analysed the Communities and Local Government Committee, *Preventing Violent Extremism* (2009–10, HC 65); Home Affairs Committee, *Roots of violent radicalisation* (2010–12, HC 1446); Home Affairs Committee, *Radicalisation: the counter-narrative and identifying the tipping point* (2016–17, HC 135).

[43] Setinar Kvale and Svend Brinkmann, *InterViews: Learning the craft of qualitative research interviewing* (2nd ed, Sage 2008) 3.

[44] Max Travers, *Understanding Law and Society* (Routledge 2010) 7–9. See further Svend Brinkmann, Michael Hviid Jacobsen and Søren Kristiansen, 'Historical Overview of Qualitative Research in the Social Sciences' in Patricia Leavy (ed), *The Oxford Handbook of Qualitative Research* (Oxford University Press 2014) 17–43; Roger Cotterrell 'Why Must Legal Ideas Be Interpreted Sociologically?' (1998) 25(2) Journal of Law and Society 171.

[45] Cotterrell (n 44) 177.

[46] Melanie Birks and Jane Mills, *Grounded Theory: A Practical Guide* (2nd edn, Sage 2015) 74–6.

[47] Robert Kahn and Charles Cannell, *The dynamics of interviewing: Theory, technique and cases* (Wiley 1957).

[48] Wilhelm Windelband, *A History of Philosophy* [1893] (Macmillan 1979).

[49] Svend Brinkmann, 'Unstructured and Semi-Structured Interviewing' in Leavy (n 44) 286.

[50] Kathy Charmaz, *Constructing Grounded Theory: A Practical Guide Through Qualitative Analysis* (2nd edn, Sage 2014) 85.

[51] Frederick J. Wertz et al, *Five Ways of Doing Qualitative Analysis: Phenomenological Psychology, Grounded Theory, Discourse Analysis, Narrative Research, and Intuitive Inquiry* (Guilford 2011) 166

[52] Charmaz (n 50) 1.

[53] Kathy Charmaz, 'The Lens of Constructivist Grounded Theory' in Wertz et al (n 51) 298.

[54] Jo Reichertz, 'Induction, Deduction, Abduction' in Uwe Flick (ed), *The SAGE Handbook of Qualitative Data Analysis* (Sage 2014) 123.

[55] Birks and Mills (n 46) 88, 106.

[56] All interviewees were invited, but some could not attend.

[57] Helen Sampson 'Navigating the waves: the usefulness of a pilot in qualitative research' (2004) 4(3), Qualitative Research 383.

[58] Charmaz (n 50) 232.

[59] For example, but not limited to: Leda Blackwood, Nick Hopkins and Steve Reicher, 'I Know Who I Am, But Who Do They Think I Am? Muslim Perspectives on Encounters with Airport Authorities' (2013) 36(6) Ethnic and Racial Studies 1090; Tufyal Choudhury and Helen Fenwick, 'The Impact of Counter-terrorism Measures on Muslim Communities' (Research Report 72,

Equality and Human Rights Commission 2011); Aziz Huq, Tom Tyler and Stephen Schulhofer, 'Mechanisms for Eliciting Cooperation in Counterterrorism Policing: Evidence from the United Kingdom' (2011) 8(4) Journal of Empirical Legal Studies 728; Lee Jarvis and Michale Lister, 'What Would You Do? Everyday Conceptions and Constructions of Counter-terrorism' (2016) 36(3) Politics 277; Therese O'Toole et al, 'Governing through Prevent? Regulation and Contested Practice in State–Muslim Engagement' (2016) 50(1) Sociology 160.

60 P2; P3; P4; P5; P12; P13; P15.

61 Iris Marion Young, 'The Logic of Masculinist Protection: Reflections on the Current Security State' (2003) 29(1) Journal of Women in Culture and Society 1; Simon Hallsworth and John Lea, 'Reconstructing Leviathan: Emerging Contours of the Security State' (2011) 15(2) Theoretical Criminology 141.

62 Edward Palmer Thompson, 'The Secret State' (1979) 20(3) Race and Class 219; Morgan (n 30).

63 Conor Gearty, *Liberty and Security* (Polity 2013)

64 Susan Marks, 'Naming Global Administrative Law' (2004) 4(4) New York University Journal of International Law and Politics 995, 995.

65 Charles Taylor, *The Ethics of Authenticity* (Harvard University Press 1991) 72.

66 For the concept of 'cultural life' we are drawing on Benjamin Goold and Liora Lazarus, 'Security and Human Rights: The Search for a Language of Reconciliation' in Benjamin Goold and Liora Lazarus (eds), *Security and Human Rights* (Hart Publishing 2007).

67 Ian Loader and Neil Walker, *Civilising Security* (Cambridge University Press 2007) 7.

68 Harry Torrance, 'Building Confidence in Qualitative Research: Engaging the Demands of Policy' (2008) 14(4) Quantitative Inquiry 507; David Taylor and Susan Balloch (eds), *The Politics of Evaluation: Participation and Policy Implementation* (Policy Press 2015); Christopher Pollitt, 'Forty Years of Public Management Reform in UK Central Government: Promises, Promises...' in Sarah Ayres (ed), *Rethinking Policy and Politics: Reflections on Contemporary Debates in Policy Studies* (Policy Press 2017) 7; Ben Middleton, 'Rebalancing, Reviewing or Rebranding the Treatment of Terrorist Suspects: the Counter-Terrorism Review 2011' (2011) 75(3) Journal of Criminal Law 225.

69 Duffy (n 7) 22.

1

The Counter-Terrorist State

In December 2018, the National Counter-Terrorism Security Office, in conjunction with the Department for Transport, announced a new scheme to 'reduce the risk of rental vehicles being used as weapons in acts of terror'.[1] The Rental Vehicle Security Scheme aims 'to promote a proactive security culture within the vehicle rental industry and individual companies' by requiring participating companies to sign up to a ten-point code of practice.[2] Among other commitments, participants should 'appoint a Recognised Security Contact' and 'train staff to identify and report suspicious behaviours'.[3]

Introduced in response to the use of a rental vehicle in the Westminster Bridge terrorist attack in March 2017, this scheme reveals the banality and reach of contemporary counter-terrorism.[4] It illustrates its expansion into policy areas traditionally unrelated to national security, and the responsibilisation of industry and private individuals as counter-terrorism actors. This is one example of how counter-terrorism has become a permanent and pervasive part of the state's operations, and of the everyday lives of people in the UK over the past five decades. Reflecting this, we term the UK a 'counter-terrorist state': a state in which counter-terrorism law, policy, discourse and operations are mainstreamed across the domains of law and government in forms that are conceptualised and designed as 'permanent' in at least some cases; in which non-state actors are responsibilised for counter-terrorism; and in which all persons are the subjects of counter-terrorism, although not to equal degrees.

In this chapter we characterise the UK as a counter-terrorist state, tracing its historical development and the processes through which counter-terrorism has become permanent in this jurisdiction. Alongside this permanence, we show how counter-terrorism pervades a wide range of fields, beyond policing and security, extending both the range of actors responsible for counter-terrorism and those subject to the state's counter-terrorist gaze. In spite of some marginal disagreement around counter-terrorism law and policy, we argue that UK politics is marked by a hegemonic consensus on the counter-terrorist state's core propositions. Finally, we attest to the fact that the counter-terrorist state is also reflected in the emergence and the stabilisation, through law, of at least some forms of counter-terrorism review. This illustrates the potential for counter-terrorism review to reinforce and legitimate the counter-terrorist state. Despite this, the combination of permanence, pervasiveness and persistent extraordinariness of counter-terrorism raises the accountability challenge with which we are concerned in this book, and which, we argue, might be met through counter-terrorism review.

Part I: Counter-insurgency, Northern Ireland, the emergence of the counter-terrorist state

Understanding how the UK has developed into a counter-terrorist state requires some familiarity with the UK's recent history of combating sub-state violence,[5] and how this has informed contemporary counter-terrorism practices. The UK's colonial past offers many potential examples of such violence, some of which were met with brutal military force, such as the American Revolution from 1775 to 1783, the attempted Irish Rebellion in 1798 and the Indian Uprising of 1857.[6] For the purposes of illustrating the influence of the UK's response to sub-state violence on counter-terrorism law and practice 'at home',[7] however, it is sufficient to trace contemporary counter-terrorism developments from the late 1960s and the start of the conflict in Northern Ireland, known as the Troubles.[8]

At that time, Northern Ireland was a self-governing region of the UK. Established in the 1920s, during which Ireland was partitioned,[9] inter-communal violence was a feature of Northern Ireland's early years.[10] The Northern Ireland Parliament responded by introducing the Civil Authorities (Special Powers) Act (Northern Ireland) 1922,[11] which granted a range of emergency powers to the Minister for Home Affairs,[12] the Royal Ulster Constabulary (RUC) and the regular armed forces garrisoned in Northern Ireland.[13] These included a power of curfew[14] and to prohibit assembly,[15] and a broad stop-and-search power.[16] Originally intended to remain in force for one year, the Act was renewed annually until 1928, then for five years, and then made permanent in 1933. Until its repeal in 1973, these powers were used frequently, particularly against members of the Catholic minority, and to suppress republican ideals and organising.[17] Abolition of 'special powers' was a core demand of the civil rights movement in Northern Ireland.

By 1969, the Northern Ireland government no longer considered the emergency powers sufficient, and requested the deployment of the British Army to support the RUC in its efforts to quell 'rioting' that had arisen out of and in response to official reactions to the activities of the civil rights movement that emerged in the late 1960s.[18] The British Army had recently returned from military campaigns in Malaya (1948–1960), Kenya (1952–1960), Cyprus (1955–1964) and Aden (1963–1967), where it had engaged in sometimes brutal counter-insurgencies against anti-colonial and independence movements.[19] By the end of the 1960s, the British Army had gained significant experience of counter-insurgency operations, and developed counter-insurgency doctrines and techniques.[20] Along with key personnel from those counter-insurgency campaigns, these were imported to Northern Ireland when the army was deployed there in August 1969.[21]

At least initially, Northern Ireland was not a counter-insurgency in the same way as those earlier campaigns. First, Northern Ireland was not a colony in the formal sense of the word, but an integral part of the Union with Great Britain whose inhabitants were entitled to British citizenship.[22] Second, the Army was deployed at the request of the Northern Irish government. Third, unlike the Kenyan Mau Mau or the Malayan National Liberation Army, the Northern Ireland Civil Rights Association was not an insurgent organisation dedicated to overthrowing the state. It sought to use a campaign of non-violent protest to secure greater civil rights for the minority Catholic community in Northern Ireland, and was, in essence, a movement for democratic reform.[23] The Army was not deployed in a counter-insurgency role, but rather to support the police and Northern Irish government to maintain peace and order in Northern Ireland. Fourth, the British Army did not face hostility from the domestic population as the minority Catholic community initially welcomed it as a bulwark against Loyalist violence and sectarian domination.[24] This phase of the British Army's deployment was short-lived. As violence began to escalate in late December 1969, the British Army began to use counter-insurgency techniques such as internment and inhuman and degrading treatment or punishment,[25] which became part of the counter-terrorist activities of the Northern Irish state.[26]

By the time direct rule was instated in 1972, Northern Ireland was experiencing significant levels of violence on a daily basis,[27] was highly militarised through the maintenance of a routinely armed police force and the active deployment of the British Army, and was still subject to emergency powers.[28] The Civil Authorities (Special Powers) Act (Northern Ireland) 1933 empowered the government 'to take all such steps and issue all such orders as may be necessary for preserving the peace and maintaining order'.[29] In other words, counter-terrorism was a key function of state activity in Northern Ireland, but contained within the traditional security apparatus of the state.

It was in these conditions that Westminster assumed responsibility for the governance of Northern Ireland, and thus for countering terrorism in the UK. Within six months, the UK Government established a commission, chaired by Lord Diplock, to review the existing policy of interning terrorist suspects, and to consider the 'arrangements for the administration of justice in Northern Ireland' that could be made in relation to 'individuals involved in terrorist activities, particularly those who plan and direct, but do not necessarily take part in, terrorist acts'.[30] Having reviewed both the policy of internment and the ordinary criminal law in Northern Ireland, the commission concluded that internment should be retained, but only for as long as the current emergency existed.[31] It also noted that no new special terrorism offences were needed. Instead, the prosecution of persons who had engaged in violent criminal activities for the purposes of terrorism could be achieved 'simply' by changes to criminal procedure in Northern Ireland.[32] The UK Parliament implemented these recommendations by repealing the Civil Authorities (Special Powers) Act (Northern Ireland) 1933. In its place, it enacted the Northern Ireland (Emergency Provisions) Act 1973, creating a system of non-jury courts to try a variety of scheduled offences,[33] allowing written evidence to be adduced in court in place of personal testimony,[34] creating new powers for the police to arrest and detain terrorist suspects for 72 hours prior to charge,[35] granting a variety of stop, search, entry and questioning powers to the police and armed forces,[36] creating a regime for proscribing organisations and a number of proscribed organisation offences,[37] and establishing an 'interim custody order' regime which allowed for terrorist suspects to be detained – or interned – without trial.[38]

The legislation applied only to Northern Ireland. However, in late 1973, the Provisional Irish Republican Army (PIRA) expanded its bombing campaign to Britain. After a year of violence, which culminated in the deaths of 21 civilians in the Birmingham pub bombings on 21 November 1974, the UK Parliament enacted new counter-terrorism legislation that, for the first time, applied to terrorist activities across the whole of the UK.[39] Although the Prevention of Terrorism (Temporary Provisions) Act 1974 included some measures applicable only to terrorism connected with Northern Irish affairs,[40] it also introduced a general power for the police to arrest without warrant and detain suspected terrorists for up to seven days.[41] The 1974 Act was intended as a temporary measure specifically to deal with the existing terrorist threat posed by PIRA's bombing campaign in Britain. As such, it incorporated a sunset clause that meant that it would expire after six months, unless the Secretary of State laid an order before Parliament to renew it.[42] In fact, it was continued in force until a new version of the Act was enacted in March 1976. Although the Prevention of Terrorism (Temporary Provisions) Act 1976 included a one-year sunset clause,[43] and in spite of its nominal temporariness, this signalled a shift towards permanent counter-terrorism in the UK.

Throughout the 1980s, it became clear that Northern Ireland was no longer the sole focus of the UK's counter-terrorism efforts. During this period, the 'exceptional' and 'temporary' legislation initially introduced to deal with the situation in Northern Ireland in the 1970s was expanded in scope and extended to new types of terrorism. In 1984, the powers of arrest and detention in the Prevention of Terrorism (Temporary Provisions) Act 1976 were extended to international, although not domestic, terrorism.[44] In 1989, a new version of the legislation was enacted, bringing international terrorism within the scope of a number of the terrorism offences.[45] The expansion reflected the steady and significant normalisation of counter-terrorism within UK law. No longer 'exceptional', counter-terrorism was to be addressed through the ordinary criminal justice system as a day-to-day part of the activities of the state, a movement that was not reversed with the passage of time and the success of the Northern Ireland Peace Process.

Part II: From temporary to permanent counter-terrorism

In the early 1990s, and following paramilitary ceasefires in Northern Ireland,[46] the UK Government commissioned Lord Lloyd to undertake a 'review of the law governing the prevention of terrorism'. Although the Peace Process was the context in which the review was instigated, its remit went beyond Northern Ireland. Lord Lloyd was asked:

> To consider the future need for specific counter-terrorism legislation in the UK if the cessation of terrorism connected with the affairs of Northern Ireland leads to a lasting peace, taking into account the continuing threat from other kinds of terrorism and the UK's obligations under international law; and to make recommendations.[47]

Following his review of both the Northern Ireland (Emergency Provisions) Act 1996 and the Prevention of Terrorism (Temporary Provisions) Act

1989,[48] Lord Lloyd concluded that, even in the context of a lasting peace in Northern Ireland, counter-terrorism legislation was needed because of the threat posed by other domestic and international terrorist organisations.[49] Accordingly, he recommended the introduction of a new, permanent law that would apply across the UK.[50] Lord Lloyd set out a proposed law, including a definition of terrorism, a variety of police powers, and a number of new offences.[51] Importantly, he also recommended that the three most contentious counter-terrorism measures that had only ever applied to Northern Ireland – non-jury courts, internment and exclusion – should be repealed and not re-enacted in the new legislation. In his estimation, such measures would not be needed in *permanent* counter-terrorism legislation; they should only be conceived of as exceptional, temporary measures for emergency situations.[52]

Some 18 months after Lord Lloyd's review was published, the Belfast Agreement was concluded, calling for the 'normalisation' of Northern Ireland across a number of policy areas, including 'security arrangements and practices'.[53] At the same time, the government initiated a consultation on how to implement the recommendations of Lord Lloyd's review,[54] leading to the publication of the Terrorism Bill 1999. This Bill incorporated a number of Lord Lloyd's core recommendations, including that new legislation should be permanent. With the enactment of the Terrorism Act 2000, the UK now had a permanent and generally applicable counter-terrorism law,[55] marking the start of a new phase in which counter-terrorism became incorporated into the general criminal justice regime in the UK.

This is not to suggest that the law mirrored what were then the existing expectations of criminal law. Instead, the Act involved the criminalisation of very remote activities,[56] the instigation in law of an extremely wide definition of terrorism,[57] and the imposition of extensive disclosure obligations on certain persons who believe or suspect that another person had committed particular terrorist offences.[58] In so doing, the Act both reflects and indicates a ramping up of the preventive turn in criminal law,[59] a trend that was only exacerbated with the introduction of programmes such as Prevent in the years following the Terrorism Act 2000. Since 2000, counter-terrorism law has primarily been pursued outside of a formally 'exceptional' or 'emergency' paradigm. Although the UK did assert a public emergency[60] and derogate from Article 5 of the European Convention on Human Rights following the terrorist attacks on the United States on 11 September 2001 ('9/11'),[61] that derogation was lifted in March 2005.[62] Apart from that, no emergency has been asserted. Rather, terrorism and counter-terrorism were, and are, the 'normal' state of affairs.

Part III: The pervasiveness of counter-terrorism

The enactment of the Terrorism Act 2000 was not only the point at which counter-terrorism legislation became permanent in the UK. It was also the point from which *counter-terrorism* in general became manifestly a pervasive part of the state's activities. This was driven in part by an initial refocusing by the UK government and the intelligence and security services on the risk of international terrorism in the aftermath of the 9/11 terrorist attacks. Subsequent fluctuations in the terrorist threat, between international, transnational and domestic risks have led to an ever-shifting focus for the UK's counter-terrorism regime. Over almost two decades the UK government has engaged in a wide range of programmes and law reform aimed at expelling suspected terrorist foreign nationals from the UK,[63] and preventing British citizens from returning following suspected involvement in terrorist activity.[64] It has also focused on countering violent extremism,[65] detaining suspected terrorists, either through incarceration[66] or orders that severely restrict a person's liberty outside of conditions of traditional detention,[67] restricting training, travel and funding related to terrorist activities,[68] undertaking communications data surveillance,[69] and more.

Further to these types of measures, which are implemented in 'conventional' national security domains, counter-terrorism has expanded into multiple policy fields, permeating a variety of sectors and industries, and responsibilising vast numbers of non-state actors. For example, the Charity Commission,[70] which regulates charities in England and Wales, has a counter-terrorism strategy to safeguard the sector from 'terrorist abuse',[71] namely, the financing or supporting of terrorist activity in the UK or abroad, whether intentional or otherwise.[72] Financial institutions are subject to legal obligations to disrupt financing imposed through domestic and international law,[73] giving rise to a significant 'political anatomy of financial surveillance'.[74] They are also required to send a 'Suspicious Activity Report' to the National Crime Agency if they know or suspect that terrorist financing is being undertaken.[75] The Treasury can also give directions to financial institutions requiring them to undertake enhanced due diligence and ongoing monitoring in relation to specified customers, to provide information or documents 'relating to transactions and business relationships' with particular customers or to cease business altogether with them.[76] While telecommunication service providers have, for a long time, been required to assist the security and intelligence agencies to intercept telephone communications,[77] increased technological capacity over the past two decades has meant that communication service providers have been required to take on further counter-terrorism activities, not least by retaining communications data in case it is needed to investigate terrorism.[78]

Counter-terrorism's sprawl also covers aviation security and immigration and citizenship decisions. Airport authorities and aviation companies operating in the UK have been incorporated into the 'chain of security,'[79] obliged to put in place security infrastructure, including land- and airside passenger screening,[80] and to collect and share data such as passenger name records,[81] for instance.[82] Changes to the British Nationality Act 1981 since 2001 have meant that the Secretary of State now has enhanced powers to deprive a person of their British citizenship, if satisfied that it is 'conducive to the public good',[83] used by the Home Office as a national security ground, including terrorism.[84] Furthermore, controversial changes were made in 2014 that allow the Secretary of State to revoke the citizenship of a naturalised British citizen even if it might make them stateless, though the Secretary of State can only do so if they have 'reasonable grounds for believing' that the person is able to acquire a second nationality.[85]

Perhaps even more surprisingly, counter-terrorism has permeated the family court system in the UK. A number of cases have been initiated in relation to allegations or suspicions that children were planning or attempting to travel to join 'Islamic State' in Syria and Iraq; that parents were planning or attempting to take their children there for the same purpose; that children were at risk of being radicalised by their parents or others; or that children were at risk of becoming involved in terrorist activities either at home or abroad. Family courts have tried to prevent the alleged risk of harm from occurring through a variety of measures, such as removing passports from parents and children to eliminate their capacity to travel, using electronic tagging devices to monitor parents suspected of attempting to remove their children from the UK, making children a ward of the Court to prevent them from being removed from the UK, and making care orders placing children outside the family home.[86]

Perhaps the initiative that best epitomises the banality of counter-terrorism in the UK today is 'Prevent', a core part of the government's counter-terrorism and counter-extremism strategy.[87] Although Prevent was created in 2003, it was not published until 2006.[88] Responsibility for the policy was initially cross-departmental, with the Department for Communities and Local Government playing a key role in delivery. At that time, Prevent was specifically concerned with tackling the radicalisation of individuals. It sought to do this at three levels: tackling disadvantage in the UK and overseas, deterring those who facilitate terrorism and challenging the ideologies that motivate terrorism.[89] The strategy initially referred only to 'Islamist' terrorism, and all of the named community programmes referred to Muslim communities.[90] That being so, it engaged and funded Muslim charities, community organisations and mosques to deliver programmes that would 'help communities protect themselves and counter the efforts of extremist radicalisers',[91] arguably co-opting them into the prevailing counter-terrorism logic, and, by implication, making non-compliant organisations susceptible to marginalising charges and treatment.[92] In addition to expanding into the community sphere, Prevent also permeated the criminal justice system. In prisons, imams received specialist training 'to support their daily work with all Muslim prisoners, including those imprisoned for terrorist-related charges'.[93] Prevent also engaged the police through activities 'focused upon addressing individual and community level risks'.[94] Prevent policing included community engagement and community intelligence generation; identifying and mounting disruptions against presenting risks; and community impact management.[95]

In 2007, the government supplemented the community-focused aspects of the Prevent programme with a pilot programme known as 'Channel'.[96] Described as 'a community-based initiative', Channel 'uses existing partnerships between the police, local authority representatives and the local community to identify those at risk from violent extremism and to support them, primarily through community based interventions'.[97] Channel was implemented across England and Wales in 2012, with the police coordinating its operation.

In 2011, Prevent was reformulated away from the community cohesion programmes that had characterised its early work towards a focus on individuals. This iteration of Prevent, which was to be delivered by local authorities and the police, stressed the perceived need to:

- respond to the ideological challenge of terrorism and the threat we face from those who promote it;
- prevent people from being drawn into terrorism and ensure that they are given appropriate advice and support; and
- work with sectors and institutions where there are risks of radicalisation which we need to address.[98]

The government listed the priority sectors and institutions as 'education, faith, health, criminal justice and charities'.[99] This strand of the Prevent Strategy was placed on a statutory footing in the Counter-Terrorism and Security Act 2015, which created a statutory duty requiring 'specified authorities' to have 'due regard to the need to prevent people from being drawn into terrorism'.[100] These specified authorities include schools and registered childcare providers, higher and further education providers, the NHS, local government, prisons and probation services, and the police.[101]

At the same time, Channel was also placed on a statutory footing,[102] cementing the police's role in Channel. Under the Act, local authorities must ensure that a multi-agency panel is in place to assess whether individuals are vulnerable to being drawn into terrorism, and to provide and monitor any support plan put in place with respect to an individual.[103] However, the Channel panel must include the chief of police for the relevant police force and, until 2019, only the chief of police could refer an individual to the panel for assessment.[104] Under the Counter-Terrorism and Border Security Act 2019, local authorities may also refer individuals to a Channel panel.[105] While participation in a Channel panel remains 'voluntary',[106] anyone who declines to participate may continue to be monitored and subject to further assessment.[107] Furthermore, if the person in question is a child, a parent or guardian's refusal of consent for their participation in Channel may result in care proceedings being initiated if the child is thought to be at risk from significant harm.[108]

Prevent reveals the scale and reach of the contemporary counter terrorist state in three key aspects. First, it demonstrates the expansion of counter-terrorism outside of the criminal justice sphere and into new fields of activity, such as education and health. In these sectors, Prevent is generally implemented through safeguarding policies and procedures,[109] albeit with attendant monitoring and sanctions that differ from 'normal' safeguarding.[110] Second, through the statutory duty imposed in 2015, Prevent has become a key technique in the expansion of counter-terrorism responsibilities and roles to new actors. A recent report by the Open Society Foundations notes that '[a]lthough the duty applies to institutions rather than individuals, individuals are likely to find themselves required by the institutions for whom they work or are otherwise associated to address the Prevent duty in the course of their work'.[111] This means, in effect, that everyone who is employed by a public authority is now a counter-terrorism actor: teachers, lecturers and nurses have all become part of the counter-terrorist state. Third, Prevent reveals the expansion of the subjects of counter-terrorism law. All children are now monitored for counter-terrorism purposes from the age at which they enter education, including early years care.[112] Monitoring continues until they leave secondary education aged 18. Indeed, any individual who uses the NHS, or attends a university or institution of further education, is also subject to counter-terrorism monitoring. In effect, we are all being counter-terrorised all the time, although probably with different levels of impact and intensity depending on whether we are perceived by those implementing the Prevent duty to be part of a 'suspect community'.[113]

As this makes clear, counter-terrorism now permeates almost every aspect of daily life. Through it, Government has responsibilised private individuals and communities as counter-terrorism actors, while also making them – us – the subjects of counter-terrorism. As well as being permanent, contemporary counter-terrorism is also pervasive; indeed, banal. This state of affairs has been achieved through the steady growth of counter-terrorism law and policy, which in turn, results from the decades long embedding in political practice of conventional wisdoms about counter-terrorism – logics of prevention, intervention, exclusion and at times rights scepticism.[114] The development and emergence of the counter-terrorist state has taken place with limited politicisation in formal, mainstream politics,[115] or at least without sufficient contestation for the direction of travel and the continuing sprawl of counter-terrorism to be resisted effectively.

Part IV: Hegemonic consensus

Security, including counter-terrorism, has long been considered a space of limited political contestation.[116] Instead, the usual practice of opposition has tended to give way to a politics of consensus and deference to the executive when it comes to the state's security activities.[117] This practice extends beyond formal politics to national and international courts,[118] and, arguably, to 'the public' and their demands for action in the face of security failures and terrorist risk.[119] The UK is no exception. Over decades, this bipartisanship has developed into a dominant consensus resulting in a dearth of the contestation necessary for justification and which underpins democratic legitimacy.[120] This consensus can be detected in a remarkable continuity in approach across Labour, Conservative and Conservative-led coalition governments, and a general consensus across political parties on the desirability, in principle, of certain approaches to responding to terrorist threats. It is also visible in the language of agreement on terrorism and counter-terrorism that can be observed in parliamentary and extra-parliamentary settings.

More terrorism, more law: the counter-terrorism legislative cycle

Prior to their general election victory in 1997, the Labour party in opposition had either voted against, or abstained on parliamentary votes to renew the temporary and emergency counter-terrorism legislation throughout the 1980s and 1990s.[121] In power, however, it adopted a responsive mode of counter-terrorism that continued throughout the first decade of the twenty-first century, and which the Conservative-led and

Conservative governments have maintained since taking power in 2010. This was to respond to terrorist incidents or perceived changes in terrorist risk and behaviours by introducing new law, often proposed and debated on an accelerated timetable.

When the Real IRA killed 29 people, one of whom was pregnant with twins, in Omagh on 15 August 1998, the Labour government recalled Parliament to enact the Criminal Justice (Terrorism and Conspiracy) Act 1998. Since 9/11, new counter-terrorism legislation has been proposed following every major new threat or attack, suggesting that the approach to terrorism is more counter-terrorism, rather than a revision of the prevailing approach to counter-terrorism. Hence, the Anti-Terrorism, Crime and Security Act 2001 was introduced in response to 9/11,[122] and the Prevent Strategy was made public in 2006 in response to the 'new' threat perceived to be posed by homegrown terrorists, demonstrated by the London bombings the preceding year.[123] The 2005 attacks also led to the enactment of the Terrorism Act 2006. Conservative governments repeated this pattern: the Counter-Terrorism and Security Act 2015 was enacted to deal with the threat posed by foreign terrorist fighters, and the Counter-Terrorism and Border Security Act 2019 was enacted in response to the multiple terrorist attacks in the UK in 2017.[124]

All of these laws were enacted with significant cross-party support and sometimes on an accelerated parliamentary timetable. The Criminal Justice (Terrorism and Conspiracy) Bill 1998, for example, was published on the evening of 1 September 1998, around two weeks after the Omagh Bombings, and proposed on 2 September 1998. The Bill was debated and concluded that day in the Commons, and considered for less than 12 hours in the Lords the following day. Royal Assent was given within minutes of the Act being passed by the Lords, at around 1:30am.[125] This was notwithstanding the criticism levied by a number of parliamentarians at the timetable imposed by the Government, although almost all went on to vote for the Bill.[126] It also disregarded the acknowledgement, even at senior levels of the civil service, that the law was a response not only to attacks but to 'a sudden crisis of public outrage' and that, in reality, some of the provisions contained within the law were neither usable nor, subsequently, much used.[127] Some counter-terrorism Bills took longer to complete their passage through Parliament. The Terrorism Act 2006, for example, was introduced on 12 October 2005, and received royal assent on 30 March 2006. In some cases, the Government was defeated on one or two provisions. Famously, for instance, Tony Blair's first defeat in the Commons was on his proposal to introduce 90-day pre-charge detention in the Terrorism Bill 2005; instead Parliament 'only' supported 28-day pre-charge detention.[128] Nevertheless, the laws themselves were largely supported and their basic propositions – that more counter-terrorism powers were needed, that detention without charge was appropriate, that data surveillance was necessary and so on – attracted considerable consensus across the aisles.

Agreement in principle on approaches to countering terrorism

Andrew Neal argues that UK parliamentarians are now more engaged with counter-terrorism, understood as part of security politics, than was previously the case. He notes that the quantity of deliberation on security has increased, and thus counter-terrorism is becoming re-politicised 'by volume'.[129] However, even Neal recognises that contestation and disagreement remain somewhat marginal, and that 'the old sovereign prerogatives of "exceptionalism" and "hard security" still exist' and side-line Parliament in qualitative ways.[130] That Parliament now deals with security and counter-terrorism more often than it did before does not trouble the claim that counter-terrorism is an area of cross-party agreement in UK politics.[131]

Even where there is disagreement between or within parties on proposed counter-terrorism law, that disagreement tends to be on the detail, not the principle. Rather than disputing the introduction of new powers, Parliament insists upon safeguards in respect of the exercise of these powers. Rather than reject the proposition that preventive and pre-charge detention is appropriate, it focuses on the length of detention, and maintains a commitment to other forms of deprivation of liberty. For example, while the replacement of control orders with Terrorism Prevention and Investigation Measures initially suggested that the Conservatives and their coalition partner the Liberal Democrats favoured a less rights-restricting approach, the use of TPIMs and their subsequent strengthening[132] indicate that the main political parties accept the propriety of restrictions on liberty for counter-terrorist purposes.[133] Indeed, across counter-terrorist law-making since 2000, we can see cross-party continuity in commitment to the preventive turn in counter-terrorism, to scepticism about the proposition that rights ought to restrict state counter-terrorist actions, and that surveillance, including mass surveillance, should be embraced for counter-terrorist purposes.[134]

Such consensus is also apparent in the main parties' manifestos from the 2017 general election. In *For the Many, Not the Few*, Labour pledged to 'always provide our security agencies with the resources and the powers they need to protect our country and keep us all safe', while 'ensur[ing] that such powers do not weaken our individual rights or civil liberties'.[135] It also pledged to engage in investigatory powers that are 'both proportionate and necessary'.[136] Labour has not abandoned the need to engage in prevention, although it indicated that it would 'address the government's failure to take any effective new measures against a growing problem of extreme or violent radicalisation'.[137] Similarly, the Conservative manifesto, *Forward Together*, privileged counter-terrorism and security funding,[138] and new criminal offences and aggravated offences to tackle extremism, singling out 'Islamist extremism' in particular.[139] Much of this was put in action by the revised CONTEST strategy, published (two years late) in 2018.[140]

The language of agreement

When it comes to parliamentary debates on counter-terrorism in the UK, we can see that across the political parties the language deployed tends to confirm the consensus rather than challenge it. For example, during the second reading debates on the Counter-Terrorism and Border Security Bill 2019, Labour MPs clearly indicated their support. Yvette Cooper MP said that 'the Home Secretary will know that I share his strong belief in taking strong action against the terrorist threat',[141] and Diane Abbott MP noted 'the Opposition broadly support [the Bill]', before going on to express somewhat more reservations than Cooper.[142] Even during a Westminster Hall debate on Prevent[143] there was a remarkable consensus between members on the overall desirability of early counter-extremism intervention of this kind, despite the specific critique of the current statutory duty as 'driving a wedge between authority and the communities'.[144] Security Minister Ben Wallace referred to representations by senior police officers as evidence that 'Prevent is working'.[145] Chairman of the Welsh Conservative Party, Byron Davies, argued it provides 'a set of guidelines that we would be floundering without'.[146] Even the Conservative backbench MP Lucy Allan, who secured the debate and whose speech was critical of it, acknowledged '[w]e all want to see extremism tackled, and the intention of Prevent is, in theory, [to do so]'.[147] Across the aisle, Naz Shah said '[a]lthough I am a critic of the implementation of Prevent, it is clear to me that we need a prevention strategy'.[148] While Prevent was described by one MP as being 'misconceived, counterproductive and [not] actually mak[ing] people any safer',[149] and thus in need of reform, the basic principle underpinning it – preventive, early intervention including by spreading responsibility for counter-terrorism to non-state actors – was broadly reinforced across the political spectrum.

Cross-party consensus is not per se undesirable; after all, in some senses democratic deliberation aspires to consensus, not least to reduce or avoid the stasis that can result from fractious political debate.[150] However, such benefits are reduced when the premises of an approach or policy are not examined and evaluated. When a consensus occurs in the counter-terrorism domain without looking at the driving principles, it reinforces rather than challenges the exceptionalist narratives that underpin repressive state activity. It enables the expansion of counter-terrorism into the everyday, into new fields of governance, and into the work of more actors. In other words, it creates the political conditions for the emergence of a counter-terrorist state, and seems to constrain opportunities for that state and its activities to be challenged. In this way, the consensus that we observe in counter-terrorism politics in the UK can be described as hegemonic. Counter-terrorism becomes and acts as the hegemon. It emerges through political consent, dominates the policy domain; pervades multiple fields of governance, comes to determine in large part the everyday experience of the state especially for 'suspect communities', and its basic premises seem largely to go undisturbed within formal parliamentary politics.

Part V: Counter-terrorism review: enabling the counter-terrorist state?

If there is a hegemonic consensus that underpins the emergence and continuation of the counter-terrorist state, how then can the emergence and operation of counter-terrorism review be understood? Counter-terrorism review has emerged alongside, and sometimes as part of, the law and policy that constitute the counter-terrorist state. Indeed, as noted earlier, the Northern Ireland (Emergency Provisions) Act 1973 was drafted following a review of the existing legal framework for countering terrorism in Northern Ireland.[151] That legislation also had counter-terrorism review built in; it contained a sunset clause that meant the Act would expire after 12 months unless the Secretary of State made an order to continue it in force and Parliament approved that order.[152] Similarly, the Prevention of Terrorism (Temporary Provisions) Act 1974 contained a sunset clause,[153] meaning that Parliament had the opportunity to review the legislation before approving any order laid by the Secretary of State to continue it in force.

As this suggests, counter-terrorism review emerged, in some forms at least, contemporaneously with the counter-terrorist state. Its development has not been systematic, but rather piecemeal, reflecting the responsive and ad hoc development of the counter-terrorist state that we have already laid out. At times, the emergence of the counter-terrorist state was facilitated by antecedent review processes. For example, in 1977, during the parliamentary debate on whether to approve the Secretary of State's order to continue the Prevention of Terrorism (Temporary Provisions) Act 1976 in force for another year, there were a number of calls for an inquiry into the operation of the Act. In response, Home Secretary Merlyn Rees promised to 'consider ways of looking at the legislation'.[154] In December that year, he announced that he had decided to initiate a review to 'assess the operation of' the legislation, 'with particular regard to' its effectiveness 'and its effect on the liberties of the subject'.[155] Following a first review in 1978,[156] Earl Jellicoe was appointed to conduct a second review in 1983. He recommended that the existing legislation should be replaced by a new Act, which should be subject to annual renewal and have a five-year life-span, after which Parliament would have the opportunity to enact new primary legislation if it considered it necessary to do so.[157] This recommendation was implemented in section 17 of the Prevention of Terrorism (Temporary Provisions) Act 1984. While both sunset clauses provided opportunities to consider the operation of counter-terrorism law, they neither prevented nor slowed the development of the counter-terrorist state. Jellicoe's further recommendation that 're-enactment should be preceded by a review of the Act's operation and consideration of suggested amendments' was not, however, implemented in statute.[158]

At other times, counter-terrorism review was established in response to political pressure. In 1984, for example, during parliamentary debate on the Prevention of Terrorism (Temporary Provisions) Bill, Lord Elton announced that the new legislation would be subject to an annual review by an independent person.[159] This was not simply a magnanimous gesture; Lord Elton was attempting to head off a House of Lords amendment that sought to incorporate a commission of inquiry into the text of the legislation.[160] This annual review mechanism subsequently developed into the Independent Reviewer of Terrorism Legislation, now operating on a statutory footing and, as we will see in Chapter 3, one of the most significant of the counter-terrorism review mechanisms in operation today, at least for our interviewees. A more recent example is the decision – after many years of government refusal – to establish an independent review of Prevent. On 22 January 2019, Security Minister Ben Wallace announced that he had 'decided that the time is now right to initiate a review of Prevent'.[161] However, he was simply conceding to the inevitable; the House of Lords had already inserted an amendment into the Counter-Terrorism and Border Security Bill 2019 that would establish a review of Prevent.[162]

Counter-terrorism review has, at times, been established to ameliorate parliamentary concerns over the enactment of new, often controversial, counter-terrorism powers. As such, it is a response to rare, but usually marginal, ruptures in the hegemonic consensus outlined above. For example, in the aftermath of 9/11, the government introduced new legislation that would enable the Secretary of State indefinitely to detain non-UK-citizen terrorist suspects who could not otherwise be deported.[163] The controversial nature of these provisions led the government to include an annual renewal sunset clause in the Anti-Terrorism Crime and Security Bill 2001.[164] However, Parliament was not persuaded that this was sufficient, and two additional counter-terrorism review mechanisms were incorporated into the legislation during its passage: annual review by the Independent Reviewer of Terrorism Legislation of the indefinite detention provisions,[165] and the establishment of a Privy Council Review Committee to review the whole Act within two years of its enactment.[166] The legislative process surrounding the enactment of the Prevention of Terrorism Act 2005 provides another example. In this case, Parliament was divided over what type of sunset clause to include in the legislation. The House of Lords and the Opposition in the House of Commons argued in favour of a clause that would lead to the expiry of the legislation after a certain period of time without any opportunity to renew it, however the government rejected this proposition.[167] This led to a lengthy 'ping pong' between the House of Commons and the House of Lords. Ultimately, Home Secretary Charles Clarke proposed a compromise that Parliament accepted: the new legislation would include a one-year sunset clause that could be renewed by the Secretary of State with the approval of Parliament.[168]

In these instances, mechanisms of counter-terrorism review were inserted as concessions to the concerns of parliamentarians and functioned to ensure the passage of the relevant law and instantiation of the powers and provisions it contained. Sunset clauses, in particular, allowed for Parliament to treat proposals as if they were temporary – as if they might lapse – even though they never did,[169] and the renewal debates were rather less than rigorous or well attended.[170] Sunset clauses allowed these measures to *appear* temporary and within the conventional exceptional paradigm of counter-terrorism law, even though in reality they operated in a permanent manner. This was not surprising: it reflected experience with sunset clauses in earlier counter-terrorism laws.[171] Furthermore, the provision for independent review in both Bills implied that any further renewal would be based on the evidence produced by those reviews. However, renewal was assured, notwithstanding concerns about the rights and societal consequences of these laws being raised in the mandated reviews.[172] In other words, in these situations, counter-terrorism review provided a form of assurance that appeared to legitimate the expansion and solidification of counter-terrorism as part of the ordinary legal landscape in the UK. These examples illustrate the potential for counter-terrorism review to bolster and legitimate the counter-terrorist state, particularly where it is cynically deployed, and when the political clamour leading to its establishment is not matched by continuing political attention and contestation.

Counter-terrorism review can also have its potential to challenge the counter-terrorist state limited by its design. The Terrorism Act 2000 provides a useful illustration. As originally enacted, this legislation required the Secretary of State to lay a report on the working of the Act before Parliament once every 12 months.[173] Parliament may avail itself of the reports laid before it in order to understand the operation of the Act, but there is no requirement for it to do anything with that information, apart from incorporate it into its everyday political activities, should a relevant debate arise, or question be tabled or asked, because the Act is permanent and not subject to a sunset clause. Such reports might feed into the work of parliamentary committees, MPs and Peers, but only at their instigation. The system of review is not designed in a way that imposes, or even especially enables, reports to have a broader impact.[174]

Even where review outputs must be considered in Parliament, the legislation that establishes them can limit the scope for this consideration to impact on the operation of the law. For instance, Lord Shackleton conducted a review of the Prevention of Terrorism (Temporary Provisions) Act 1974 and the Prevention of Terrorism (Temporary Provisions) Act 1976 in 1978.[175] The opportunity for this review to be discussed was the debate on the annual renewal of the Prevention of Terrorism (Temporary Provisions) Act 1976 in March 1979.[176] However, in that debate the only matter for Parliament to determine was whether to continue the law in force, or allow it to lapse; it was not possible to lay amendments to the law based on the findings of the review. Parliament was left only with the 'nuclear' option of allowing the law to lapse if it wished to implement improvements based on the review's findings; an outcome that was then, and is now, likely too politically unpalatable for most politicians seriously to consider. The recommendations from Lord Shackleton's report that required an amendment to the Act were never implemented.

Similarly, parliamentary time and schedules might be arranged, or, indeed, manipulated, so as to limit the effect of a mandated review or sunset clause, by requiring renewal based on the affirmative resolution procedure. That is what tended to happen with the annual renewal debates on the Prevention of Terrorism Act 2005.[177] Section 13 of that

Act required each House of Parliament to approve any draft order made by the Secretary of State. If it was not approved within 40 days of the order being laid, the legislation would cease to have effect.[178] Furthermore, if the sunset clause was due to expire within the 40-day period allowed by the affirmative resolution procedure, and Parliament did not vote to renew the legislation, the Act would cease to have effect on that date.[179] In the case of the Prevention of Terrorism Act 2005, the legislation would expire on 11 March in any given year if not continued in force. The Secretary of State consistently timed the renewal debates for well within this 40-day period. The earliest any of these renewal debates took place, which was the first renewal debate, was 15 February in the House of Commons, less than a month from the expiry date. The latest was a House of Lords debate that was scheduled for 8 March, just three days before the legislation would expire.[180] As debates on this law showed, leaving so little time to debate renewal and demand accountability of ministers is a technique of simultaneously legitimating the counter-terrorist state (by renewing its laws following parliamentary debate) and exploiting the risks of security failure that may follow a failure to renew (by leaving members and Peers so little time that they considered they not could reasonably vote against renewal as there would not be enough time to replace it before it lapsed).[181]

Conclusion

This critical redescription of the state of counter-terrorism in the UK shows that, even if parliamentarians and politicians continue to use the language of exception when making counter-terrorism law,[182] that exception is no longer temporary; the counter-terrorism powers of the state are no longer limited to the classical domains of 'security'; and the counter-terrorism enterprise is now truly a social one, spread (by law, by policy and by political expectation) across the polity into schools, hospitals, communities, even families. Counter-terrorism has become part of the everyday experience of living in the UK, from welfare officers in sports clubs having to do 'Prevent training',[183] to automated messages reminding us to 'see it, say it, sorted' on public transport.[184] The quotidian, pervasive and socialised nature of counter-terrorism is such that it must be understood as the ordinary state of affairs, even if – judged against the law in the first half of the twentieth century – it may seem extraordinary. What we have shown in this chapter is that this state – the counter-terrorist state – has emerged slowly but steadily over recent decades, reflected and enabled in legislation that, even when called 'temporary', has rarely lapsed with the passage of time. Instead, it has been approved, retained, continued in force and applied through a cross-party consensus that reflects the hegemonic nature of narratives of counter-terrorism in the UK.

This counter-terrorist state uses a mixture of conventional, indirect and regulatory coercion to pursue its security goals and, in doing so, can intrude on individuals and communities, as well as extending the reach of the state's power in significant ways. These shifts in state form and in the modes of the state's operation raise the kinds of questions about how accountability can be ensured that we canvassed in the Introduction. As we have seen, at least some forms and mechanisms of counter-terrorism review emerged alongside the counter-terrorist state: the Independent Reviewer of Terrorism Legislation, the use of sunset clauses, and closed proceedings, for example. Although counter-terrorism review might bolster the power of the counter-terrorist state, it also has the potential to provide a route to ensuring its accountability. We now turn to assessing whether that potential is fulfilled.

Notes

1   National Counter Terrorism Security Office, 'Vehicle Hire Companies to Reduce Terrorism Risk' (17 December 2018) www.gov.uk/government/news/vehicle-hire-companies-to-reduce-terrorism-risk [Accessed 8 February 2019].

2   Department for Transport, *UK Rental Vehicle Security Scheme (RVSS) Code of Practice & Supporting Guidance* (Crown Copyright 2018) 6.

3   Ibid 9.

4   We are not the first to make the observation that continuing expansion of counter-terrorism in the UK has tones of banality. Charlotte Heath-Kelly and Erzsébet Strausz note that Prevent is presented as the 'banal' extension of safeguarding in much official narrative: Charlotte Heath-Kelly and Erzsébet Strausz, 'The Banality of Counterterrorism "After, After 9/11"? Perspectives on the Prevent Duty from the UK Health Care Sector' (2019) 12(1) Critical Studies on Terrorism 89.

5   We are interested here in the types of violence waged by organisations seeking to change the status of their constitutional relationship with the UK, not in violence occasioned by traditional warfare, such the First and Second World Wars, or in NATO campaigns, such as in the conflict in the former Yugoslavia.

6   Also known as the Indian Rebellion, the War of Independence of 1857, the First War of Indian Independence, the Revolt of 1857 and (often pejoratively) the 'Indian Mutiny of 1857'. At the time, the British used the term 'the Indian Insurrection' to describe the events. See generally the seven-volume Crispin Bates (ed), *Mutiny at the Margins: New Perspectives on the Indian Uprising of 1857* (Sage Publishing 2003–17) and the AHRC-funded project from which it emerged. Available from: www.csas.ed.ac.uk/mutiny/index.html [Accessed 28 March 2019].

7   This is not to suggest a complete isolation of experience and approach between approaches 'at home' and 'in Empire'. Caroline Kennedy-Pipe, *The Origins of the Present Troubles in Northern Ireland* (Routledge 1997).

[8]   Niall Ó Dochartaigh, *From Civil Rights to Armalites: Derry and the Birth of the Irish Troubles* (2nd edn, Palgrave Macmillan 2005); Simon Prince, *Northern Ireland's '68: Civil Rights, Global Revolt and the Origins of the Troubles* (Irish Academic Press 2007).

[9]   The Government of Ireland Act 1920 established separate parliaments for 'Southern Ireland' and 'Northern Ireland' (s 1(1)), and a legal division between 'the six counties' and the rest of Ireland was recognised (s 1(2)). When the Irish Free State was established (by the Articles of Agreement for a Treaty between Great Britain and Ireland 1921), Northern Ireland was given the right to withdraw from the Free State, which it did. Partition continues today.

[10] See: Jonathan Tonge, *Northern Ireland: Conflict and Change* (2nd edn, Pearson Publishing 2002) ch 2.

[11] This Act substantially re-enacted many of the emergency powers originally introduced in the Restoration of Order in Ireland Act 1920, which was enacted to combat the violence which emerged as the Irish War of Independence. The 1920 Act was itself based on the Defence of the Realm Acts 1914–1915, which were enacted during the First World War to ensure public safety and the 'defence of the realm'. See: Colm Campbell, *Emergency Law in Ireland, 1918–1925* (Clarendon Press 1994).

[12] Section 12(1) of the Civil Authorities (Special Powers) Act (Northern Ireland) 1922 incorporated a one-year sunset clause; however, the legislation was renewed annually until 1928, when it was extended for a further five years as the Civil Authorities (Special Powers) Act (Northern Ireland) 1928. In 1933, a new version of the Act was made permanent and the Civil Authorities (Special Powers) Act (Northern Ireland) 1933 remained on the statute books for a further 40 years. For a full history of the development of special powers in Northern Ireland, see: Laura K. Donohue, *Counter-Terrorist Law and Emergency Powers in the UK 1922–2000* (Irish Academic Press 2007).

[13] The RUC was routinely armed and supported by the Ulster Special Constabulary, an auxiliary paramilitary reserve force. For a history of the development of policing in Northern Ireland, see: Graham Ellison and Jim Smyth, *The Crowned Harp: Policing Northern Ireland* (Pluto Press 2000) 18–31.

[14] Schedule to the Civil Authorities (Special Powers) Act (Northern Ireland) 1922, s 1.

[15] Ibid s 4.

[16] Ibid s 3(4)(b).

[17] Laura K. Donohue, 'Regulating Northern Ireland: The Special Powers Acts, 1922–1972' (1998) 41(4) The Historical Journal 1089.

[18] On the development of the civil rights movement, the emergence of violence, and the state response see for example David McKittrick and David McVea, *Making Sense of the Troubles: A History of the Northern Ireland Conflict* (Penguin 2012).

[19] For example: Karl Hack, 'The Malayan Emergency as Counter-Insurgency Paradigm' (2009) 32(3) Journal of Strategic Studies 383; Huw Bennett, *Fighting the Mau Mau: The British Army and Counter-Insurgency in the Kenya Emergency* (Cambridge University Press 2013); Preston Jordan Lim, *The Evolution of British Counter-Insurgency during the Cyprus Revolt 1955–1959* (Palgrave Pivot 2018); Spencer Mawby, *British Policy in Aden and the Protectorates 1955–67: Last Outpost of a Middle East Empire* (Routledge 2005). For a broad critical perspective see for example Brian Drohan, *Brutality in an Age of Human Rights: Activism and Counterinsurgency at the End of the British Empire* (Cornell University Press 2017).

[20] Drohan (n 19).

21 For example, the first General Officer Commanding Northern Ireland, Lieutenant General Sir Ian Henry Freeland, who commanded 2nd Battalion during the Cyprus Emergency and General Sir Frank Kitson, who served during the Kenyan, Malayan, and Cyprus emergencies before being posted to Northern Ireland in 1970. Kitson's *Low Intensity Operations: Subversion, Insurgency, Peacekeeping* (Faber and Faber 1970), had some influence on British Army counter-insurgency doctrine and informed his approach to the Troubles in Northern Ireland.

22 People born in Northern Ireland are now also entitled to Irish citizenship in recognition of their 'birthright' to identify as either Irish or British: Northern Ireland Office, *The Belfast Agreement: An Agreement Reached at the Multi-Party Talks on Northern Ireland* (Cm 3883, 1998) 2.

23 Northern Ireland Civil Rights Association, *'We Shall Overcome'…The History of the Struggle for Civil Rights in Northern Ireland 1968–1978* (Northern Ireland Civil Rights Association 1978).

24 Paul Dixon, *Northern Ireland: The Politics of War and Peace* (2nd edn, Palgrave 2008) 102.

25 The Northern Ireland Government reintroduced internment in August 1971. Over a two-day period, the British Army arrested and interned 342 suspected terrorists, killing ten people during the violence that this provoked. For a timeline of internment in Northern Ireland see: Martin Melaugh, 'Internment – A Chronology of the Main Events' (Conflict Archive on the Internet Web Service, 6 February 2019). Available from: https://cain.ulster.ac.uk/events/intern/chron. htm [Accessed 17 March 2019].

26 Such punishment included the use of the 'five techniques', 'developed since the [Second World] War to deal with a number of situations involving internal security' including 'counter insurgency operations in Palestine, Malaya, Kenya and Cyprus': Lord Parker of Waddington, *Report of the Committee of Privy Councillors Appointed to Consider Authorised Procedures for the Interrogation of Persons Suspected of Terrorism* (Cmnd 4901, 1972) 3. The European Court of Human Rights held that the five techniques constitute inhuman or degrading treatment or punishment: *Ireland v United Kingdom* (1979–80) 2 EHRR 25. See also Sir Edmund Compton, *Report of the Enquiry into Allegations against the Security Forces of Physical Brutality in Northern Ireland Arising out of Events on the 9th August 1971* (Cmnd 4823, 1971) 71.

27 David McKittrick et al (eds), *Lost Lives: The Stories of the Men, Women and Children who Died as a Result of the Northern Ireland Troubles* (Mainstream Publishing 2007) 139–72.

28 In 1970, the RUC, which had been routinely armed since it was founded on 1 June 1922, was disarmed in accordance with the Police Act (Northern Ireland) 1970 in order to implement recommendations of Baron Hunt, *Report of the Advisory Committee on Police in Northern Ireland* (Cmd 535, 1969). With the deterioration of the security situation in the early 1970s, the RUC was gradually rearmed.

29 This 1933 Act replicated the measures in the Civil Authorities (Special Powers) Act (Northern Ireland) 1922. The quote comes from the preamble of the Act.

30 Lord Diplock, *Report of the Commission to Consider Legal Procedures to Deal with Terrorist Activities in Northern Ireland* (Cmnd 5185, 1972) 1.

31 Ibid 14.

32 Ibid 5–6.

33 The term 'scheduled offences' refers to the list of offences in Schedule 4 of the Act, that is offences that were to be tried by the court without a jury. They included murder, manslaughter, various offences relating to damage to property

and causing harm to persons, offences relating to explosive substances and making bombs, and firearms offences: Northern Ireland (Emergency Provisions) Act 1973, s 2 and sch 4.

34 Ibid s 5.

35 Ibid s 10.

36 Ibid ss 13–17.

37 Ibid ss 19–23.

38 Ibid sch 1.

39 In 1939, shortly before the outbreak of the Second World War, the UK Parliament enacted the Prevention of Violence (Temporary Provisions) Act 1939, to counter an IRA bombing campaign in Britain. The Act granted the Secretary of State the power to exclude or prohibit IRA suspects from entering the UK, but did not legislate for terrorism in the round.

40 Prevention of Terrorism (Temporary Provisions) Act 1974, s 1: introducing a new proscription regime to replicate and complement (although not replace) that which operated in Northern Ireland under the Northern Ireland (Emergency Provisions) Act 1973; Prevention of Terrorism (Temporary Provisions) Act 1974, s 3 empowering the Secretary of State to exclude Northern Irish terrorist suspects from Great Britain.

41 The police could detain a person arrested under the Act for an initial 48 hours, after which the Secretary of State could extend their detention for a period no longer than a further five days: ibid s 7(2).

42 Ibid s 12.

43 Ibid s 17.

44 Ibid s 12(3)(b).

45 Ibid s 9, 11, 12.

46 PIRA declared a ceasefire on 31 August 1994, followed shortly thereafter by the main loyalist and other republican paramilitary organisations. The IRA ceasefire was broken from February 1996 until July 1997, when a further IRA ceasefire was announced. Since then ceasefires have largely remained in place, although sectarian and paramilitary violence still occur. See for example Roger Mac Ginty, Orla T. Muldoon and Neil Ferguson, 'No War, No Peace: Northern Ireland after the Agreement' (2007) 28(1) Political Psychology 1; Peter Shirlow and Colin Coulter, 'Northern Ireland: 20 Years after the Cease-Fires' (2014) 37 Studies in Conflict and Terrorism 713.

47 Lord Lloyd of Berwick, *Inquiry into Legislation against Terrorism* (Cm 3420, 1996).

48 As with the Prevention of Terrorism (Temporary Provisions) Act 1974, the Northern Ireland (Emergency Provisions) Act 1973 was also amended, extended, and re-enacted on several occasions throughout the 1970s, 1980s and 1990s. The Northern Ireland (Emergency Provisions) Act 1996 was the version of the Act that was in force when Lord Lloyd commenced his review.

49 Lord Lloyd of Berwick (n 47) 23–4.

50 Ibid 24–5.

51 Ibid 173–6.

52 Ibid 99–102.

53 Northern Ireland Office (n 22) 21.

54 Home Office, *Legislation against Terrorism: A Consultation Paper* (Cm 4178, 1998).

55 The exception was Part 7, which created a temporary emergency regime for Northern Ireland that required annual renewal and that would expire at the end of five years: Terrorism Act 2000, s 112.

[56] For example it is an offence, without reasonable excuse, to collect or make a record of information 'of a kind likely to be useful to a person committing or preparing an act of terrorist', or to possess a document containing such information: Terrorism Act 2000, s 58.

[57] Ibid s 1. See also *R v Gul* [2013] UKSC 64; Alan Greene, 'The Quest for a Satisfactory Definition of Terrorism: *R v Gul*' (2017) 77(5) Modern Law Review 780.

[58] Terrorism Act 2000, ss 19–22A.

[59] Andrew Ashworth and Lucia Zedner, *Preventive Justice* (Oxford University Press 2014). See also Steve Hewitt, 'Great Britain: Terrorism and Counter-terrorism since 1968' in Andrew Silke (ed), *Routledge Handbook of Terrorism and Counter-Terrorism* (Routledge 2019) 540–51.

[60] That is, within the meaning of European Convention on Human Rights (ECHR) art 15.

[61] Derogation contained in a Note Verbale from the Permanent Representation of the UK, dated 18 December 2001, registered by the Secretariat General on 18 December 2001.

[62] Ibid, withdrawn by a Note Verbale from the Permanent Representation of the UK, dated 16 March 2005, registered at the Secretariat General on 16 March 2005.

[63] This is well illustrated by the policy of deportation with assurances, on which see David Anderson and Clive Walker, *Deportation with Assurances* (Cm 9462, 2017).

[64] Temporary Exclusion Orders were introduced by the Counter-Terrorism and Security Act 2015, s 2.

[65] This is both through the Prevent strategy (the first published version of which is HM Government, *Countering International Terrorism: The United Kingdom's Strategy* (Cm 6888, 2006)) and the United Kingdom's Counter Extremism Strategy (HM Government, *Counter-Extremism Strategy* (Cm 9148, 2015)).

[66] Anti-Terrorism, Crime and Security Act 2001, s 23.

[67] Control orders were introduced by the Prevention of Terrorism Act 2005.

[68] Terrorism Act 2000, ss 15–17 and 54–5; Terrorism Act 2006, s 6; Counter-Terrorism and Security Act 2015, pt 1.

[69] Investigatory Powers Act 2016.

[70] Charities Act 2006, ch 1. Prior to 2006, the Charity Commission had no legal existence as a body: Charities Act 2006, explanatory notes paras 37–41.

[71] Charity Commission, *Counter-Terrorism Strategy* (Revised September 2015/First published July 2008).

[72] Ibid.

[73] In the UK much of this is through EU Directives implemented by primary and secondary law, especially Directive (EU) 2015/849 of the European Parliament and of the Council of 20 May 2015 on preventing the use of the financial system for money laundering or terrorist financing (4th Anti-Money-Laundering Directive) transposed into UK law by the Money Laundering, Terrorist Financing and Transfer of Funds (Information on the Payer) Regulations 2017, SI 2017/692. This supplements primary legislation including the Proceeds of Crime Act 2002 and Criminal Finance Act 2017.

[74] Anthony Amicelle, 'Towards a "New" Political Anatomy of Financial Surveillance' (2011) 4(2) Security Dialogue 161. Serious questions about the effectiveness of the prevailing approach to countering terrorist financing prevail: see for example Michael Levi, 'Combating the Financing of Terrorism: A History and Assessment

of the Control of "Threat Finance'" (2010) 50(4) British Journal of Criminology 650.

75 Terrorism Act 2000, pt 3; Proceeds of Crime Act 2002, pt 7; Money Laundering, Terrorist Financing and Transfer of Funds (Information on the Payer) Regulations 2017, SI 2017/692, s 104.

76 Counter-Terrorism Act 2008, sch 7, pt 3.

77 See: Interception of Communications Act 1985 (repealed); Regulation of Investigatory Powers Act 2000, pt 1, ch 1 (repealed).

78 Initially enabled by the EU Data Retention Directive (EC) 2006/24 of the European Parliament and of the Council of 15 March 2006 on the retention of data generated or processed in connection with the provision of publicly available electronic communications services or of public communications networks and amending Directive 2002/58/EC, temporarily enabled through the Data Retention and Investigatory Powers Act 2014 (DRIPA) following Joined Cases C-293/12 and C-594/12 *Digital Rights Ireland and Seitlinger v Minister for Communications, Marine and Natural Resources* [2014] ECR I–238, [2014] 2 All ER (Comm) 1, now the Investigatory Powers Act 2016, pts 3 and 4.

79 Marieke de Goede, 'The Chain of Security' (2018) 44(1) Review of International Studies 24.

80 Regulation (EC) 2320/2002 of the European Parliament and of the Council of 16 December 2002 establishing common rules in the field of civil aviation security (Text with EEA relevance) – Interinstitutional declaration; Commission Regulation (EC) 622/2003 of 4 April 2003 laying down measures for the implementation of the common basic standards on aviation security; Commission Regulation (EC) 1217/2003 of 4 July 2003 laying down common specifications for national civil aviation security quality control programme; Commission Regulation (EC) 1486/2003 of 22 August 2003 laying down procedures for conducting Commission inspections in the field of civil aviation security; Regulation (EC) No 300/2008 of the European Parliament and of the Council of 11 March 2008 on common rules in the field of civil aviation security and repealing Regulation (EC) 2320/2002.

81 Directive (EU) 2016/681 of the European Parliament and of the Council of 27 April 2016 on the use of passenger name record (PNR) data for the prevention, detection, investigation and prosecution of terrorist offences and serious crime. This has been implemented in the UK by Passenger Name Record Data and Miscellaneous Amendments Regulations 2018.

82 See generally: Louise Butcher, 'Aviation: Security' (House of Commons Library Standard Note SN/BT/1246, 14 June 2011).

83 British Nationality Act 1981, s 40(2).

84 HM Government, *HM Government Transparency Report 2018: Disruptive and Investigatory Powers* (Cm, 2018) 26–7.

85 British Nationality Act 1981, s 40(4A).

86 See: Sir James Munby, 'Radicalisation Cases in the Family Courts' (*Courts and Tribunal Judiciary*, 8 October 2015), Available from: www.judiciary.uk/wp-content/uploads/2015/10/pfd-guidance-radicalisation-cases.pdf [Accessed 12 February 2019]; Rachel Taylor, 'Religion as Harm? Radicalisation, Extremism and Child Protection' (2018) 30(1) Child and Family Law Quarterly 41.

87 Clive Walker, 'Counter-terrorism and Counter-extremism: the UK Policy Spirals' [2018] Public Law 725; Amrit Singh, *Eroding Trust: The UK's PREVENT Counter-*

Extremism Strategy in Health and Education (Open Society Justice Initiative 2016); Joint Committee on Human Rights, *Counter Extremism: Second Report of Session 2016–17* (2016–17, HL 39, HC 105).

88 The first published version of the Prevent strategy is in: HM Government, *Countering International Terrorism* (n 65).

89 Ibid 1–2.

90 Ibid para 25 and paras 47–63.

91 Ibid 13.

92 See for example the different approach of the Muslim Council of Britain compared with Cage as noted in the Home Affairs Committee, *Radicalisation, the Counternarrative and Identifying the Tipping Point* (HC 2016–17, 135) paras 106 and 89–90. See further Singh (n 87); Christina Pantazis and Simon Pemberton, 'From the "Old" to the "New" Suspect Community: Examining the Impacts of Recent UK Counter-Terrorist Legislation' (2009) 49(5) British Journal of Criminology 646.

93 HM Government, *Countering International Terrorism* (n 65) 13.

94 Martin Innes et al, *Assessing the Effects of Prevent Policing: A Report to the Association of Chief Police Officers* (Cardiff University 2011) 3.

95 Ibid.

96 Singh (n 87) 22.

97 Ibid 23.

98 HM Government, *Prevent Strategy* (Cm 8092, 2011) 7.

99 Ibid 63.

100 Counter-Terrorism and Security Act 2015, s 26.

101 Ibid sch 6.

102 Ibid pt 5, ch 2.

103 Ibid ss 36(1); 36(4).

104 Ibid s 37(1)(b); ibid s 36(3).

105 Counter-Terrorism and Border Security Act 2019, s 20.

106 Counter-Terrorism and Security Act 2015, s 36(4)(b).

107 Ibid s 36(4)(e).

108 HM Government, *Channel Duty Guidance: Protecting Vulnerable People from Being Drawn into Terrorism: Statutory Guidance for Channel Panel Members and Partners of Local Panels* (Crown Copyright 2015) para 79. The concept of 'significant harm' is defined by reference to the Children Act 1989.

109 Notably, Charlotte Heath-Kelly and Erzsébet Strausz find that NHS safeguarding professionals do see Prevent as different to 'normal' safeguarding: 'Counter-Terrorism in the NHS: Evaluating Prevent Duty Safeguarding in the NHS' (*University of Warwick*, 2018), Available from: https://warwick.ac.uk/fac/soc/pais/research/researchcentres/irs/counterterrorisminthenhs/ [Accessed 17 March 2019].

110 Higher Education and Research Act 2017, pt 1, ss 15–21 and 77; HM Government, *Prevent Duty Guidance: for Further Education Institutions in England and Wales* (Home Office 2015) para 30.

111 Singh (n 87) 27.

112 Counter-Terrorism and Security Act 2015, sch 6, pt 1. On the implications and operation of Prevent in educational settings see: Rights Watch UK, *Preventing Education? Human Rights and UK Counter-Terrorism Policy in Schools* (Rights Watch UK 2016); Joel Busher et al, *What the Prevent Duty Means for Schools and Colleges in England: An Analysis of Educationalists' Experiences* (July 2017), Available from:

http://azizfoundation.org.uk/wp-content/uploads/2017/07/What-the-Prevent-Duty-means-for-schools-and-colleges-in-England.pdf [Accessed 17 March 2019].

[113] Paddy Hillyard, *Suspect Community: People's Experience of the Prevention of Terrorism Acts in Britain* (Pluto Press 1993); Pantazis and Pemberton (n 92); Mary Hickman et al, '"Suspect Communities"? Counter-Terrorism Policy, the Press, and the Impact on Irish and Muslim Communities in Britain' (*London Metropolitan University*, 2011), Available from: www.city.ac.uk/__data/assets/pdf_file/0005/96287/suspect-communities-report-july2011.pdf [Accessed 17 March 2019].

[114] Lydia Morgan and Fiona de Londras, 'Is there a Conservative Counter-Terrorism?' (2018) 29(2) King's Law Journal 187.

[115] Politicisation here is understood as controversy and contestation in policy fields, vital to accountability and publicity. This borrows the notion from political science. See: Matthew Wood, 'Politicisation, Depoliticisation and Anti-Politics: Towards a Multilevel Research Agenda' (2016) 14(4) Political Studies Review 521; Laura Jenkins, 'The Difference Genealogy Makes: Strategies for Politicisation or How to Extend Capacities for Autonomy' (2011) 59(1) Political Studies 156.

[116] See for example Claudia Aradau, 'Security and the Democratic Scene: Desecuritization and Emancipation' (2004) 7(4) Journal of International Relations and Development 388; Jef Huysmans, *Security Unbound: Enacting Democratic Limits* (Routledge 2014); Ole Wæver, 'Politics, Security, Theory' (2011) 42(4–5) Security Dialogue 465.

[117] See: Andrew W. Neal, *Security as Politics: Beyond the State of Exception* (Edinburgh University Press 2019).

[118] For an overview of the debates on this in legal scholarship see Fergal F. Davis and Fiona de Londras, 'Counter-Terrorist Judicial Review: Beyond Dichotomies' in Fergal F. Davis and Fiona de Londras (eds), *Critical Debates on Counter-Terrorism Judicial Review* (Cambridge University Press 2014).

[119] See generally Fiona de Londras, *Detention in the 'War on Terror': Can Human Rights Fight Back?* (Cambridge University Press 2011), ch 1; Isabelle Duyvesteyn and Bart Schuurman 'Popular Support and (Counter) Terrorism' in Silke (n 59) 416–24.

[120] This is not to conflate parliamentary politics with democracy; the concepts are not coterminous, particularly in the UK where Parliament's role has historically been 'to facilitate legitimate government': Alexandra Kelso, *Parliamentary Reform at Westminster* (Manchester University Press 2009) 15.

[121] HC Deb 14 March 1996, vol 273, col 1133.

[122] See generally Helen Fenwick, 'The Anti-Terrorism, Crime and Security Act 2001: A Proportionate Response to 11 September?' (2002) 65(5) Modern Law Review 724.

[123] HM Government, *Countering International Terrorism* (n 65) 11.

[124] When introducing the second reading in the Commons, Home Secretary, Sajid Javid MP, said 'as we know all too well, there were five terrorist attacks last year. Thirty-six people were murdered, and many more are still grieving or coming to terms with life-changing injuries as a result of the terrorist atrocities in London and Manchester. We owe it to the victims and survivors to do our very best to prevent such attacks from happening again […] This is what the wide-ranging Counter-Terrorism and Border Security Bill is all about; it is about keeping the people of this country safe.' HC Deb 11 June 2018, vol 642, col 630.

[125] For analysis of the Act itself see Clive Walker, 'The Bombs in Omagh and their Aftermath: The Criminal Justice (Terrorism and Conspiracy) Act 1998' (1999) 62(6) Modern Law Review 879.

126 See the debate on the business motion introducing the Bill and its timetable in the House of Commons on 2 September 1998: HC Deb 2 September 1998, vol 317, cols 713–36.

127 Remarks of Sir John Chilcot to the Constitution Committee, reported in Constitution Committee, *Fast-Track Legislation: Constitutional Implications and Safeguards Volume 1: Report* (HL 2008–9, 116-I) para 75; ibid paras 72–6.

128 28-day detention was introduced by 323 votes to 290, whereas 90-day detention was defeated by 322 to 291. Terrorism Act 2006, ss 23–5.

129 Andrew W. Neal, 'Parliamentary Security Politics as Politicisation by Volume' (2018) 5(3) European Review of International Studies 70.

130 Ibid 90.

131 See generally Morgan and de Londras (n 114) for discussion.

132 Counter-Terrorism and Security Act 2015, pt 2.

133 Helen Fenwick, 'Terrorism and the Control Orders/TPIMs Saga: a Vindication of the Human Rights Act or a Manifestation of "Defensive Democracy"?' [2017] Public Law 609–26; Adrian Hunt, 'From Control Orders to TPIMs: Variations on a Number of Themes in British Legal Responses to Terrorism' (2014) 62(3) Crime, Law and Social Change 289; Clive Walker, *Blackstone's Guide to the Anti-Terrorism Legislation* (3rd edn, Oxford University Press 2014) 274.

134 For detailed discussion across administrations and topics see Morgan and de Londras (n 114).

135 Labour Party, *For the Many, Not the Few: The Labour Party Manifesto 2017* (Labour Party 2017) 77.

136 Ibid.

137 Ibid.

138 Conservative Party, *Forward Together: The Conservative and Unionist Party Manifesto 2017* (Conservative Party 2017) 44.

139 Ibid 55.

140 HM Government, *CONTEST: The United Kingdom's Strategy for Countering Terrorism* (Cm 9608, 2018).

141 HC Deb 11 June 2018, vol 642, col 633.

142 Ibid col 639.

143 HC Deb 1 February 2017, vol 620, col 356WH.

144 Ibid.

145 Ibid col 380WH.

146 Ibid col 364WH.

147 Ibid, col 358WH.

148 Ibid col 371WH.

149 Ibid col 375WH.

150 Joshua Cohen, 'Procedure and Substance in Deliberative Democracy' in Thomas Christiano (ed), *Philosophy and Democracy: an Anthology* (Oxford University Press 2003); Amy Gutmann and Dennis Thompson, *Democracy and Disagreement* (Belknap Press 1996) 162, 199; Chantal Mouffe 'Which Public Sphere for a Democratic Society' (2002) 49(99) Theoria: A Journal of Social and Political Theory 55.

151 Lord Diplock (n 30).

152 Northern Ireland (Emergency Provisions) Act 1973, s 30.

153 Prevention of Terrorism (Temporary Provisions) Act 1974, s 12(1).

154 HC Deb 9 March 1977, vol 927, col 1566. The full debate is at cols 1472–570.

155 HC Deb 12 December 1977, vol 941, cols 15–16W.

[156] Lord Shackleton, *Review of the Operation of the Prevention of Terrorism (Temporary Provisions) Acts 1974 and 1976* (Cmnd 7324, 1978).

[157] Earl Jellicoe, *Review of the Operation of the Prevention of Terrorism (Temporary Provisions) Act 1976* (Cmnd 8803, 1983) 6.

[158] Ibid 7.

[159] HL Deb 8 March 1984, vol 449, cols 404–6.

[160] Ibid.

[161] HC Deb 22 January 2019, vol 653, col 171.

[162] Ibid.

[163] Anti-Terrorism Crime and Security Bill 2001, pt 4.

[164] Ibid clause 28.

[165] Ibid.

[166] The provision requiring review by a committee of Privy Councillors was proposed and incorporated during the committee stage in the House of Lords. See: HL Deb 29 November 2001, vol 629, col 460. See also the discussion of the Newton Committee in Chapter 4.

[167] See Lord Lloyd of Berwick's description of the enactment process on the sunset clause: HL Deb 15 February 2006, vol 678, col 1221.

[168] Ibid.

[169] In fact, the Part 4 indefinite detention provisions of the Anti-Terrorism Crime and Security Act 2001 were repealed with effect from 14 March 2005: Prevention of Terrorism Act 2005, ss 16(2)(a) and 16(3). The control order powers in the Prevention of Terrorism Act 2005 were subsequently repealed by the Terrorism Prevention and Investigation Measures Act 2011, s 1.

[170] For example, in a 2003 House of Lords debate on whether to renew the indefinite detention provisions of the Anti-Terrorism, Crime and Security Act 2001 just four Peers spoke. This included the Minister who had introduced the renewal order: HL Deb 11 March 2003, vol 645, cols 1291–300.

[171] Referring to the renewal debates on the Prevention of Terrorism (Temporary Provisions) Act 1976 in the 1980s, Clive Walker has noted that there was a 'general lack of parliamentary interest, with the result that the debates tended to be short, poorly attended and conducted late at night': Clive Walker, *The Prevention of Terrorism in British Law* (Manchester University Press 1992) 35.

[172] Lord Carlile's reports on Part 4 of the Anti-Terrorism, Crime and Security Act 2001 and the Prevention of Terrorism Act 2005 supported continuation of those laws in general, but raised a number of concerns. With regards to Part 4 of the Anti-Terrorism Crime and Security Act 2001, Lord Carlile was particularly concerned about the conditions of detention of the detainees, as well as the special advocate system. See: Lord Carlile, *Anti-Terrorism, Crime and Security Act 2001, Part IV Section 28 Review 2003* (Stationery Office 2003) 20–2, 27–9; Lord Carlile, *Anti-Terrorism, Crime and Security Act 2001, Part IV Section 28 Review 2004* (Stationery Office 2004) 28–32, 35–6. In respect of the Prevention of Terrorism Act 2005, Lord Carlile was concerned that individual control orders should not be extended beyond two years. See for example: Lord Carlile, *Third Report of the Independent Reviewer Pursuant to Section 14(3) of the Prevention of Terrorism Act 2005* (Stationery Office 2008) 18; Lord Carlile, *Fourth Report of the Independent Reviewer Pursuant to Section 14(3) of the Prevention of Terrorism Act 2005* (Stationery Office 2009) 20; Lord Carlile, *Fifth Report of the Independent Reviewer Pursuant to Section 14(3) of the Prevention of Terrorism Act 2005* (Stationery Office 2010) 45;

Lord Carlile, *Sixth Report of the Independent Reviewer Pursuant to Section 14(3) of the Prevention of Terrorism Act 2005* (Stationery Office 2011) 23.

[173] Terrorism Act 2000, s 126.

[174] See further the discussion in Chapter 5 of the paucity of parliamentary attention and time for counter-terrorism review activities.

[175] Lord Shackleton (n 156).

[176] HC Deb 21 March 1979, vol 964, cols 1505–624.

[177] Prevention of Terrorism Act 2005, s 13(4).

[178] Ibid s 13(6).

[179] Ibid s 13.

[180] HC Deb 15 February 2006, vol 442, cols 1499–523; HL Deb 8 March 2011, vol 725, cols 1585–604.

[181] HL Deb 5 March 2007, vol 690, col 22; HC Deb 3 March 2009, vol 488, col 744.

[182] See for example parliamentary debates on the Terrorism Prevention and Investigation Measures Act 2011 in which MPs objected to Minister James Brokenshire seeming to suggest that TPIMs were 'business as usual', insisting that they were 'exceptional'. HC Deb 5 September 2011, vol 532, cols 91–2.

[183] This is usually undertaken as part of safeguarding training. See for example the Lawn Tennis Association's rules on the safeguarding training that is acceptable for LTA club welfare officers, which includes 'Local Authority safeguarding training (as long as it includes information about anti-radicalisation'), Available from: https://helpcentre.lta.org.uk/hc/en-gb/articles/115007663368-What-safeguarding-training-is-accepted-by-the-LTA-for-Welfare-Officers [Accessed 28 March 2019].

[184] British Transport Police, 'See It. Say It. Sorted' http://www.btp.police.uk/about_us/our_campaigns/see_it_say_it_sorted.aspx [Accessed 28 March 2019].

2

The Practice and Potential of Counter-Terrorism Review

The UK Government says that it is committed to the '[o]versight, scrutiny and transparency of our counter-terrorism work', which it considers to be 'world-leading'.[1] According to *CONTEST: The United Kingdom's Strategy for Countering Terrorism*, this 'includes the reports we publish, the involvement of independent judges who review government agencies' use of intrusive powers and government applications for TEOs and TPIMs, an independent reviewer of terrorism legislation, and accountability to Parliament'.[2] In order to 'listen and respond to improve our approach to keeping the public safe', the Government says it will 'continue to engage extensively with the public, civil society, academia and Parliament, and through community outreach'.[3]

As it stands, this is as close to a complete account of the Government's understanding of counter-terrorism review as exists. Yet it is not comprehensive. Judges do far more in counter-terrorism review than review agencies' use of intrusive powers or applications for counter-terrorism orders. They also preside over criminal trials and appeals relating to terrorism offences and hear applications for judicial review and applications under the Human Rights Act 1998. Alongside the Independent Reviewer of Terrorism Legislation, there is an Independent Reviewer of the Justice and Security (Northern Ireland) Act 2007, and the Counter-Terrorism and Border Security Act 2019 provides for an independent review of Prevent. Parliamentary accountability includes the everyday work (including committee work) of the legislature, but also specific forms of counter-terrorism review and accountability. These largely comprise approving (via affirmative resolution) or not annulling (via negative resolution) orders laid before Parliament under counter-terrorism legislation, such as creating various codes of practice, proscribing and de-proscribing terrorist organisations, and continuing temporary counter-terrorism laws in force. Furthermore, just as counter-terrorism is now part of the quotidian business of statehood, so too is counter-terrorism review part of the everyday business of the organs of state: the Executive, Parliament and the courts. Here we refer to how the constitutional labour of these branches may be applied to counter-terrorism outside of specific and mandated reviews of counter-terrorism laws and policies. Civil society's role in counter-terrorism review is multifaceted and can include publishing reports on particular counter-terrorism laws or policies, feeding into state-initiated reviews and initiating legal proceedings to challenge counter-terrorism laws and policies.

The Government's account is also not comprehensive when it comes to identifying relevant actors in what we call the counter-terrorism review assemblage. It neglects to mention, for example, that general regulatory bodies – such as the Independent Office for Police Conduct (IOPC) – have a role inasmuch as they regulate the exercise of counter-terrorism powers. NHS and education sector regulators are similarly drawn in because, as we saw in Chapter 1, their regulatees are engaged through Prevent as counter-terrorist actors.

In short, the counter-terrorism review assemblage is more complex than the picture presented by the government of its 'world-leading' oversight, scrutiny and accountability framework. Moreover, it is not clear what the Government's claim that its approach is 'world-leading' rests on: is it the scale of the counter-terrorism review assemblage, or the quality of the review processes themselves? In this chapter, we use two examples to illustrate the ways in which this account of relevant counter-terrorism review actors and their roles is inadequate, and show that, considered against an understanding of counter-terrorism review as a web of accountability, questions about the excellence of current practice arise. We do this through a descriptive analysis of the review of Prevent and TPIMs.

In Chapter, 1 we saw how Prevent is illustrative of important characteristics of the counter-terrorist state: sprawl of counter-terrorism into non-conventional domains, expansion of counter-terrorism to include countering extremism, and counter-terrorist responsibilisation of new actors. Prevent is, thus, a critical part of the infrastructure of the counter-terrorist state, but also among its most controversial. We focus specifically on its application in education to illustrate the ways in which it has (or has not) been subject to review. TPIMs align more to what might be expected of conventional counter-terrorism law. Although somewhat exceptional within the criminal law, TPIMs are restrictive 'temporary' measures, said to enable counter-terrorism to be pursued through both preventive and investigative routes.

In each case, we identify the review mechanisms that exist 'on paper', focusing on the relevant legislation. We then identify reviews that developed alongside the UK's counter-terrorism laws and policies, but which are not prescribed by statute. Finally, we consider the counter-terrorism reviews that take place as part of the ordinary everyday business of statehood – that is, the variety of reviews conducted by the executive, legislature, judiciary, regulators and civil society. These include reviews that, on the face of it, relate to individual cases, but which may identify systemic issues relating to the impact or operation of a law or policy. This process provides a sense of the potential scale of the counter-terrorism review assemblage, but it does not reveal the extent to which that potential is actualised. If, as we suggested in the Introduction, counter-terrorism review is a mechanism of trying to optimise accountability in the counter-terrorist state, then its success requires at a minimum that review would actually take place. Therefore, in addition to describing the counter-terrorism review assemblage that attaches to Prevent and TPIMs, we also identify the reviews that have been undertaken over the five-year period from 1 January 2014 to 31 December 2018. For each of these, we consider the standards against which these reviews evaluated the law or programme, which we have identified by close textual analysis of the reviews themselves.

Part I: Reviewing Prevent

Prevent is one strand of the UK government's counter-terrorism strategy, CONTEST, and has already been described in Chapter 1. Given that, it is sufficient at this stage to note that in England, Wales and Scotland the strategy has been augmented with a statutory Prevent Duty, enacted in the Counter-Terrorism and Security Act 2015. The duty requires specified authorities to have 'due regard to the need to prevent people from being drawn into terrorism' in the exercise of their functions.[4]

Reviews established in counter-terrorism legislation

A number of statutory reviews exist, relating variously to the Prevent Strategy as a whole, to parts of the Counter-Terrorism and Security Act 2015, and to the application of Prevent to individuals.

In spite of persistent calls for Prevent as a whole to be reviewed,[5] no statutory provision mandating such a review existed until the Counter-Terrorism and Border Security Act 2019 was enacted in February of that year. Within six months of the Act's enactment, the Secretary of

State must 'make arrangements for an independent review and report on the Government strategy for supporting people vulnerable to being drawn into terrorism'.[6] That report must be laid before both Houses of Parliament within 18 months of the Act's enactment,[7] and must be accompanied by a statement by the Secretary of State responding to each recommendation made as part of the independent review.[8] The legislation only mandates this one review of the Prevent Strategy; unlike in respect of other counter-terrorism powers, it does not provide for annual or repeat reviews.[9] Shortly before publication of this book, Lord Carlile of Berriew, former Independent Reviewer of Terrorism Legislation, was appointed to conduct the independent review of Prevent. That appointment has proved controversial, with one civil society organisation, Rights Watch UK, initiating proceedings to challenge the Home Secretary's decision to appoint Lord Carlile.[10]

Within the Counter-Terrorism and Security Act 2015 there are four different situations in which parliament is required to approve, by the affirmative resolution procedure, a draft statutory instrument relating to Prevent that is laid before it by the Secretary of State, all of which provide opportunities for review. These arise where the Secretary of State seeks to: add 'specified authorities'[11] to Schedule 6 of the Act,[12] issue guidance to specified authorities about the exercise of their duty under the Act,[13] change the definition of a 'local authority'[14] in section 41 of the Act,[15] and amend the list of 'partners of local panels'[16] in Schedule 7 of the Act.[17] Parliament's reviewing role is therefore only engaged if and when the Secretary of State lays an order before it under the Act. To date, two such statutory instruments have been laid before Parliament for approval: the Counter-Terrorism and Security Act 2015 (Risk of Being Drawn into Terrorism) (Amendment and Guidance) Regulations 2015, and the Counter-Terrorism and Security Act 2015 (Risk of Being Drawn into Terrorism) (Guidance) Regulations 2015.[18]

In essence, these statutory instruments outline how the Prevent Duty is to operate in practice, and were formulated following a substantial consultation and pre-legislative scrutiny (albeit on an accelerated timetable) by the Joint Committee on Statutory Instruments and the Secondary Legislation Scrutiny Committee.[19] Presenting these statutory instruments, Government centred the nature of contemporary terrorist activity and presented the Prevent Duty and this guidance as enabling a consistent and appropriate response to this threat that could be applied across the country. For example, presenting the Counter-Terrorism and Security Act 2015 (Risk of Being Drawn into Terrorism) (Amendment and Guidance) Regulations 2015 in the House of Lords, the Parliamentary Under-Secretary of State for the Home Office, Lord Bates, said:

The intelligence agencies tell us that the threat now is worse than at any time since 9/11. It is serious and it is growing. The threat has changed and so must our response. As part of that response, we need to continue to combat the underlying ideology that feeds, supports and sanctions terrorism, and prevent people from being drawn onto that path. The Prevent duty will ensure that such activity is consistent across the country and in all those bodies whose staff work on the front line with those at risk from radicalisation.[20]

The debate that ensued in the Lords lasted for a little over an hour, and focused largely on significant questions about the primary legislation (such as the definition of non-violent extremism, or infringements on freedom of speech) rather than the Guidance per se. No Peer quibbled with the implication from Lord Bates' speech that 'fit' of a measure to a threat as defined by intelligence agencies was the appropriate standard by which to consider the Guidance. Indeed, a number of Peers spoke about how important it was to ensure appropriate fit to avoid 'do[ing] things which are counterproductive',[21] or that 'giv[e] extremists victories',[22] so that even when respect for rights was discussed, it was presented largely as a matter of operational strategy or success rather than rights protection per se. Similar debates took place on the Counter-Terrorism and Security Act 2015 (Risk of Being Drawn into Terrorism) (Amendment and Guidance) Regulations 2015, although in that case only three Peers spoke in addition to Lord Ashton who introduced the Regulations, and the debate concluded in 42 minutes. Interestingly, there had been some speculation that the Lords might not approve these Regulations, so they were then tabled for after 5pm on a Thursday evening in mid-September. As Lord Rosser said, 'revolution does not normally come during last business on a Thursday afternoon before a three-week recess'.[23]

The Secretary of State's power to delegate an authority to be a 'monitoring authority' for the purposes of monitoring compliance of further and higher education authorities with the Prevent Duty is subject to a negative resolution procedure.[24] The Counter-Terrorism and Security Act 2015 (Monitoring of Further Education Bodies) (England) Regulations 2016 were made by the Secretary of State on 29 June 2016 and laid before Parliament the next day.[25] Parliament did not, on this occasion, use its review function to debate whether the order should be annulled. It entered into force on 1 August 2016.[26]

Compliance monitoring can have some review-like elements; it is a means of gathering evidence (that is, of 'engaging with reality'), which in turn can feed into evaluation of merits and perhaps proposals for improvement. Compliance monitoring is undertaken differently in higher and further education than in other sectors. The Counter-Terrorism and Security Act 2015 specifically states that the Secretary of State, or 'a person to whom the Secretary of State delegates the function' will monitor institutions of further and higher education.[27] These functions have indeed been delegated: to the Office for Standards in Education, Children's Services and Skills (Ofsted),[28] and the Higher Education Funding Council for England (HEFCE), and then the Office for Students when it became operational in April 2018.[29] In the healthcare sector, compliance monitoring appears to have been delegated to a sub-group of NHS England's National Safeguarding Steering Group,[30] the NHS Wales National Safeguarding Team (itself overseen by the National Independent Safeguarding Board[31]) and the Scottish Government NHS Resilience Unit.[32]

The Secretary of State issues guidance, which may include monitoring and compliance guidance, to these specified authorities.[33] The *Revised Prevent Duty Guidance for England and Wales* centres compliance monitoring in the Home Office and requires specified authorities 'to maintain appropriate records to show compliance with their responsibilities and provide reports when requested'.[34] Where there is already an existing inspection regime for a sector, support and monitoring for the Prevent Duty is to be provided there.[35] This is the case for compliance monitoring in the NHS, in prisons, in probation services and in the police. All other sectors are formally subject to compliance monitoring by the Home Secretary and covered by the *Revised Prevent Duty Guidance*.[36]

In addition to these reviews of Prevent as a whole, there is one review mechanism built into the Counter-Terrorism and Security Act 2015 that relates to the individual application of Prevent. Section 36 provides for assessment and support to be provided by local multi-agency panels to individuals who, following an assessment, are deemed to be vulnerable to being drawn into terrorism. This is the Channel Duty. If a support plan has been put in place, the local panel must 'keep under review the giving of support to an identified individual under a support plan'.[37] Between April 2015 and March 2018 there were 1,107 individuals in respect of whom support plans were required to be kept under review by local panels.[38] Little information is available about how these plans are reviewed. The Channel Duty Guidance suggests that '[i]ndividuals receiving support should be reassessed at least every three months to ensure that the progress being made in supporting the individual is being captured', although more frequent assessment is permitted if appropriate.[39] Presumably, the panel assesses whether the support plan is working to fulfil the programme's aims of 'reducing [the individual's] vulnerability to being drawn into terrorism'. When someone 'exits' Channel, they are to be reviewed after six and again after 12 months,[40] and the Government claims to take ensuring this happens seriously.[41] Again, there is little information about how these reviews are conducted, or the criteria against which 'remaining vulnerabilities' will be assessed, although we might once again assume that the panel will essentially be concerned with whether Channel has worked to reduce an individual's vulnerability to being drawn into terrorism. Local authorities do not publish information on these reviews. It is not clear whether they feed into any larger systemic review or monitoring of Channel.

Non-statutory reviews

The UK's counter-terrorism strategy has been revised on a number of occasions since it was first established in 2003. On each occasion the government of the day has considered how the strategy is working, and made suggestions to revise it. In other words, it has reviewed it. When the Conservative-led Coalition Government came to power in 2010, it instigated a wide-ranging review of national security, including Prevent, as part of its Programme for Government.[42]

Aligned to this review, the Government commissioned a former Independent Reviewer of Terrorism Legislation, Lord Carlile of Berriew QC, to review its proposed new Prevent Strategy.[43] Lord Carlile drew on experiences of Prevent and its operation to date, and reached overwhelmingly positive conclusions, although he did suggest that in the future, evaluation of the Strategy might be enhanced 'if all events in the project ... were evaluated even subjectively on a simple effectiveness scale' and that overall 'a more permanent and methodological overview of governance is required'.[44] While recognising the need to comply with 'civil liberties',[45] Lord Carlile framed his analysis primarily around questions of operational effectiveness, and lent his public support to the new strategy. Indeed, the Home Secretary expressly referred to his support in her forward to the new strategy.[46] Lord Carlile himself wrote the preface to the *Prevent Strategy*,[47] and his report is available side by side with it on the Government website.[48]

The revised CONTEST Strategy, published in 2018, was informed by the outcome of several reviews including the National Security Capability Review, which was established shortly after the 2017 General Election to identify how to 'develop, deliver and deploy our considerable national security capabilities to maximum collective effect'.[49] That review was commissioned following the National Security Strategy and Strategic Defence and Security Review 2015,[50] undertaken by the National Security Council. Finally, the Government reviewed the existing CONTEST Strategy, taking into account various other 'reviews and lessons learned exercises' which were 'undertaken by government departments, Counter-Terrorism Policing, the security and intelligence agencies and Parliament'.[51] None of these reviews was independent or external, all were operationally focused,[52] and the CONTEST strategy does not explain how and according to what criteria the previous strategy was evaluated.

In 2011, the Government committed to providing annual reports on CONTEST, assessing it 'against a set of performance indicators, complemented by deeper evaluation of specific programmes ... supported by wider research and horizon scanning' and 'publishing data where security classification allows'.[53] The 2018 version of CONTEST made the same commitment.[54] While CONTEST 2011 included what appeared to be headline performance indicators,[55] the 2018 version of CONTEST does not, and when it comes to Prevent, the reports have tended largely to be statistical.[56] Furthermore, because the 2011 CONTEST Strategy was only intended to be a five-year programme, and because the most recent iteration of CONTEST was published two years late (in 2018), no annual reports were published for 2017 and 2018, although CONTEST continued to operate. This suggests a minimal compliance approach with the Government's own commitment to evaluation and publication, at least under the 2011 iteration.

As well as annual reports, the Home Office has published annual statistics on Prevent since April 2015.[57] These statistical bulletins provide a general picture of the numbers of individuals formally referred to and supported though Prevent, disaggregated by a number of factors, including the individuals' age, gender, region and 'type of concern', meaning whether they were referred for 'Islamist' extremism or right-wing extremism. They also include information on the sector from which an individual was referred (such as education, the police or a local authority), and the outcome of the referral. While these statistical snapshots are useful, they only capture *formal* referrals and their approach is strictly descriptive and operational. They do not capture information on persons about whom referral was considered or in respect of whom an informal conversation on whether to refer took place with Prevent authorities.[58] These reports do not contain any evaluation, make claims of the appropriateness or necessity of the programme, or note whether referral to Prevent was a proportionate response to the concerns raised about each individual.

The Prevent Oversight Board is a non-statutory body established in 2011.[59] The 2011 version of the CONTEST Strategy identified the existence of a 'CONTEST Board' that was 'responsible for developing and monitoring implementation of the strategy',[60] with 'sub-Boards ... responsible for Pursue, Prevent, Protect and Prepare'.[61] It is not clear whether the Prevent Oversight Board is the sub-board mentioned here, especially as the 2011 *Prevent Strategy* notes:

> The board will be permanent, with strong, independent membership, but not statutory. Reflecting the importance of local partnerships – and recognising the important connections between Prevent and the wider work referred to above – it will be jointly chaired by the Home Secretary and the Secretary of State for Communities and Local Government. Membership of the board is still under consideration.[62]

After 2011 there was little information on the oversight board until the instigation of the statutory Prevent Duty in 2015. The Prevent Duty Guidance notes that the Home Office will 'support the Prevent Oversight Board, chaired by the Minister for Immigration and Security, which may agree on further action to support implementation of the duty. Where a specified body is not complying with the duty, the Prevent Oversight Board may recommend that the Secretary of State use the power of direction under section 30 of the Act.'[63] By January 2017, it seems, the Prevent Oversight Board had been co-opted into the Home Office. A parliamentary question by Lord Carlile elicited the following response:

> The Prevent Oversight Board provides scrutiny and independent oversight to the Prevent Programme. It is chaired by the Home Secretary, and membership includes Secretaries of State responsible for the relevant sectors within which Prevent operates including Education, Health, Local Communities and Justice. The Prevent Oversight Board also includes a number of independent members.
>
> Following consideration of the evolving threat and the growing focus on Prevent, the Home Secretary's decision in September last year to chair the Prevent Oversight Board recognises its essential and ongoing role in driving delivery and scrutinising the Prevent programme to ensure it continues to effectively safeguard people vulnerable to radicalisation.[64]

There is no mention of the Prevent Oversight Board at all in the 2018 iteration of CONTEST, although it appears still to function: in December 2018, Lord Carlile mentioned that he was a member of the Board, and stated that it had recently met for the first time in 18 months as two earlier meetings had been cancelled.[65] Our Freedom of Information request seeking information on the Prevent Oversight Board's mandate and terms of reference was denied, predominantly on the grounds of national security,[66] so we have not been able to identify what criteria the Board uses to assess effectiveness. No other information on what the Board evaluates, or how, is publicly available.

Reviews undertaken as part of the everyday business of statehood

As with all areas of state activity, Parliament has significant capacity to review Prevent within its general business of committee work, parliamentary questions, motions and debates, and pre-legislative scrutiny that includes consideration of the operation of predecessor laws and strategies.

A number of parliamentary committees have initiated inquiries into the Prevent Strategy and Prevent Duty. These include the Joint Committee on Human Rights (JCHR), Home Affairs Committee, Education Committee, and Intelligence and Security Committee of Parliament.[67] As part of its pre-legislative scrutiny, the JCHR initiated a review of the Prevent Duty elements of the Counter Terrorism and Security Bill 2014.[68] The Committee held oral evidence sessions with, amongst others, the then Independent Reviewer of Terrorism Legislation, David Anderson QC,[69] and Minister for Security, James Brokenshire.[70] These sessions focused on the compatibility of the Prevent Duty with academic freedom,[71] as well as on questions of safeguards, oversight and scrutiny.[72] Focusing on rights and proportionality, the final report included consideration of the duty's compatibility with existing rights[73] (particularly free speech and academic freedom in universities[74]), the role given to Parliament for oversight of the Secretary of State's power to issue guidance,[75] and whether the introduction of a statutory duty was necessary.[76] The Committee subsequently established an inquiry into freedom of speech in universities, which considered the Prevent duty against a legality standard (respect for the right to freedom of expression).[77] The Home Affairs Committee has considered Prevent in three reports since 2014, evaluating it against a range of standards, including appropriateness, necessity and effectiveness.[78] It also considered the need for independent review of and increased transparency in respect of Prevent.[79] As part of its report into the 2017 terrorist attacks in the UK, the Intelligence and Security Committee considered the Prevent Strategy, the Prevent Duty and the Channel

Duty. It focused primarily on questions of operational effectiveness, with particular emphasis on situations where multiple members of the same family were under consideration, and reiterated its earlier criticism about failure to refer individuals who are 'Subjects of Interest'.[80]

A number of questions have been asked in Parliament in relation to the Prevent Programme and its two associated statutory duties.[81] These have focused on the effectiveness[82] and 'value for money' of Prevent,[83] as well as whether the Prevent programme has struck the correct balance between preventing terrorism and protecting people from Islamophobia.[84] In February 2017, Conservative MP Lucy Allan initiated a Westminster Hall debate on the Prevent strategy. Introducing the debate, she noted: 'There is now a level of disquiet, which it would be wrong to ignore, about how the Prevent duty is working in practice and its impact on community cohesion.'[85] Several of those who engaged in the debate, particularly Government Ministers and Conservative back-benchers, claimed that Prevent was both necessary and working.[86] Those claims of necessity were tempered by general concerns about the negative perception of Prevent in, and the stigmatisation of, Muslim communities,[87] the unintended consequences of the Prevent strategy,[88] questions of over-compliance,[89] a lack of trust and its implications for effectiveness.[90] However, the underlying logic of prevention was not under challenge. Naz Shah MP perhaps summed the character of the debate up best when she said: 'Although I am a critic of the implementation of Prevent, it is clear to me that we need a prevention strategy.'[91] The Prevent Strategy and the Prevent Duty were also subject to debate during the passage of new counter-terrorism legislation, in particular the Counter-Terrorism and Security Bill 2014, which sought to set the existing Prevent Strategy on a statutory footing, and the Counter-Terrorism and Border Security Bill 2019, which led to the establishment of an independent review of Prevent in the Counter-Terrorism and Border Security Act 2019.

The second reading debate in the House of Commons on the Counter-Terrorism and Security Bill 2014 is illustrative of the types of evaluation with which Parliament was concerned. The debate that followed the Home Secretary's introductory speech focused on three main issues:[92] the necessity of putting Prevent on a statutory footing,[93] the impact it would have on free speech in higher education,[94] and whether the concentration on preventing individuals from being drawn into terrorism (rather than a 'collective responsibility'[95] to challenge the narrative of extremism) was sufficient. Although some MPs questioned the decision to put the programme on a statutory footing, and the reduction of funding for some programmes,[96] there was general cross-party support for the Prevent Strategy. Hazel Blears MP who as 'a former counter-terrorism Minister',[97] had played a lead role on Prevent under the Labour Government, noted that while she 'supported action against non-violent extremism as well as violent extremism',[98] she had concerns about how the Prevent programme had been, and the Prevent Duty would be, evaluated:

> A crucial part of this will be the evaluation of its effectiveness. When the Government did their review of Prevent three and a half years ago, they said that there were not sufficient measures of effectiveness, that there were no metrics, and that they were not able to measure the impact. What progress have the Government made in measuring the impact of the Prevent strategy, because I have seen no metrics, no valuation and no evidence on that score? If we are going to spend significant amounts of public money, as we have done and as I hope we will continue to, we must ensure that it is making a difference. Evaluation is therefore important.[99]

Similar concerns were raised at the second reading of the Counter-Terrorism and Border Security Bill 2019 in the House of Commons. For example, four members (Diane Abbott MP, Gavin Newlands MP, Sir Edward Davey MP and John Hayes MP) made extensive contributions on Prevent and for all of them the key focus was effectiveness; it was whether or not Prevent 'works' against the objectives that underpin it.[100] Among MPs who contributed on Prevent there was near unanimity that it be independently reviewed to evaluate its operational effectiveness.[101] At that same debate, and responding to the calls for review of Prevent, Minister Ben Wallace's speech indicated neatly how the Government can deploy review to underpin proposed new powers. He said:

> There is often pressure after such attacks to have new legislation – something must be done – and I am proud that this Government did not rush to legislation. We set up several significant reviews that were consolidated into four main reviews. The operational review produced a classified report of some 1,300 pages that went into every single decision, piece of intelligence and bit of work that went on in the lead-up to some of the attacks. I read all 1,300 pages not just because I am incredibly interested and because it is my duty, but because only then could I learn what legislation will put right, what is reasonable to be asked by our security services and police and what should not necessarily need to be placed on the statute book.

We also had the Home Office's counter-terrorism legislative review, and we reviewed Contest, pausing its relaunch to see whether anything needed to be handled. Several of those reviews were "oversighted" by David Anderson, the former independent reviewer of terrorism legislation, or Max Hill, the current reviewer, who reviewed how police used their powers in the aftermath. That gentle but solid consideration is why we are here today with legislation that hopefully helps to answer some of the challenges we face.[102]

As already mentioned, litigation can fulfil a review function, although in respect of Prevent there is only one reported case since 2014.[103] Having been identified as a 'hate speaker' by the Home Office's Extremism Analysis Unit, Salman Butt was named in a press release announcing the *Revised Prevent Duty Guidance for Higher Education Institutions in England and Wales*. Butt denied that he was a 'hate speaker' and sought judicial review of the decision to classify him as such, arguing *inter alia* that the Guidance was unlawful both because it was *ultra vires* the powers established in the Counter-Terrorism and Security Act 2015, and because it resulted in violations of the right to freedom of expression protected by Article 10 of the European Convention on Human Rights.[104] While the human rights claims did not succeed, Butt was successful in establishing that, in making the Prevent Guidance, the Secretary of State had failed to have 'due regard to the need to prevent people from being drawn into terrorism' as required by Section 26 of the Act. This is because the Guidance also required higher education institutions to 'consider carefully whether the views being expressed, or likely to be expressed, constitute extremist views that risk drawing people into terrorism or are shared by terrorist groups' and, if so, 'the event should not be allowed to proceed except where [relevant higher education bodies] are entirely convinced that such risk can be fully mitigated without cancellation of the event'.[105] As far as the Court of Appeal was concerned, this Guidance was 'not sufficiently balanced and accurate to inform the decision-maker' in a higher education body of their obligation to ensure freedom of speech when deciding whether to host a visiting speaker.[106] The current Prevent Guidance was, therefore, unlawful, although as of August 2019, it had not been formally revised in light of this judgment. Importantly, this case does not call into question the lawfulness of Prevent, or establish that either Prevent or analysis by the Extremism Analysis Unit violates human rights law; rather, it finds that in developing its Guidance on the Act, the Home Secretary failed properly to adhere to the duties imposed on the office by the text of the primary legislation itself.

Regulatory reviews

As outlined above, monitoring compliance with the Prevent Duty is either undertaken or delegated by the Home Secretary. We have already noted that it is widely delegated, and in higher education the delegee is the Office for Students (formerly HEFCE). We focus on that example to illustrate how compliance monitoring does (or does not) constitute review as we understand it.

In a general sense, universities and institutions of higher education monitor themselves for compliance, and report their implementation of the Prevent Duty to the Office for Students by means of an annual reporting process. The Office for Students provides guidance on the contents of those reports,[107] which it then reviews in order to prepare its own periodic report for the Home Office and Department for Education. When the Office for Students receives institutional reports, its Prevent advisers undertake an initial assessment and they contact the provider if there are any queries or concerns about the report. Where 'Prevent-related serious incidents' arise the practice is to report these to the Office for Students outside of the normal reporting cycle.[108] An institution's annual report ought to include information about their risk assessment and action plan; partnership with relevant bodies; leadership; implementation of Prevent in respect of external speakers and events, welfare, IT policies and pastoral care; staff training; student engagement; and areas of good practice and those where further support may be required.[109]

As a general matter, the regulatory regime appears to consider that the role of higher and further education institutions is simply to implement the Prevent Guidance, albeit by means of a 'risk-based and proportionate approach to monitoring providers' implementation of the Prevent duty'.[110] It appears from both the guidance documents and from interviews we undertook with persons working with Prevent in higher education, that the general perception of the regulator's and regulatees' role is that they implement and to some extent enforce the Prevent Duty, rather than that they engage in review activities.[111] While there was some sense that the Home Office might use the reporting materials in its own review and revision processes, higher and further education workers we spoke to did not generally sense that their role was evaluative.[112] It is not clear whether these reporting processes act as or lead to review processes, especially since the nature and scope of internal review processes that may be undertaken in the Home Office or by bodies such as the Prevent Oversight Board are, as already mentioned, largely beyond the reach of the public.

Civil society review

Given the ways in which Prevent expands the reach of the counter-terrorist state, and the fact that until 2019 there was no indication that the Government would subject it to comprehensive evaluative review, it is unsurprising that it has received significant civil society attention.[113] This includes calls for Prevent to be subjected to independent review,[114] and attempts by civil society actors (including the Muslim Council of Britain) to bring qualitative evidence about the societal impact of Prevent to the attention of Government through, for example, engagement with the Independent Reviewer of Terrorism Legislation,[115] and the submission of briefings during pre-legislative scrutiny processes.[116]

Civil society organisations have also commissioned and undertaken significant evaluative review of Prevent on their own initiative. A number of examples are illustrative.[117] In 2016, Rights Watch UK published a study of Prevent in schools, based on desk-research and 26 interviews, which concluded that Prevent both violated the human rights of young people and 'risks being counter-productive' by disincentivising children from discussing issues relating to terrorism and identity in the classroom, driving those discussions 'online where simplistic narratives are promoted and go unchallenged'.[118] JUST Yorkshire undertook research, including 36 interviews, that also led them to conclude that various human rights abuses were facilitated by and taking place in the context of Prevent, with particular discriminatory impacts on Muslims, and that the instigation of the Prevent Duty in statute meant that 'a "policing culture" is now noticeable, particularly within higher education institutions'.[119] In *Eroding Trust*, the Open Society Justice Initiative found that the Prevent Duty as it currently operates in health and education heightens risks of discrimination and results in rights violations including the right to privacy and the rights of children. Again, this was based on interview data, this time with 'more than 87 people'.[120]

In all of these cases, the analysis was undertaken largely by reference to human rights standards, but with implications for the likely effectiveness of Prevent being drawn from this analytical framework, meaning that Prevent was evaluated against standards of legality and operational effectiveness. Importantly, however, these civil society reviews also tackled the assumptions on which Prevent is based, largely arguing that the entire programme and approach are based on flawed understandings of radicalisation and extremism,[121] on stereotypical views of Muslims, and on discriminatory securitisation logics.[122] These reports provide a useful example of both radical challenge to the logics of the counter-terrorist state and engagement with legal standards as an evaluative framework, although few recommend abandonment of Prevent rather than its recalibration (including repeal of the statutory Prevent Duty,[123] or revision of how higher education institutions implement Prevent[124]) and review.[125]

Part II: Terrorism Prevention and Investigation Measures

Following a government review of counter-terrorism in 2010,[126] and in light of previous attempts to restrict the liberty of suspected, but not convicted, terrorists,[127] the Terrorism Prevention and Investigation Measures Act 2011 received Royal Assent in December 2011. This established TPIMs, which can be used to impose obligations, restrictions and other provisions on individuals suspected of terrorism, including restrictions on liberty.[128] Breach of any measure specified in a TPIM is a criminal offence punishable by a maximum sentence of five years' imprisonment.[129]

The Secretary of State may only make a TPIM if five conditions are met.[130] 'Condition A is that the Secretary of State is satisfied, on the balance of probabilities,[131] that the individual is, or has been, involved in terrorism-related activity'.[132] 'Condition B is that some or all of the relevant activity is new terrorism-related activity'. 'Condition C is that the Secretary of State reasonably considers that it is necessary, for purposes connected with protecting members of the public from a risk of terrorism, for terrorism prevention and investigation measures to be imposed on the individual'. 'Condition D is that the Secretary of State reasonably considers that it is necessary, for purposes connected with preventing or restricting the individual's involvement in terrorism-related activity, for the specified terrorism prevention and investigation measures to be imposed on the individual', and finally, Condition E is that either 'the court gives the Secretary of State permission' to make a TPIM,[133] or 'the Secretary of State reasonably considers that the urgency of the case requires terrorism prevention and investigation measures to be imposed without obtaining such permission'.[134]

Although a TPIM can only be imposed for one year, the Secretary of State may renew it once if conditions A, C and D are met.[135] The Secretary of State may by notice revoke or vary a TPIM, and an individual subject to a TPIM may also apply to the Secretary of State for the TPIM to be varied or revoked.[136] It is only on the extension or variation of a TPIM that the individual subject to it can appeal the decision of the Secretary of State to impose the order; there is no right of appeal on the imposition of the original order.[137] In conducting that appeal, the Court is limited to the principles of judicial review; it cannot decide the appeal on the substantive facts of the case.[138] Furthermore, appeal proceedings are subject to special rules of the Court, which are outlined in Schedule 4 of the Terrorism Prevention and Investigation Measures Act 2011. These rules can prevent the disclosure of relevant material to the person subject to a TPIM as well as their legal representative, require the TPIM subject and their lawyer to be excluded from the proceedings and provide for a Special Advocate to be involved in any closed material proceedings.[139]

Reviews established in counter-terrorism legislation

The Terrorism Prevention and Investigation Measures Act 2011 includes a number of review provisions relating to both individual TPIM cases and the legislative regime itself.

Reviews relating to individual TPIMs

In terms of individual TPIM cases, the Executive and judiciary are involved in review-like activity from the start. Except in urgent cases,[140] the Secretary of State must apply to the Court for prior permission to impose measures on an individual.[141] The function of the Court is to use the 'principles applicable on an application for judicial review',[142] in order 'to determine whether the relevant decisions of the Secretary of State are obviously flawed'.[143] If they are not, then the Court must give permission for the TPIM to be imposed.[144] If the Court gives that permission then it must set a date for a 'directions hearing',[145] the purpose of which is to give directions for a 'review hearing to be held as soon as reasonably practicable'.[146] The purpose of the review hearing is for the Court to 'review the decisions of the Secretary of State that the relevant conditions were met and continue to be met'.[147] Again, the Court must apply judicial review principles in determining such questions.[148] At a review hearing, the Court has the power to quash the TPIM in its entirety, to quash individual measures specified in the TPIM, or to give directions to the Secretary of State to revoke or vary any measure specified in the TPIM.[149] If it does not take one of these actions, then the Court 'must decide that the TPIM is to continue in force'.[150] Since 2014, there have been three reported cases of statutory review hearings.[151] In each case, the Court upheld the Secretary of State's decision to impose a TPIM against the relevant individual, although minor variations to some of the measures were made in relation to four of those individuals.[152]

After a TPIM has been imposed, there are three further review mechanisms that apply to individual cases. First, the individual subject to a TPIM can appeal against it. Second, the Secretary of State must keep under review whether she reasonably considers that it is necessary for a TPIM to be imposed on the individual, and that the particular measures specified in the TPIM notice are necessary.[153] Third, the chief officer of the appropriate police force must keep under review whether there is sufficient evidence to bring a prosecution against the individual for a criminal offence relating to terrorism.[154]

An individual may appeal against a TPIM notice, but not during the first year of its operation unless the Secretary of State has varied the measures within the TPIM, or denied the individual's application for the measures to be varied or revoked.[155] If the Secretary of State uses her powers to extend the TPIM by up to one year,[156] or to revive an expired or revoked TPIM,[157] the individual may appeal that decision, and the Court will review the Secretary of State's assessment of whether the statutory conditions for extension or revival 'were met and continue to be met'.[158] Importantly, the Court may not substitute its decision for whether the conditions themselves are met; rather it reviews the Home Secretary's decision against the 'principles applicable on an application for judicial review'.[159] The Court can quash the extension or revival of the TPIM, quash any individual measure specified in the TPIM or give directions to the Secretary of State to revoke or vary any of the measures specified in the TPIM.[160] If it does not take one of these actions, the Court must dismiss the appeal.[161] There is no further appeal, 'except on a question of law'.[162]

There have been two reported appeals in relation to TPIMs since 1 January 2014. Both cases involved an appeal against the Secretary of State's refusal to vary the measures in the TPIM,[163] although one of these was combined with the statutory review hearing.[164] In both cases, the overall appeal was lost, although the measures were varied, and in one the requirement for the individual to wear an electronic tag was quashed on the grounds that it caused deterioration in his mental health.[165]

For as long as a TPIM is in force, the Secretary of State must keep under review whether Conditions C and D continue to be met.[166] Although the contents of the conditions themselves tell us what evaluative standards the Secretary of State is to apply, the Act provides no further guidance on what form this review must take, how frequently it must occur in relation to the individual TPIM that is in force or what the outcome would be if either or both of the conditions ceased to be met. We might assume that it is intended to feed into decisions about whether to continue, vary or extend a TPIM, but to date no Home Secretary appears to have published any information about the reviews conducted under this mechanism. As a result, we cannot ascertain with certainty whether this ongoing review is in fact undertaken, or the use to which it is put.

As the name suggests, TPIMs ought to be investigatory as well as preventive.[167] The Chief Officer of the appropriate police force must 'secure that the investigation of the individual's conduct, with a view to a prosecution of the individual for an offence relating to terrorism, is kept under review throughout the period the TPIM notice is in force'.[168] There is no information in the Terrorism Prevention and Investigation Measures Act 2011 as to the frequency of these reviews, although the Chief Officer must provide a report on any review to the Secretary of State.[169] These reports have not been made public; however, in 2013 the then Independent Reviewer of Terrorism Legislation, David Anderson QC gave some insight into them:

> That duty is discharged through reports which are made known to the CPS [Crown Prosecution Service]. In practice, most discussion tends to be of the subject's compliance with the terms of his TPIM notice, and the feasibility of prosecution for breach. I am told that if evidence were to come to light of engagement in [Terrorism-Related Activity] prior to or during the currency of a TPIM notice, the mechanisms exist to ensure that the CPS would be asked to supplement its advice on the feasibility of prosecution. This is, however, not common in practice.[170]

This suggests that even though the police are required to keep the possibility of initiating a prosecution against an individual subject to a TPIM under review, this is not happening in practice. The opportunity for the police to consider whether, in their view, the TPIM remains necessary and appropriate, is thus being missed.

Reviews relating to the TPIM regime

In addition to reviews of individual TPIM cases, the Terrorism Prevention and Investigation Measures Act 2011 provides for four mechanisms of reviewing the TPIM regime as a whole. First, the Secretary of State must prepare and lay before Parliament quarterly reports on the exercise of the TPIM powers.[171] Successive Home Secretaries have fulfilled their obligation under the Act by publishing a written ministerial statement in both Houses of Parliament.[172] These reports include information only on the exercise of the powers; they are simply statistical accounts of the use of TPIMs in each three-month period. The reports tend to include information on the number of TPIM notices in force, the number in respect of British citizens, the number of TPIMs extended, revoked or revived during the reporting period, the number of applications to vary TPIM measures, the number of variations made to measures specified in TPIMs and the number of individuals who were relocated as part of their TPIM.[173] In addition to the exercise of the TPIM powers, recent written ministerial statements have also contained information on any TPIM proceedings that have taken place during the reporting period (such as review hearings or appeals), whether any individuals have been charged with the offence of breaching a TPIM in the reporting period, and the dates of any meetings of the TPIM Review Group (which we discuss below). Up to July 2019, written ministerial statements had been published on every three-month period, although publication was not always prompt.[174]

The second and third review mechanisms relate to the same review process: the sunset clause in section 21 of the Terrorism Prevention and Investigation Measures Act 2011. This provides for the expiry of the 'Secretary of State's TPIM powers ... at the end of 5 years beginning with the day on which this Act is passed'.[175] The Secretary of State may seek to renew the legislation beyond five years. However, to do so she must first consult with the Independent Reviewer of Terrorism Legislation, the Investigatory Powers Commissioner, and the Director General of the Security Service,[176] and then lay an order before Parliament to continue the legislation in force for a further period not exceeding five years,[177] which must be approved by a resolution of both Houses.[178] Thus, the sunset clause instigates two potential but connected reviews: that of the Home Secretary in deciding whether to seek renewal, and that of Parliament should she actually seek the continuation in force of the legislation.

In 2016 when the Terrorism Prevention and Investigation Measures Act 2011 was due to expire, then Home Secretary Amber Rudd opted to seek renewal. The Minister for Security confirmed in the House of Commons that '[i]n accordance with section 21 of the TPIM Act, the director general of MI5, the independent reviewer of terrorism legislation and the intelligence services commissioner have all been consulted, and they all recommend the continuation of the Secretary of State's powers'.[179] Baroness Chisholm of Owlpen made an identical statement in the equivalent debate in the House of Lords.[180] No further information on the consultation was provided, but nor was there any obligation on the Secretary of State to make the advice received from the consultation public, even in redacted form.[181] Furthermore, none of those consulted (the Independent Reviewer of Terrorism Legislation, the Investigatory Powers Commissioner and the Director General of the Security Service) published information on the advice they provided. Little is known about what form the consultation took, and so the standards applied by this review to evaluate whether to continue the legislation for another five years are, therefore, unknown.

When the renewal order – the Draft Terrorism Prevention and Investigation Measures Act 2011 (Continuation) Order 2016 – was laid before the Houses of Parliament, responsibility for reviewing the statutory instrument was entrusted to the Third Delegated Legislation Committee of the House of Commons. The Order was to be subject to the affirmative resolution procedure, in respect of which there are no set criteria for evaluation. It was thus up to the Committee to decide how to proceed. On 26 October 2016, the Committee spent just 32 minutes considering the Order before recommending its approval, focusing on the question of the effectiveness of the TPIM regime in preventing terrorism.[182] Five days later, without any debate at all, the House of Commons agreed to approve the order.[183] On 24 November 2016, the House of Lords took its turn at reviewing the statutory instrument. After only 17 minutes of debate, involving just three speakers (including the Peer who introduced the motion), the House of Lords approved the Draft Terrorism Prevention and Investigation Measures Act 2011 (Continuation) Order 2016.[184] The lack of meaningful debate becomes all the more concerning when we recall that MPs, including those sitting on the Committee, made their decision without up-to-date information about the operation of TPIMs: the Home Secretary had fulfilled her obligation to publish quarterly statistics by publishing her ministerial statement on the morning that the debate took place in the Committee. It seemed that some MPs were not aware of this, with Rupa Huq MP, for example, stating that 'we are down to just one TPIM' and having to be corrected by James Brokenshire MP, who informed her that '[t]here are now six'.[185]

The final review mechanism built into the Terrorism Prevention and Investigation Measures Act 2011 is review by the Independent Reviewer of Terrorism Legislation.[186] A report on the outcome of the review is to be submitted to the Secretary of State,[187] who, upon 'receiving' it, must lay a copy before Parliament.[188] Until 12 April 2015, the review had to take place annually,[189] but under the Counter-Terrorism and Security Act 2015 the Independent Reviewer now has discretion to decide whether to review the Act annually or less often.[190] The Independent Reviewer has undertaken two reviews since 2014, the first of which was conducted under the statutory obligation to review the law annually.[191] That report, published in March 2015, was remarkably brief, in part because no new

TPIMs had been made during the reporting period, and only one TPIM remained in force.[192] It focused instead on outlining the changes made to the TPIM regime under the Counter-Terrorism and Security Act 2015, including the changes that the Independent Reviewer had proposed as part of a non-statutory review, which we discuss below.[193] No further statutory review of TPIMs took place until Max Hill QC carried out a thematic review of executive powers, including TPIMs, in his report on the Terrorism Acts in 2017, which was published in October 2018.[194] Hill did not evaluate the TPIM regime itself against any particular standards. Instead he highlighted the role of the TPIM Review Group (which we also discuss further below) and the courts in scrutinising individual TPIMs, including the 'interference in the ordinary rights of TPIM subjects (and by extension, their immediate family members)'.[195] Hill concluded that the TPIM regime 'continues to survive robust scrutiny as to the necessity and proportionality of the many interferences with the rights of TPIM subjects which go hand in hand with every measure made'.[196]

Non-statutory reviews

A number of review mechanisms have developed in tandem with TPIMs. Two of these apply to the regime as a whole. The first is the annual CONTEST report, discussed above. The 2014 report included no evaluation of TPIMs, but merely a description of the changes brought about by the Counter-Terrorism and Security Act 2015.[197] The 2015 report provided much the same information, as well as stating that two TPIMs were in force at the end of the reporting period.[198] These reports provided little evaluation of the TPIM regime or its place in the wider CONTEST strategy, and it is difficult to identify within it any case in which TPIMs were assessed 'against a set of performance indicators' as the 2011 CONTEST strategy suggested.

The second is a 'snapshot' review undertaken by the Independent Reviewer pursuant to a request from the Home Secretary on 11 September 2014.[199] She asked him to consider whether

> the operational objectives for the management of TPIM subjects could be met through the sole use of exclusion zones (either under the existing legislative framework or through amendment of the legislation to allow more extensive use), or whether some form of relocation power would be needed and if so what form the new power should take.[200]

This particular review was commissioned to inform the government's planned legislation to counter the threat from foreign terrorist fighters. It had been signalled in a speech by then Prime Minister David Cameron on 1 September 2014,[201] but the Counter-Terrorism and Security Bill was not introduced into Parliament until 26 November 2014. It followed David Anderson QC's review of TPIMs, which was completed on 17 September 2014, but not made public.[202] Anderson's attempts to include a redacted version of the review in his report on TPIMs in 2014 were unsuccessful, and the only information that has been made public is a summary of the recommendations, published first on the Independent Reviewer of Terrorism Legislation's website,[203] and subsequently as part of the 2014 TPIMs report.[204]

Two review mechanisms have been established in relation to individual TPIMs. The TPIM Review Group was established when the Terrorism Prevention and Investigation Measures Act 2011 replaced the Prevention of Terrorism Act 2005.[205] What little is known about this Group has been published by the Independent Reviewer of Terrorism Legislation. In his report on TPIMs in 2012, the Independent Reviewer said the Group's terms of reference were 'to bring together the departments and agencies involved in making, maintaining and monitoring TPIM notices on a quarterly basis to keep all cases under frequent, formal and audited review'.[206] This includes review of the necessity and proportionality of individual TPIMs, as well as their impact on each TPIM subject and their family.[207]

As the minutes of meetings are not made public, we only know that meetings have in fact taken place because we are told that they have in the written ministerial statements made under section 11 of the Terrorism Prevention and Investigation Measures Act 2011. Recent statements have included information on the number of times and dates on which the TPIM Review Group has met. For example, the statement made by Home Secretary Sajid Javid on 31 October 2018 noted that '[t]he second quarter TRG [TPIM Review Group] meetings took place on 6, 7, 11, 22 and 25 June 2018 and 3 and 5 July 2018. The most recent TRG meetings took place on 12, 14, 18, 25 and 27 September 2018. The next round of TRGs will take place during December 2018.'[208] In contrast, earlier statements tended just to note the month of the next TPIM Review Group meeting and that it kept 'every TPIM notice under regular and formal review'.[209]

In addition to the TPIM Review Group, since 2013 a new TPIM Strategy Meeting has taken place on a quarterly basis. As with the TPIM Review Group, it has no statutory basis or formal terms of reference. According to David Anderson QC, membership of the Quarterly TPIM

Strategy Meeting consists of the head of the Pursue Disruptions Unit at the Home Office's Office for Security and Counter-Terrorism (who chairs the meeting), as well as representatives from MI5, the Metropolitan Police Service, the Prevent team in the Office for Security and Counter-Terrorism, and the CPS.[210] It meets after the TPIM Review Group meetings 'to discuss strategic issues concerning the operation and future use of TPIMs'.[211] As for the TPIM Review Group, the outcomes of the TPIM Strategy Meeting are not published, so it is not possible to know what role the views of its members on whether a TPIM should continue have in terms of the Secretary of State's decision-making in relation to individual TPIMs, or what standards are applied when considering strategic questions of TPIMs' continued use.

Reviews undertaken as part of the everyday business of statehood

In addition to these designated routes to review of TPIMs, it is always open to the Government to initiate an ad hoc review of any counter-terrorism measure, including TPIMs. One such review has taken place. In October 2016, the Home Office provided a 'Memorandum to the Home Affairs Committee' as part of its post-legislative scrutiny of the Terrorism Prevention and Investigation Measures Act 2011.[212] According to the Home Office, the 'memorandum provides a preliminary assessment of the Terrorism Prevention and Investigation Measures Act 2011'.[213] It purports to do so by 'setting out the policy intention/objectives and the impact these powers have had over the five year period'.[214] The memorandum, however, focuses heavily on the operational use of TPIMs, with little analysis of impact, except inasmuch as it asserts their effectiveness as a preventive counter-terrorism measure. The Home Office's ultimate assessment was that 'the Act has met its intended objectives'.[215]

As ever, Parliament has a considerable potential role in reviewing TPIMs, especially as they seem to come within the remit of a number of parliamentary committees. However, in practice only the Joint Committee on Human Rights (JCHR) and the House of Commons Select Committee on Home Affairs have conducted reviews of TPIMs since 1 January 2014.[216] One of these – the JCHR's post-legislative scrutiny of the Act – focused specifically on TPIMs as the subject of inquiry. In it, the Committee assessed how the TPIM regime was 'functioning in practice, in terms of its human rights implications, and of the continued necessity for it'.[217] The JCHR evaluated the impact of TPIMs on the individual concerned and their family members,[218] and the fairness of TPIM proceedings.[219] Two further reports considered TPIMs as just one part of a broader review of counter-terrorism. In 2015, the JCHR examined TPIMs in its pre-legislative scrutiny of the Counter-Terrorism and Security Bill, then making its way through Parliament.[220] It noted that in the absence of sufficiently detailed information about the terrorist threat picture, it could not evaluate whether particular changes to the legislation were in fact necessary. It did, however, raise questions about the impact on family life and the potential for TPIMs to cause 'extreme resentment in certain minority communities who felt victimised by its use against members of those communities'.[221] It thus engaged both rights and effectiveness as evaluative standards. Also in 2015, the House of Commons Select Committee on Home Affairs evaluated TPIMs as part of its review into the government's response to foreign terrorist fighters. Its main concern was the effectiveness of TPIMs, in particular in providing for the deradicalisation of individuals subject to them.[222]

On rare occasions, parliamentary questions on TPIMs have been asked. Since 1 January 2014, these questions have largely sought information on the number of TPIMs in existence, the number of TPIMs applying to returned foreign terrorist fighters or supporters of Islamic State, and the cost of legal aid spent on TPIMs.[223] Questions were typically answered within a week,[224] but where the information sought related to the number of TPIMs in existence, the reply tended to point the enquirer to the most recent written ministerial statement presented to Parliament by the Home Secretary.[225] In the same period, ministers have been asked oral questions,[226] again predominantly relating to the number of individuals subject to a TPIM,[227] as well as the government's approach to TPIM individuals once their TPIM had expired,[228] and the effectiveness of TPIMs.[229] Questions about TPIMs have also been raised in a number of parliamentary debates on a variety subjects, including primary legislation (whether specifically terrorism-related or otherwise)[230] and statutory instruments,[231] the European Council,[232] terrorist attacks,[233] and security in the Middle East.[234] Since 1 January 2014, two debates relating to TPIMs have been initiated in Parliament. On 21 January 2014, Yvette Cooper MP moved a motion on TPIMs that resulted in a two and half hour debate in the House of Commons.[235] Cooper, who contributed extensively to the debate, was concerned about the government's claims that TPIMs were 'working' and the effectiveness of the TPIM regime as a whole, particularly in comparison to the predecessor control order regime.[236] This was because the TPIMs in relation to six individuals were due to expire that month.[237] A month later, the Grand Committee in the House of Lords considered a question relating to the assessment that the government had made 'of the effectiveness of counterterrorism practices; and what measures they will adopt to reduce any harm caused by ineffective or provocative practices'.[238] Questions about TPIMs, in particular their effectiveness in preventing individuals subject to them from absconding, were raised as part of this short debate.[239]

Finally, TPIMs were discussed as part of the pre-legislative scrutiny of the Counter-Terrorism and Security Act 2015. That Act made a number of changes to the TPIM regime. For the most part, these implemented recommendations that had been in the Independent Reviewer's ad hoc review, discussed above.[240] The most controversial of these changes was the introduction of a power to relocate individuals subject to a TPIM up to 200 miles from their ordinary residence.[241] This type of relocation measure had previously been included in the control order regime under the Prevention of Terrorism Act 2005,[242] but its removal was one of the liberalising aspects of the change to TPIMs in 2011. Much of the parliamentary debate in relation to TPIMs during the passage of the Counter-Terrorism and Security Act 2015 focused on the introduction of a relocation measure into the Terrorism Prevention and Investigation Measures Act 2011. Labour politicians, in particular, were keen to stress that the existing TPIM regime (minus the relocation measure) was ineffective, because a number of TPIM subjects had managed to abscond and that the Conservative-led Coalition government had erred in excluding relocation from the Terrorism Prevention and Investigation Measures Act 2011.[243] Yvette Cooper MP summed these arguments up neatly, when she stated:

> On TPIMs, the Home Secretary knows that we have called for some time for the Government to bring back the relocation powers that were abolished a few years ago. We are glad that she has finally done so. It is clear that the police and the agencies had concluded that TPIMs were no longer useful in their previous form. I hope that this Bill will change that and make them useful again.[244]

Questions of effectiveness were also raised by non-Labour politicians, but there was a divide between those who supported the introduction of a relocation power to ensure the effectiveness of the TPIM regime,[245] and those who questioned how relocation could effectively manage the threat posed by individuals subject to a TPIM.[246] Others were, however, concerned about the impact on rights and liberties of those subject to TPIMs,[247] and the importance of safeguards attaching to the regime.[248] In the House of Lords there was concern about the potential impact of the relocation measure on families,[249] although for some the concern was largely about whether the approach might be counter-productive and harmful in the longer term.[250] As the Lord Bishop of Durham put it:

> [T]here must be concern for those separated from a parent
> made to move under a TPIM. Breaking up a family, as could
> occur, could create longer-term harm even, at one extreme,
> sowing the seeds of the next generation of terrorists in young
> children. Great care needs to be taken with any form of what
> amounts to internal exile that leaves children wondering what
> has happened to their parent.[251]

Litigation relating to TPIMs, beyond the specified proceedings discussed above, is also possible. However, there has been no judicial review of TPIMs since 1 January 2014, and only one Human Rights Act 1998 challenge has been reported since 1 January 2014. In *DD v Secretary of State for the Home Department*,[252] the Court held an expedited hearing on the preliminary issue of 'whether the imposition of a TPIM on DD is a breach of his rights under art.3 ECHR, and consequently a breach of s6 HRA'. It held that the hardship imposed by the TPIM did not meet the minimum threshold of severity required to find a violation of Article 3 of the European Convention on Human Rights.[253]

Civil society reviews

Three reviews of TPIMs have been undertaken by civil society organisations, two by Liberty and one by Justice.[254] Two further briefing notes – by Amnesty International and Big Brother Watch respectively – were also released during the debate stages of the Counter-Terrorism and Security Bill in 2014.[255] These reviews evaluated TPIMs against the criteria of whether they were fair,[256] effective,[257] sufficiently distinct from and an improvement on control orders,[258] and the impact they had on both the TPIM subject and their family.[259] On fairness, Justice said:

> TPIMs and its predecessor control orders are the antithesis of
> common law fairness ... They involve severe restrictions being
> imposed on individuals, who have never been charged with or
> convicted of a criminal offence ... The more draconian the
> controls, the greater the case must be for the higher criminal
> standard of proof to apply.[260]

As both Justice and Liberty pointed out, the relevant controls had been lowered. Liberty also indicated that the limited use of TPIMs to date did not represent a successful policy, but a refusal to consider alternative measures.[261] In the same briefing, Liberty also highlighted how the 2015 amendments to TPIMs, which were intended to be more rights-respecting than control orders, meant that the regime would be 'identical with the previous Control Order regime – reintroducing its most punishing and unjust feature, the overnight residence requirement'.[262] The relocation power, as we have already seen, was of particular concern because of the additional impact of a TPIM on the subject and their family.[263] In their briefing on the Counter-Terrorism and Security Bill in 2014, Amnesty said 'adding the internal exile of forced relocation to the already unfair TPIM regime is another measure which causes significant concern for basic freedoms'.[264]

Conclusion: meaningful accountability through review?

Both Prevent and TPIMs are among the most controversial parts of the counter-terrorist state. A close consideration of the (possible and actual) reviews of these measures can, thus, act as a useful illustration of whether, when and against what standards the counter-terrorism review assemblage evaluates counter-terrorism.

While the legislative matrix of review can appear turgid – requiring multiple reporting exercises, authorisations, judicial reviews, Independent Reviewer reports and so on – once the maze of provisions is stripped back, we can see that review takes place against a remarkably narrow range of standards. The questions that are asked are largely about operational effectiveness by reference to the objectives of the measures themselves, or about lawfulness (whether that is adherence to statutory requirements, compliance with the Human Rights Act 1998 or satisfaction of judicial review standards). Within the reviews that are undertaken or mandated by the organs of the state and their delegees (including the Independent Reviewer), there is far less focus on qualitative questions of societal impact and unforeseen consequences than on effectiveness. In some cases, processes that have capacity to act as review (for example, required reporting on the operation of a measure) become simple information provision exercises: placing statistical data on the record rather than engaging in evaluative analysis. In others they become a matter of compliance monitoring, if not enforcement, with little or no review component at all. While civil society reviews seem more engaged with qualitative realities and with fundamental questions of design, it is questionable whether these reviews impact on Government action or influence parliamentary accountability work in significant ways.

As these two case studies suggest, there seems to be little engagement by Parliament in maximising its accountability-enhancing role in the counter-terrorist state. We have seen that when reporting is undertaken as a statistical, rather than evaluative, exercise, Parliament does not seem to do much to make these data do more evaluative work or to use them to ground more evaluative review processes. As we discuss more in Chapter 4, this suggests that for all the reliance on review as a safeguard in counter-terrorism legislation, Parliament's historical tendency not robustly to challenge security narratives from Government is remarkably resilient. While these mandated reviews do take place (and non-mandated or discretionary reviews seem to be less frequent), their success in evaluating the measures, engaging in reality and showing capacity for action is questionable.

This is especially important because, as we show here, Parliament has a very significant role in review, at least 'on paper'. It certainly has far more opportunities for review-type interventions in the counter-terrorist state than does the Independent Reviewer, even though – as we will show in Chapters 3 and 4 – he is extremely prominent when those working within the counter-terrorism review assemblage are asked to reflect on review. In spite of this, it is not entirely clear that the reviews undertaken by Parliament contribute effectively to meaningful accountability in the counter-terrorist state. Rather, what these examples of reviews as actually undertaken in the UK seem to suggest is that while we know that Prevent and TPIMs are being used, we do not know whether they 'work' effectively to counter terrorism. Nor do the organs of state seem to be especially interested in finding that out, or in addressing concerns that, in fact, these measures may be counter-productive when a longer-term view of countering terrorism is taken.

Notes

[1] HM Government, *Contest: The United Kingdom's Strategy for Countering Terrorism* (CM 9608, 2018) para 333.

[2] Ibid.

[3] Ibid.

[4] Counter-Terrorism and Security Act 2015, s 26.

[5] Including from, amongst others, the Independent Reviewer of Terrorism Legislation: David Anderson QC, 'David Anderson QC: 'Prevent Strategy Can Work Against Radicalisation ... If It Is Trusted' (*Evening Standard*, 15 February 2017) and civil society: Rights Watch UK and Liberty, 'Briefing on the Higher Education and Research Bill: an independent review of Prevent' (March 2017).

[6] Counter-Terrorism and Border Security Act 2019, s 20(8).

[7] Ibid s 20(9).

[8] Ibid s 20(10).

[9] Some reviews undertaken by the Independent Reviewer of Terrorism Legislation fall into this category: Terrorism Act 2006, s 36; Counter-Terrorism and Security Act 2015, s 45.

[10] Jamie Grierson, 'Home Office faces legal battle over Prevent reviewer' (*The Guardian*, 29 August 2019).

[11] Specified authorities are the authorities specified in Schedule 6 of the Counter-Terrorism and Security Act 2015.

[12] Counter-Terrorism and Security Act 2015, s 27(4).

[13] Ibid s 29(5).

[14] Under section 36 of the Counter-Terrorism and Security Act 2015, 'local authorities' are responsible for ensuring that a panel is in place to assess 'the extent to which identified individuals are vulnerable to being drawn into terrorism' and prepare a plan to support them.

[15] Counter-Terrorism and Security Act 2015, s 39(5).

[16] The list of 'partners of local panels' in Schedule 7 of the Act includes, for example: Ministers of the Crown, a government department, a local authority, a governor of a prison, the governing body of an institution in the further education sector, an NHS trust or foundation, or a chief officer of a police force in England and Wales. It is the role of the partners of a local panel to 'so far as appropriate and reasonably practicable, act in co-operation with – (a) the panel in the carrying out of its functions; (b) the police in the carrying out of their functions in connection with' a panel. Ibid s 38(1).

[17] Ibid s 39(5).

[18] The Counter-Terrorism and Security Act 2015 (Risk of Being Drawn into Terrorism) (Guidance) Regulations 2015 SI 2015/928; The Counter-Terrorism and Security Act 2015 (Risk of Being Drawn into Terrorism) (Amendment and Guidance) Regulations 2015, SI 2015/1697.

[19] HL Deb 23 March 2015, vol 760, cols 1232–51.

[20] Ibid col 1234.

[21] Ibid col 1239.

[22] Ibid col 1240.

[23] HL Deb 17 September 2015, vol 764, col 2051.

[24] Counter-Terrorism and Security Act 2015, s 32(4)(b) and (6).

[25] Counter-Terrorism and Security Act 2015 (Monitoring of Further Education Bodies) (England) Regulations 2016, SI 2016/683.

[26] Ibid.

[27] Counter-Terrorism and Security Act 2015, s 32(4).

[28] Counter-Terrorism and Security Act 2015 (Monitoring of Further Education Bodies) (England) Regulations 2016, SI 2016/683, 2; Office for Students, *Prevent duty: Framework for monitoring in higher education in England 2018–19 onwards* (12 September 2018), para 19. Available from: https://www.officeforstudents.org. uk/media/3e9aa5d3-21de-4b24-ac21-18de19b041dc/ofs2018__35.pdf [Accessed 29 March 2019].

[29] A search of legislation.gov.uk in relation to statutory instruments related to the Counter-Terrorism and Security Act 2015 reveals no statutory instrument formally undertaking this delegation, but it is confirmed by both the Office for Students, ibid and Education Secretary Damian Hinds, 'Counter-Terrorism and Security Act 2015: Delegation of Monitoring Authority Function to the Office for Students' (2018). Available from: https://www.officeforstudents.org.uk/media/1301/ prevent-ofs-delegation-letter.pdf [Accessed 29 March 2019].

[30] See for example, NHS Contract Team, 'NHS Standard Contract 2017/18 and 2018/19 Particulars (Full Length) May 2018 Edition' (May 2018).

[31] Established by the Social Services and Well-being (Wales) Act 2014.

32 NHS Resilience Scotland, *Playing Our Part Implementing the Prevent Strategy: Guidance for Health Boards* (January 2015).

33 Counter-Terrorism and Security Act 2015, s 29.

34 HM Government, *Revised Prevent Duty Guidance for England and Wales* (Crown Copyright 2015) 5.

35 Ibid.

36 Issued pursuant to section 29 Counter-Terrorism and Security Act 2015.

37 Counter-Terrorism and Security Act 2015, s 36(4)(c).

38 Deduced from analysis of Home Office, *Individuals referred to and supported through the Prevent Programme, April 2015 to March 2016 Statistical Bulletin 23/17* (Crown Copyright 2017) 4; Home Office, *Individuals referred to and supported through the Prevent Programme, April 2016 to March 2017 Statistical Bulletin 06/18* (Crown Copyright 2018) 4; Home Office, *Individuals referred to and supported through the Prevent Programme, April 2017 to March 2018 Statistical bulletin 31/18* (Crown Copyright 2019) 4.

39 HM Government *Channel Duty Guidance Protecting vulnerable people from being drawn into terrorism Statutory guidance for Channel panel members and partners of local panels* (Crown Copyright, 2015) 18.

40 Ibid.

41 Home Office *Prevent Duty Toolkit for Local Authorities and Partner Agencies Supplementary Information to the Prevent Duty Guidance for England and Wales* (7 September 2018), Available from: https://assets.publishing.service.gov.uk/government/uploads/system/uploads/attachment_data/file/736759/Prevent_Duty_Toolkit_for_Local_Authorities.pdf [Accessed 26 March 2019].

42 HM Government, *The Coalition: Our Programme for Government* (Crown Copyright 2010) 11, 24.

43 HM Government, *Report to the Home Secretary of Independent Oversight of Prevent Review and Strategy* (Crown Copyright 2011).

44 Ibid paras 25 and 63

45 Ibid paras 6 and 42.

46 HM Government, *Prevent Strategy* (Cm 8092, 2011) 2.

47 Ibid 3–4.

48 Home Office, 'Prevent Strategy 2011' (7 June 2011), Available from: https://www.gov.uk/government/publications/prevent-strategy-2011 [Accessed 24 March 2019].

49 HM Government, 'National Security Capability Review' (March 2018), Available from: https://assets.publishing.service.gov.uk/government/uploads/system/uploads/attachment_data/file/705347/6.4391_CO_National-Security-Review_web.pdf [Accessed 29 March 2019].

50 HM Government, *National Security Strategy and Strategic Defence and Security Review 2015 A Secure and Prosperous United Kingdom* (Cm 9161, 2015).

51 HM Government (n 1) 26.

52 For example, we are told that the National Security Capability Review 'found CONTEST to be a well-organised and comprehensive response to terrorism, with strengths in terms of powers, resources, reach and resilience'. Quoted in HM Government (n 1) 6.

53 HM Government, *CONTEST: The United Kingdom's Strategy for Countering Terrorism* (Cm 8123, 2011), 15 and 109.

54 HM Government (n 1) 87.

55 In the 2011 iteration of CONTEST, the apparent indicators for Prevent were (i) public support in the UK and overseas for terrorism (ii) proportion of priority

local areas in which prevent is "on track", (iii) the numbers of people participating in Prevent and percentage assessed to be at reduced risk of supporting or engaging in terrorism-related activity after completing the programme, (iv) popularity of terrorism-related website and disruption of terrorist content online, and (v) radicalisation in prisons: HM Government (n 53) 117.

56 HM Government, *CONTEST The United Kingdom's Strategy for Countering Terrorism Annual Report for 2014* (Cm 9048, 2015) 15-17; HM *Government, CONTEST The United Kingdom's Strategy for Countering Terrorism Annual Report for 2015* (Cm 9310, 2016) 15–17.

57 Home Office (n 38).

58 One higher education representative described informal interactions with the relevant Police Counter-Terrorism Unit Link. This is a dedicated officer who might be approached informally to ask 'can you give us a bit of advice on a student?' who might then indicate that 'there's no CT concern here' precluding the need for a formal referral (P16). Another interviewee with an in-depth knowledge of the Prevent Duty also explained that they felt there is 'a vast number of referrals that don't make it to the Prevent case management tracker because they've been dealt with at the primary level of triage' so are not represented in the Police collated data (P8). According to this participant, the Home Office statistical reports are 'only the tip of iceberg' (P8).

59 In Parliament in December 2018, Lord Carlile stated: 'The board was established during the coalition Government, and was accepted by the coalition Government, in response to the review that I conducted – on behalf of the coalition Government – of the Prevent strand of counterterrorism policy.' HC Deb 17 December 2018, vol 794, col 1638. Lord Carlile's report, however, suggests that it was the government that proposed the new board: 'The strategy provides for the establishment of a permanent, nonexecutive Prevent board to oversee Prevent strategy and its local implementation.' HM Government, *Report to the Home Secretary of Independent Oversight of Prevent Review and Strategy* (Crown Copyright, 2011).

60 HM Government (n 53) 110.

61 Ibid.

62 HM Government (n 46) 96.

63 HM Government (n 34) 5.

64 Home Office, *Prevent Oversight Board: Written Question – 4388* (HL 2016–17, 4388).

65 HL Deb, 17 December 2018, vol 794, col 1638. On this, Lord Carlile said 'One of the points made at the most recent meeting was that, if the board is to be effective, it must meet more frequently'.

66 Home Office, FOI Response 48090 (14 June 2018), Available from: https://counterterrorismreview.files.wordpress.com/2018/07/foi-response-48090-lydia-morgan-final.pdf [Accessed 26 March 2019].

67 Joint Committee on Human Rights, *Legislative Scrutiny: Counter-Terrorism and Security Bill* (2014–15, HL 8, HC 85); Joint Committee on Human Rights, *Freedom of Speech in Universities* (2017–19, HL 111, HC 58); Home Affairs Committee, *Counter-Terrorism* (2013–14, HC 231); Home Affairs Committee, *Counter-Terrorism: Foreign Fighters* (2014–15, HC 933); Education Committee, *Extremism in Schools: The Trojan Horse Affair* (2014–15, HC 47); Intelligence and Security Committee of Parliament, *Report on the Intelligence Relating to Fusilier Lee Rigby* (2014–15 HC 795); Intelligence and Security Committee of Parliament, *The 2017 Attacks: What Needs to Change?* (2018–19, HC 1694).

[68] Joint Committee on Human Rights, *Legislative Scrutiny* (n 67)

[69] Joint Committee on Human Rights, *Uncorrected Transcript of Oral Evidence with David Anderson* (2014–15, HC 859).

[70] Joint Committee on Human Rights, *Uncorrected Transcript of Oral Evidence with James Brokenshire* (2014–15, HC 859).

[71] Joint Committee on Human Rights (n 69), 16; (n 70) 22–3, 27–8, 31.

[72] Joint Committee on Human Rights (n 69); (n 70).

[73] Joint Committee on Human Rights, *Legislative Scrutiny* (n 67) para 6.7.

[74] Ibid paras 6.10–6.11. The JCHR recommended that the duty not be applied to Universities or, that at the very least a provision about academic freedom be added to the Bill.

[75] Ibid para 6.13. See also recommendations 25–9.

[76] Ibid para 6.7.

[77] Joint Committee on Human Rights, *Freedom of Speech in Universities* (n 67).

[78] Home Affairs Committee, *Counter-Terrorism* (n 67); Home Affairs Committee, *Counter-Terrorism: Foreign Fighters* (n 67); Home Affairs Committee, *Radicalisation: the Counter-Narrative and Identifying the Tipping Point* (2016–17, HC 135).

[79] Home Affairs Committee, *Radicalisation* (n 78) paras 11–15.

[80] Intelligence and Security Committee of Parliament, *The 2017 Attacks: What Needs to Change?* (HC 2018–19, 1694).

[81] Ministry of Justice, *Prisoners: Radicalism: Written Question – 1769* (HL 2015–16, 1769); Home Office, *Radicalism and Religiously Aggravated Offences: Written Question – 44664* (HC 2016–17, 44664);

[82] Home Office, *Counter-terrorism: Written Question – 51248* (HC 2016–17, 51248).

[83] HC Deb 9 February 2015, vol 592 col 541.

[84] Home Office (n 81).

[85] HC Deb 1 February 2017, vol 620, col 356WH.

[86] Ibid cols 368WH, 371WH, 372WH, 373–4WH, 376–7WH.

[87] Ibid cols 370–1WH, 373WH. Similar concerns have been raised in the House of Lords. In a debate on counter-terrorism in communities, Lord Sheikh noted: 'The Government need to understand the Muslim community's concern about the Prevent strategy and its effectiveness. Muslims are not convinced that the Government's counterterrorism strategy is working. It needs to be overhauled, with participation from the Muslim community.' HL Deb 26 November 2015, vol 767, col 878.

[88] Ibid col 358WH.

[89] Ibid.

[90] Ibid col 365WH, 368WH, 370WH, 371WH.

[91] Ibid 371WH.

[92] HC Deb 2 December 2014, vol 589, cols 207–73. There were four days of debate in the Commons on the Bill with substantive debate on the first and fourth days. Substantial debate also took place in the Lords. See: HL Deb 13 January 2015 Vol 758 cols 661–772.

[93] HC Deb 2 December 2014, vol 589, cols 215–16, 219–20, 240.

[94] Ibid vol 589, cols 215–16, 235, 239–40, 247.

[95] Ibid vol 589, col 219.

[96] Ibid vol 589, cols 207, 219, 220, 247.

[97] Ibid vol 589, col 238.

[98] Ibid vol 589, col 241.

[99] Ibid col 240.

100 HC Deb 11 June 2018 vol 642, cols 640–1, 646, 648–9, 671.

101 Ibid cols 640, 641, 647, 671, 677, 681.

102 Ibid col 682.

103 *R on the application of Salman Butt v Secretary of State for the Home Department* [2019] EWCA Civ 256.

104 Ibid, [53].

105 HM Government (n 34) para 11.

106 [2019] EWCA Civ 256 [177].

107 Institutions are provided with reporting guidance by the Office for Students. For example Office for Students, 'Guidance for Prevent Annual Reports 2016–17', Available from: https://www.officeforstudents.org.uk/media/1080/guidance_for_prevent_annual_reporting1617.pdf [Accessed 25 March 2019].

108 Office for Students, 'Prevent-related serious incidents guidance' (15 October 2018), Available from: https://www.officeforstudents.org.uk/media/29154421-d3e7-4989-9e53-94413fd013f9/ofs-prevent-related-serious-incident-guidance.pdf [Accessed 29 March 2019].

109 Office for Students (n 107) para 13.

110 Ibid para 8.

111 P8; P16; P17; P21.

112 P16; P17.

113 This was so prior to the instigation of the Prevent Duty in 2015 as well, although we focus on reviews under the new statutory scheme. See for example Arun Kundnani, *Spooked! How Not to Prevent Violent Extremism* (Institute of Race Relations 2009).

114 For example in November 2018 Amnesty International, Article 19, Committee on the Administration of Justice, Human Rights Watch, Index on Censorship, Liberty, Medact and Rights Watch (UK) issued a joint call for an amendment to be inserted in the Counter-Terrorism and Border Security Bill that would require an independent review of Prevent (Open letter on the UK's 'Prevent' Counter-Terrorism Strategy, 16 November 2018). See also British Muslims for Secular Democracy, *Democracy, Integration and Freedom in the Age of Prevent: Report* (2017), calling for Prevent to be reviewed every two years.

115 See Muslim Council of Britain, 'Meeting between David Anderson QC and the MCB: Concerns on Prevent' (2015), Available from: https://www.mcb.org.uk/wp-content/uploads/2015/10/20150803-Case-studies-about-Prevent.pdf [Accessed 25 March 2019], reporting on this meeting which took place on 28 July 2015 and in which the MCB shared case studies that they claimed established that Prevent was resulting in Muslim young children being viewed through a security lens, leading to over-reporting, discriminatory application of the law, and consequential self-censorship by young children.

116 Liberty, *Liberty's Second Reading briefing on the Counter-Terrorism and Security Bill in the House of Lords* (2015); Justice, *Counter-Terrorism and Security Bill House of Commons Second Reading* (2014).

117 In addition to the illustrative examples later in this chapter, a number of other organisations have completed (largely sector-specific) reviews since 2014. See Nikita Malik, *Radicalising Our Children An Analysis Of Family Court Cases Of British Children At Risk Of Radicalisation, 2013–2018* (Henry Jackson Society Centre on Radicalisation and Terrorism 2019); Emma Webb, *For Our Children: An Examination of Prevent in the Curriculum* (HJS Centre for the Response to Radicalisation and Terrorism Policy Paper No. 10 2017); Rupert Sutton, *Myths and*

Misunderstandings: Understanding Opposition to The Prevent Strategy (Centre for the Response to Radicalisation and Terrorism 2016); Cage, 'Separating Families: How PREVENT Seeks the Removal of Children' (2018) Available from: https://www. cage.ngo/separating-families-2 [Accessed 25 March 2019]; Cage, 'The "science" of pre-crime: The secret "radicalisation" study underpinning PREVENT' (2016) Available from: https://cage.ngo/wp-content/uploads/2016/09/CAGE-Science-Pre-Crime-Report.pdf [Accessed 25 March 2019].

[118] Rights Watch UK, *Preventing Education? Human Rights and UK Counter-Terrorism Policy in Schools* (2016), 4. Along similar lines the Institute of Race Relations found that Prevent 'undermines' children's rights under the UN Convention on the Rights of the Child, although it drew this conclusion from a review of existing research and opinion, rather than an autonomous doctrinal analysis (Institute of Race Relations, *Prevent and the Children's Rights Convention* (2016).

[119] JUST Yorkshire, *Rethinking Prevent: A Case for an Alternative Approach* (2017) 1 and 20.

[120] Open Society Justice Initiative, *Eroding Trust: The UK's PREVENT Counter-Extremism Strategy in Health and Education* (Open Society Foundations 2016) 11.

[121] For example, Rights Watch UK (n 118) 12; Open Society Justice Initiative, ibid 33–50.

[122] JUST Yorkshire (n 119); ibid.

[123] For example, Open Society Justice Initiative (n 120).

[124] For example, Index on Censorship, *Uncomfortable but Educational: Freedom of Expression in UK Universities* (2018).

[125] Although JUST Yorkshire does call for the 'immediate withdrawal' of Prevent. JUST Yorkshire (n 119).

[126] HM Government, *Review of Counter-Terrorism and Security Powers: Review Findings and Recommendations* (Cm 8004, 2011).

[127] This included detention without charge under the Anti-Terrorism, Crime and Security Act 2001, pt 4, and control orders established in the Prevention of Terrorism Act 2005, pt 5.

[128] Terrorism Prevention and Investigation Measures Act 2011, s 2(2). A list of the measures available is included in Schedule 1 of the Terrorism Prevention and Investigation Measures Act 2011.

[129] Terrorism Prevention and Investigation Measures Act 2011, s 23.

[130] Ibid s 3.

[131] On enactment, the threshold test for imposing a TPIM was reasonable belief, but this was amended via the Counter-Terrorism and Security Act 2015, s 20(1).

[132] 'Terrorism-related activity' is defined as: 'the commission, preparation or instigation of acts of terrorism'; 'conduct which facilitates the commission, preparation or instigation of such acts, or which is intended to do so'; 'conduct which gives encouragement to the commission, preparation or instigation of such acts, or which is intended to do so'; or 'conduct which gives support or assistance to individuals who are known or believed by the individual concerned to be involved in' the commission, preparation or instigation of acts of terrorism. Terrorism Prevention and Investigation Measures Act 2011, s 4(1).

[133] See ibid s 6.

[134] See ibid s 7 and sch 2. In urgent cases, the Secretary of State must refer the imposition of measures to the Court 'immediately after serving the TPIM notice'.

[135] Ibid s 5(3), s 5(2).

136 Ibid s 13, s 12(1), s 12(2), 13(3).

137 Ibid s 16.

138 Ibid s 16(6).

139 Ibid sch 4; CPR 80 (TPIMs).

140 In this situation, the Secretary of State 'must refer to the court the imposition of the measures on the individual' 'immediately after serving the TPIM notice'. The Court uses the same test as when it considers giving the Secretary of State prior permission to impose a TPIM on an individual; it must 'consider whether the relevant decisions of the Secretary of State were obviously flawed.' Terrorism Prevention and Investigation Measures Act 2011, sch 2.

141 In England and Wales, the relevant court is the High Court, in Scotland it is the Outer House of the Court of Session, and in Northern Ireland, it is the High Court in Northern Ireland: ibid s 30(1), s 6.

142 Ibid s 6(6).

143 Ibid s 6(3)(a).

144 Ibid s 6(8).

145 Ibid s 8.

146 Ibid ss 8(4) and (5).

147 Ibid s 9(1).

148 Ibid s 9(2).

149 Ibid s 9(5).

150 Ibid s 9(6).

151 *Secretary of State for the Home Department v EC and EG* [2017] EWHC 795 (Admin); *Secretary of State for the Home Department v IM, JM and LG* [2017] EWHC 1529 (Admin); *Secretary of State for the Home Department v LF* [2017] EWHC 2685 (Admin).

152 *Secretary of State for the Home Department v IM, JM and LG* [2017] EWHC 1529 (Admin); *Secretary of State for the Home Department v LF* [2017] EWHC 2685 (Admin).

153 Terrorism Prevention and Investigation Measures Act 2011, s 11.

154 Ibid s 10(5).

155 Ibid s 16(2), s 16(3), s 16(4).

156 Ibid s 5(2)

157 Ibid s 13(6)

158 Ibid s 16(1).

159 Ibid s 16(6).

160 Ibid s 16(7).

161 Ibid s 16(8).

162 Ibid s 18(1).

163 *DD v Secretary of State for the Home Department* [2015] EWHC 1681 (Admin); *Secretary of State for the Home Department v EB* [2016] EWHC 1970 (Admin).

164 *Secretary of State for the Home Department v EB* [2016] EWHC 1970 (Admin).

165 *DD v Secretary of State for the Home Department* [2015] EWHC 1681 (Admin) [41]–[69].

166 Terrorism Prevention and Investigation Measures Act 2011, s 11.

167 In his report on TPIMs in 2012, David Anderson identified the inherent tension in measures being designed as both *investigatory* and *preventive*. He noted that this emerged from 'the different preoccupations of different constituencies in the political debate', highlighting that for the majority, the purpose of TPIMs was to prevent terrorism-related activity (TRA), while the minority hoped that 'they

would afford investigative opportunities that could result in criminal charges'. Anderson's conclusion was that '[b]oth constituencies could not be right. Put simply, if the existence of a TPIM prevents TRA, there will be no TRA to investigate.' David Anderson, *Terrorism Prevention and Investigation Measures in 2012* (Stationery Office 2013) 86.

[168] Defined as 'the police force – (a) that is investigating the commission of any ... offence [relating to terrorism] by the individual, or (b) by which it appears to the Secretary of State that the commission of any such offence by the individual would fall to be investigated.' Terrorism Prevention and Investigation Measures Act 2011, s 10(3), s 10(5)(a).

[169] Ibid s 10(5)(b).

[170] David Anderson (n 167) 68.

[171] Terrorism Prevention and Investigation Measures Act 2011, s 19(1).

[172] Home Office, *Terrorism Prevention and Investigation Measures: Written Statement – HCWS1549* (HC2018–19, HCWS1549); Home Office, *Terrorism Prevention and Investigation Measures: Written Statement – HCWS1547* (HC2018–18, HCWS1547); Home Office, *Terrorism Prevention and Investigation Measures: Written Statement – HCWS1050* (HC 2018–18, HCWS1050); Home Office, *Terrorism Prevention and Investigation Measures: Written Statement – HCWS851* (HC 2018–18, HCWS851); Home Office, *Terrorism Prevention and Investigation Measures: Written Statement – HCWS850* (HC 2017–18, HCWS850); Home Office, *Terrorism Prevention and Investigation Measures: Written Statement – HCWS411* (HC 2017–18, HCWS411); Home Office, *Terrorism Prevention and Investigation Measures: Written Statement – HCWS173* (HC 2017–18, HCWS173); Home Office, *Terrorism Prevention and Investigation Measures: Written Statement – HCWS98* (HC 2017–17, HCWS98); Home Office, *Terrorism Prevention and Investigation Measures: Written Statement – HCWS80* (HC 2016–17, HCWS80); Home Office, *Terrorism Prevention and Investigation Measures: Written Statement – HCWS362* (HC 2016–16, HCWS HCWS262); Home Office, *Terrorism Prevention and Investigation Measures: Written Statement – HCWS220* (HC 2016–16, HCWS220); Home Office, *Terrorism Prevention and Investigation Measures: Written Statement – HCWS92* (HC 2016–16, HCWS92); Home Office, *Terrorism Prevention and Investigation Measures: Written Statement – HCWS603* (HC 2015–16, HCWS603); Home Office, *Terrorism Prevention and Investigation Measures: Written Statement – HCWS382* (HC 2015–15, HCWS382); Home Office, *Terrorism Prevention and Investigation Measures: Written Statement – HCWS206* (HC 2015–15, HCWS206); Home Office, *Terrorism Prevention and Investigation Measures: Written Statement – HCWS826* (HC 2015–15, HCWS26); Home Office, *Terrorism Prevention and Investigation Measures: Written Statement – HCWS384* (HC 2014–15, HCWS384); Home Office, *Terrorism Prevention and Investigation Measures: Written Statement – HCWS287* (HC 2014–15, HCWS287); Home Office, *Terrorism Prevention and Investigation Measures: Written Statement – HCWS97* (HC 2014–14, HCWS97); Home Office, *Terrorism Prevention and Investigation Measures: Written Statement – HCWS46* (HC 2014–15, HCWS46); Home Office, *Terrorism Prevention and Investigation Measures: Written Statement – HCWS64* (HC 2014–15, HCWS64); Home Office, *Terrorism Prevention and Investigation Measures: Written Statement – HCWS50* (HC 2013–14, HCWS50)

[173] See, for example Home Office, *Terrorism Prevention and Investigation Measures: Written Statement – HCWS1050* (HC 2018–19, HCWS1050).

[174] The reports are usually published within two months of the end of the reporting period, but the report for 1 December 2016–28 February 2017 (*Terrorism*

Prevention and Investigation Measures (HCWS80 19 July 2017) was not published until 19 July 2017, the day before the next quarterly report was published (Home Office, *Terrorism Prevention and Investigation Measures: Written Statement – HCWS98* (HC2017–18, HCWS98)). Similarly, the reports for 1 September 2018–30 November 2018 and 1 December 2018–28 February 2019 were both published on the same day (9 May 2019): Home Office, *Terrorism Prevention and Investigation Measures: Written Statement – HCWS1547* (HC2018–18, HCWS1547); Home Office, *Terrorism Prevention and Investigation Measures: Written Statement – HCWS1549* (HC2018–19, HCWS1549).

[175] Terrorism Prevention and Investigation Measures Act 2011, s 21(1).

[176] Ibid s 21(3).

[177] Ibid s 21(2)(c).

[178] Ibid s 21(4).

[179] Third Delegated Legislation Committee (Draft Terrorism Prevention and Investigation Measures Act 2011 (Continuation) Order 2016) HC Deb 26 October 2016, col 5.

[180] HL Deb 24 November 2016, vol 776, col 2137.

[181] See the comments of Rupa Huq MP in this respect: 'I note that the 2011 Act does not require the Government to publish the advice given by the independent reviewer ... during the consultation. There may be national security issues here, but I wonder whether the Minister is willing to make that advice public, perhaps in redacted form so that nothing too sensitive slips out'. Third Delegated Legislation Committee (n 179) col 6.

[182] Ibid, cols 1–12.

[183] HC Deb 31 October 2016, vol 616, col 743.

[184] HL Deb 24 November 2016, vol 776, cols 2136–9.

[185] Third Delegated Legislation Committee (n 179) col 7.

[186] Terrorism Prevention and Investigation Measures Act 2011, s 20.

[187] Ibid s 20(4).

[188] Ibid s (5).

[189] Ibid s 20(2).

[190] Counter-Terrorism and Security Act 2015, s 45(3)

[191] David Anderson, *Terrorism Prevention and Investigation Measures in 2014* (Stationery Office 2015).

[192] Ibid, 4.

[193] Ibid 9–19. Anderson had, in an earlier review, evaluated TPIMs against the standards of whether they were effective and fair: Anderson (n 167).

[194] Max Hill, *The Terrorism Acts in 2017* (Stationery Office 2018).

[195] Ibid 66.

[196] Ibid 69.

[197] HM Government, *CONTEST The United Kingdom's Strategy for Countering Terrorism Annual Report for 2014* (n 56) 13.

[198] HM Government, *CONTEST The United Kingdom's Strategy for Countering Terrorism Annual Report for 2015* (n 56) 11.

[199] The term 'snapshot' is that used on the website of the Independent Reviewer of Terrorism Legislation to describe the non-statutory reviews that have been referred or self-initiated: 'Non-statutory functions', Available from: https://terrorismlegislationreviewer.independent.gov.uk/about-me/#non_stat_functions [Accessed 28 November 2018].

[200] Anderson (n 191) 15.

[201] HC Deb 1 September 2014 vol 585, cols 23–7.

[202] Anderson (n 191) 16.

[203] David Anderson, 'Relocation Relocation Relocation' (25 November 2014), Available from: https://webarchive.nationalarchives.gov.uk/20170301155827/https://terrorismlegislationreviewer.independent.gov.uk/relocation-relocation-relocation/ [Accessed 3 December 2018].

[204] Anderson (n 191) 16.

[205] A Control Order Review Group had existed in relation to Control Orders under the Prevention of Terrorism Act 2005.

[206] Anderson (n 167). According to Max Hill the agencies involved in TPIM Review Group meetings include: the Home Office, which chairs the TPIM Review Group meetings, as well as relevant representatives from the Security Service, the Home Office, the Counter Terrorism Command of the Metropolitan Police Service and officers from the Counter-Terrorism Unit in the area selected for the TPIM subject to reside if relocated. Max Hill (n 194), 59. The Independent Reviewer of Terrorism Legislation has also tended to attend the meetings in their capacity to review TPIMs.

[207] Anderson (n 167) 130. For further information on the functioning of the TPIM Review Group see: ibid 68–70 and Hill (n 194) 59–62.

[208] Home Office, *Terrorism Prevention and Investigation Measures: Written Statement – HCWS1050* (HC 2018–19, HCWS1050).

[209] Home Office, *Terrorism Prevention and Investigation Measures: Written Statement – HCWS97* (HC 2014–14, HCWS97).

[210] David Anderson, *Terrorism Prevention and Investigation Measures in 2013* (Stationery Office 2014) 28.

[211] Ibid 28.

[212] Home Office, *Memorandum to the Home Affairs Committee Post-Legislative Scrutiny of the Terrorism Prevention and Investigation Measures Act 2011* (Cm 9348, 2016).

[213] Ibid 1.

[214] Ibid 9.

[215] Ibid 30.

[216] Joint Committee on Human Rights, *Post-Legislative Scrutiny: Terrorism Prevention and Investigation Measures Act 2011* (2013–14, HL 113, HC 1014); Joint Committee on Human Rights, *Legislative Scrutiny: Counter-Terrorism and Security Bill* (2014–15, HL 86 HC 859); Home Affairs Committee, *Counter-Terrorism Foreign Fighters* (n 67).

[217] Joint Committee on Human Rights, *Post-Legislative Scrutiny* ibid 9.

[218] Ibid 19–21.

[219] Ibid 21–2.

[220] Joint Committee on Human Rights, *Legislative Scrutiny* (n 216).

[221] Ibid 19.

[222] Home Affairs Committee, *Counter-Terrorism Foreign Fighters* (n 67) 13–14.

[223] Home Office, *Terrorism Prevention and Investigation Measures: Written Question – 216939* (HC 2014–15, 216939); Home Office, *Terrorism Prevention and Investigation Measures: Written Question – 49882* (HC 2016–17, 49882); Home Office, *Terrorism Prevention and Investigation Measures: Written Question – 625* (HC 2017–18, 625); Home Office, *Terrorism Prevention and Investigation Measures: Written Question – 586* (HC 2017–18, 586); Home Office, *Terrorism Prevention and Investigation Measures: Written Question – 1213* (HC 2017–18, 1213); Home Office, *Terrorism Prevention and Investigation Measures: Written Question – 123734* (HC 2017–18, 123734).

224 With one exception; question 216939 of 2 December 2014 was answered 13 days later: Home Office, *Terrorism Prevention and Investigation Measures: Written Question – 216939* (HC 2014–15, 216939).

225 See, for example Home Office, *Terrorism Prevention and Investigation Measures: Written Question – 586* (HC 2017–18, 586).

226 HC Deb 9 January 2014, vol 573, col 467; HC Deb 27 January 2014, vol 574, cols 643–6; HC Deb 13 October 2014, vol 586, col 19

227 HC Deb 9 January 2014, vol 573, col 467; HC Deb 27 January 2014, vol 574, cols 643–6.

228 HC Deb 27 January 2014, vol 574, cols 643–6.

229 HC Deb 13 October 2014, vol 586, col 19.

230 HL Deb 15 July 2014, vol 755, col 559; HC Public Bill Committee Sixth Sitting, 14 April 2016.

231 HC Deb 10 March 2015, vol 594, col 230.

232 HC Deb 5 January 2016, vol 604, cols 36, 60; HC Deb 1 September 2014, vol 585, cols 26. 33, 38 47–8.

233 HL Deb 14 January 2015 vol 758, col 786; HC Deb 22 June 2017, vol 656, cols 197–8; HC Deb 14 January 2015, vol 590, col 872.

234 HC Deb 26 November 2016, vol 602, col 1525; HC Deb 1 September 2014, vol 585, col 26; HC Deb 10 September 2014, vol 585, col 916.

235 HC Deb 21 January 2014 vol 574, cols 221–63.

236 Ibid 221.

237 Ibid.

238 HL Deb 27 February 2014, vol 752, col 400.

239 Ibid cols 408–10.

240 For further detail, see: Jessie Blackbourn, Deniz Kayis and Nicola McGarrity, *Anti-Terrorism Law and Foreign Terrorist Fighters* (Routledge, 2018) 52–3.

241 Counter-Terrorism and Security Act 2016.

242 Prevention of Terrorism Act 2005, s 1.

243 HC Deb 2 December 2014, vol 589, col 208, 221–3, 247, 266; HC Deb 7 January 2015, Vol 590 col 342; HL Deb 13 January 2015 vol 758 cols 666, 764.

244 HC Deb 7 January 2015, vol 590 col 342.

245 HL Deb 13 January 2015 vol 758, cols 692, 717, 741.

246 HL Deb 13 January 2015 vol 758, col 747.

247 HC Deb 2 December 2014, vol 589 col 254–6, 262; HL Deb 13 January 2015 vol 758, col 687.

248 HC Deb 2 December 2014, vol 589 col 262.

249 HL Deb 13 January 2015 vol 758, col 747.

250 HL Deb 13 January 2015 vol 758, cols 675, 686.

251 HL Deb 13 January 2015 vol 758, col 675.

252 [2014] EWHC 3820 (Admin)

253 *DD v Secretary of State for the Home Department* [2014] EWHC 3820 (Admin), [136].

254 Liberty (n 116); Justice (n 116).

255 Amnesty International UK press release, 'Counter-terrorism Bill: "Dangerous to Rush Through this Grab-bag of Measures"' (Amnesty International UK, 26 November 2014), Available from: https://www.amnesty.org.uk/press-releases/counter-terrorism-bill-dangerous-rush-through-grab-bag-measures [Accessed 25 March 2019]; Big Brother Watch, *Briefing Note, Terrorism Prevention and Investigation Measure* (2014), Available from: https://www.bigbrotherwatch.org.uk/

wp-content/uploads/2014/09/Terrorism-Prevention-and-Investigation-Measures-Briefing.pdf [Accessed 25 March 2019].

[256] Justice (n 116) paras 21–3, 27, 32.

[257] Liberty, *Liberty's Briefing on the Proposed Renewal of Terrorism Prevention and Investigation Measures (TPIMs)* (2016) paras 6–8.

[258] Ibid para 3; Liberty (n 116), para 34.

[259] Ibid paras 9–11.

[260] Justice (n 116) para 32.

[261] Liberty (n 257) paras 5 and 13.

[262] Ibid para 3.

[263] Ibid para 12; Liberty (n 116) para 13; Justice (n 116) para 22.

[264] Amnesty International UK (n 255).

3

The Prevailing Approach
to Review

In the decade up to March 2018, a total of 725,194 people were 'examined' at ports and airports in the UK to determine whether they were or are 'concerned in the commission, preparation or instigation of acts of terrorism'.[1] The stops took place under Schedule 7 of the Terrorism Act 2000.[2] Before 2009, review of Schedule 7 was light, focusing on the overuse of 'intuitive stops' without reference to compatibility with rights.[3] Later reviews by civil society,[4] researchers,[5] parliamentary committees,[6] the Home Office,[7] and the Independent Reviewer of Terrorism Legislation[8] highlighted the rights- and discrimination-related concerns that these powers gave rise to. However, it seemed that the Government, politicians and the media had 'not the slightest interest in Schedule 7' until David Miranda was stopped at Heathrow Airport in the midst of the Snowden revelations.[9] Miranda challenged the use of Schedule 7, with the Court of Appeal finding that the powers were partly incompatible with the European Convention on Human Rights.[10] It was only after this judgment that the Government appeared to take seriously the need for change, even though numerous reviews had identified problems of rights, equality and procedure in respect of Schedule 7. Our interviewees told us how a number of different review mechanisms in the counter-terrorism review assemblage worked together to take advantage of the opportunity presented by the Court of Appeal finding in order to try to bring about change.

The story of Schedule 7 suggests that, even where review reveals significant flaws, a government that is committed to a certain counter-terrorism law or policy is 'obviously not going to listen until something dramatic happens'.[11] It indicates that different review mechanisms can amplify and support one another, building a case for change, but that a 'hard nudge', such as an adverse court decision or change in political priorities, might be needed for that change to happen. It underlines how, as the material in this chapter will show, politics, personality, media attention and professional cultures all influence how review takes place and how it is received.

The semi-structured interviews we undertook for this research sought to illuminate these ideas and to assess how far the practice of counter-terrorism review meets, exceeds or falls short of optimising accountability in the counter-terrorist state. In doing so, we draw out the perceptions and experiences of counter-terrorism review that go beyond what can be discerned from looking only at reviews 'on paper', complementing Chapter 2 to provide a fuller, experience-based picture of counter-terrorism review in the UK.

In this chapter, we present a thematic analysis of 24 interviews with actors we identified as undertaking, participating in or interacting with counter-terrorism review.[12] As outlined in the Introduction, the interviewees include former Home Secretaries, former Independent Reviewers of Terrorism Legislation, high-level political actors, representatives of regulators and complaints bodies, civil servants, lawyers and representatives from a range of civil society organisations.

From this rich material we have identified five themes, which we consider across Parts I to III of this chapter. In Part I, looking at the *purposes* of review, we draw out what counter-terrorism review actors thought they should be or were doing. Building on this, we consider the *pursuit* of these purposes, outlining how the processes of review actors create a variety of approaches to review. We consider whether this multi-part assemblage can be understood as an organic whole, with a neat division of labour, or whether it is better seen as a disharmonious, imperfect but nevertheless functioning jumble of mechanisms. We also ask whether there is a danger that divisions and/or competition between review mechanisms might be manipulated by political agendas or inhibit the assemblage's contribution to accountability. In Part II, we discuss the *values* the interviewees indicated underpin review and the relationship these have with accountability in general. In so doing, we justify our view of counter-terrorism review as an imperfect but functioning assemblage. However, we also show that, to function, such an assemblage is dependent on the implementation and realisation of these values. Finally, in Part III, we consider what the interviews might tell us about the impact of review. We argue that, while this experiential perspective suggests that counter-terrorism review can increase accountability, the pathways to impact are diffuse and difficult to manipulate, and political realities may require a more pragmatic approach from reviewers than may be considered optimal. We end the chapter with a broad analysis of what the interviews suggest about counter-terrorism review in the UK, and how they trouble or seem to reinforce our claim that counter-terrorism review can play an accountability function in the counter-terrorist state.

Part I: Purposes

It is our contention that, in theory, counter-terrorism review may contribute to accountability in the contemporary counter-terrorist state. To ascertain whether that view is shared across the assemblage, in this section we outline the purposes of counter-terrorism review that our interviewees identified, and discuss them in relation to the ways in which those purposes are pursued in practice.

The purposes of review

The counter-terrorism review assemblage is 'a densely populated landscape',[13] comprising a multiplicity of review mechanisms. While one might expect that multiple mechanisms of review would mean that there are many different purposes for review across the assemblage, we found that, when the purposes identified by interviewees were interrogated, there was far less variety than anticipated. Our interviewees indicated different starting propositions about what counter-terrorism review is for. For example, both former Home Secretaries to whom we spoke began their response to our question about the nature and purpose of counter-terrorism review by highlighting the importance of being able to ensure that the law 'matches' the perceived threat. As one put it:

> there will be times when you will review your counter-terror legislation and policy because an event has happened that means that you need to reconsider whether or not it's adequate, or the threat level has changed, or your understanding of the nature of the threat has changed and, therefore, you need to think about the way in which your counter terror activity, and particularly the legislation, is operating.[14]

This suggests that, for these actors, a significant purpose of review is to consider the adequacy of counter-terrorism from an operational perspective and, if it is found to be inadequate, to change or add to it. However, other interviewees seemed to perceive counter-terrorism review more as a 'checking' mechanism. As one explained:

> the primary thing ... is the checks and balances to see is the power required, and if so, is it at the right level? ... Is the power not achieving what it needs to be? And are those affected by it able to properly challenge it?[15]

Put somewhat more viscerally, for these interviewees, review should seek to 'identify flaws in the existing system, to identify anything that's unlawful about it, anything that's discriminatory'.[16] Such perspectives were not necessarily in tension with the operational sense of counter-terrorism review that the interviews with former Home Secretaries revealed. They too indicated that review has a 'checking' function, speaking about the importance of striking the right balance.[17] While different interviewees may have different ideas of what the 'right' balance is, almost all saw striking it as important, and counter-terrorism review as having a role in trying to achieve that.

Bearing in mind the levels of apparent agreement this seems to suggest across interviewees, there were five purposes identifiable from the interviews:

- assessing levels of threat and adequacy of the response;[18]
- scrutinising the justification,[19] necessity[20] and proportionality[21] of counter-terrorism law and policy;
- analysing the lawfulness of individual counter-terrorism decisions and actions;
- identifying and challenging flaws, discrimination and procedural unfairness in practice;[22]
- evaluating effectiveness,[23] identifying areas for improvement,[24] and informing Parliament.[25]

Broadly speaking, we can see that these purposes connect to operational, policy-related and legalistic concerns about counter-terrorism, but all are evaluative. They indicated a surprisingly narrow range of purposes. There may be some separation between law-related and politics-related purposes of review: scrutinising necessity and proportionality, analysing lawfulness of individual decisions and actions, and identifying and challenging discrimination are broadly legalistic concerns, while assessing threat levels or the adequacy of a response, evaluating effectiveness, and identifying areas for improvement are ostensibly political and practical questions. For example, our interviews suggested that policy reviews completed by the Executive, internal agencies, and to some extent Select Committees, tend to assess the quality of the counter-terrorism frameworks in the light of current threats and the political climate.[26] In contrast, judicial (and quasi-judicial) reviews tend to look at the lawfulness of and justification for 'decisions that interfere with the rights of the individual',[27] and whether counter-terrorism actors are fulfilling their statutory obligations. Similarly, pre-legislative reviews and reviews accompanying sunset clauses evaluate the operation of the legislative provisions.[28] Some review mechanisms cut across both policy and legal enquiry, such as those completed by the Independent Reviewer of Terrorism Legislation, but this has as much to do with how the office-holder interprets the role as it does with the mandate of the Independent Reviewer.[29]

Although narrower than we might have anticipated, the purposes interviewees indicated suggest that counter-terrorism reviews may be undertaken in distinct ways. These are determined to a significant degree by what the review mechanism perceives the purpose to be. In other words, the review mechanism's sense of the purpose of review may determine what questions it pursues, and how it goes about gathering the evidence required to answer them. Some review mechanisms focus on how to improve the quality of counter-terrorism,[30] or on the adequacy and relevance of current powers and laws.[31] Others question whether the powers and laws are being misused and whether there are adequate safeguards against such misuse.[32] Some look at why counter-terrorism policy is being pursued in a particular way,[33] and others at whether a particular counter-terrorism power, law or approach can continue to be justified. Furthermore, review mechanisms are not necessarily static as they may take different approaches across different reviews, and subject their own activities and approaches to review and revision.[34]

Some of these questions and approaches are more amenable to considering counter-terrorism's unintended consequences than others. A narrow review that asks, for example, whether a law achieves its own objectives might be limited in its scope. Whereas a broader review that asks, for example, about the impact of Prevent on freedom of speech and on universities' ability to identify and support vulnerable students may be able to consider the unintended consequences of counter-terrorism policies and legislation in more depth.[35] These reviews can advance our understanding of the counter-terrorist state and enable broader debate and contestation, including on the impact of UK counter-terrorism outside of the UK.[36] For one of our interviewees, the variation in approaches to review across the assemblage suggests that 'there are different aspects of scrutiny at different levels'.[37] This is important, not only because under current rules relating to classification of materials some reviews can only be conducted with appropriate security clearance, but also because counter-terrorism review involves asking knotty questions that can only be answered by undertaking hands-on work with communities to see how they are being affected and whether there is any kind of unintended consequences, or alternatively how the intended consequences might actually be damaging to individuals and their longer-term relationship with the state, and in turn damaging to any objectives that are designed to better deter acts of terrorism.[38]

Multiple purposes; plural assemblage?

We have already noted that our interviewees saw counter-terrorism review as an extensive assemblage with many different elements. As we discuss in Part II of this chapter, such diversity is reflected in how the different mechanisms and reviewers tend to go about review; that is, how they pursue the purposes of the review exercise. But first, it is worth reflecting on whether, for our interviewees, the counter-terrorism review assemblage is fragmented,[39] pluralistic or something between the two.

One of our interviewees indicated that there were 'clear delineations of responsibility' within the counter-terrorism review assemblage.[40] However, that was a minority view. While most saw the assemblage as enabling specialist consideration in some areas of counter-terrorism review, there was a general sense that the current assemblage makes it difficult to achieve an 'overview' of how the different elements of counter-terrorism operate. There was a clear desire for a 'holistic stocktake' and an evidence-based understanding of counter-terrorism taken as a whole,[41] even if interviewees considered that this might not be deliverable in practice,[42] not least because of concerns about feasibility and access to confidential materials. That none of the existing review mechanisms did, or perhaps could, deliver such an overview was generally thought to reflect the somewhat piecemeal emergence of counter-terrorism review, mirroring the emergence of the counter-terrorist state itself. As different powers and responsibilities were created, review mechanisms to consider them were either established or had their remits expanded, such as happened with the Independent Reviewer. In addition, institutional innovations were put in place to allow existing processes to be used as routes for accountability in counter-terrorism, such as the use of Special Advocates in closed material proceedings.[43] Some existing entities with broad regulatory powers had their regulatory functions expanded to include the monitoring of counter-terrorism activities by their existing regulatees, such as the Office for Students. A number of our interviewees suggested that, in at least some cases, reviews had been mandated for instrumental reasons,[44] such as sunset clauses inserted into legislation as a conciliatory gesture,[45] or reviews established with narrow terms of reference, seemingly to produce outcomes that will legitimate desired government action.[46] This implies that, for our interviewees, the counter-terrorism review space is emergent rather than 'designed'. As a result, it is not surprising that some overlap exists between what the different review mechanisms do, and the purposes they attempt to pursue. Nor is it surprising that there might be places where counter-terrorism review is absent or sub-optimal.

The counter-terrorism review assemblage may be imperfect in this respect, but that does not mean that it is not functioning. As our interviewees made clear, the number and nature of review mechanisms does not, alone, capture the ways in which the assemblage operates in practice. In particular, it tells us little about whether and how these mechanisms coordinate, cooperate and compete, and whether accountability is optimised through their operation. Ascertaining this requires us to be attentive to scale, time, relational distance and access. In particular, we need to ask whether and, if so how, the different elements of the counter-terrorism review assemblage are able to navigate these dimensions such that the difficulties they pose to securing accountability are mitigated.

The question of scale

A key question is whether the counter-terrorism review assemblage matches the scale of the counter-terrorist state. This plays out in a number of ways. In the first instance, it causes us to consider whether the full range of provisions and powers available to the counter-terrorist state are being evaluated. Furthermore, seeing 'scale' as a question of depth and reach as well as extent, raises questions about whether the impact and operation of counter-terrorism across different timescales, actors and contexts is reviewed across an appropriate range of standards. In the absence of one overarching mechanism engaging in review across all of these scales, achieving appropriate review may require different modes and mechanisms of review. This is important because, as we showed in the Introduction, evaluation requires us to engage with evidence not only on frequency of use but also on the purposes for which powers are used, which actors are using them, what if any implications the use of one power had for other parts of counter-terrorist activity, and their intended and unintended consequences and impacts. The range of different review types, triggers and mandates, which one interviewee called the 'suite of tools',[47] may well be the way in which the scale of counter-terrorism can be matched in counter-terrorism review.

Time

Time and timeliness are also important.[48] For some reviews time is a critical factor. If, as one of our interviewees suggested, a particular review is about assessing whether counter-terrorism is adequate to address a terrorist threat at any given time, 'the question of review for the situation today may be different from what it was ten years ago, and may be different from what it is ten years in the future'.[49] Such an approach to review is primarily an operational one, so it is perhaps unsurprising that this view emanated from a former Home Secretary. It was shared by the other former Home Secretary we spoke with, who thought that reviewing counter-terrorism is about asking:

> whether or not [counter-terrorism is] adequate, or the threat level has changed, or your understanding of the nature of the threat has changed and, therefore, you need to think about the way in which your counter terror activity, and particularly the legislation, is operating.[50]

In such a review, timeliness is important because the threat picture changes over time, meaning the question of adequacy cannot be answered once and for all. It requires contemporaneous consideration against the risk as it exists at a given time. However, for most of our interviewees time played a different role. They considered it important that some time would have passed between the introduction of the counter-terrorism power or policy being reviewed and the review being undertaken, because the laws or policies being reviewed might have been introduced 'when some very difficult decisions may have been taken in times of very high emotion'.[51] The passage of time meant that these might be reviewed in a calmer and less pressurised context than the one in which they were introduced; this was a view shared across the people to whom we spoke, including the former Home Secretaries.[52] Rather than taking 'a stab in the dark at a time of very heightened emotion and anxiety',[53] review undertaken at a temporal remove may be more rigorous. The review will be undertaken with the benefit of seeing how the law has operated, bearing in mind that it takes 'a considerable period of time for any new piece of legislation to bed in'.[54] In the context of counter-terrorism, this hindsight is vital because pre-legislative processes can often be expedited and less robust than might be hoped. As one interviewee remarked, the 'challenge with Bills is that you don't have much time to read the information and do the call for evidence, to have the witnesses and produce the report, before your report becomes time-critical and is then too late and just not relevant anymore'.[55] From a parliamentary perspective there is insufficient time for MPs and Peers to embark on a 'holistic stocktake of the status quo: what's out there, how useful is it?' before they have to vote on adding more counter-terrorism law to the existing legislation, regulation and policy.[56]

For some of our interviewees time was also a structural factor that influences how review is undertaken by review mechanisms. Interviewees from regulatory agencies and former Independent Reviewers explained that reviews must be completed according to a specific, often tight, timeframe. The workload and the realities of staffing,[57] as well as the parameters of the review itself, produce a shortage of time.[58] Further, the longer a review takes, the more difficult it may be to maintain the interest of the public and of decision-makers in the process and its outcome.[59] The Government's power to delay publication of the outcome of a counter-terrorism review, or even not to publish it at all, is relevant here. Some interviewees engaged in legal practice and civil society activity perceived this power as a way for Government to manage the fall-out from reviews, potentially diminishing their effectiveness.[60] Across the counter-terrorism review assemblage, time and timeliness play different roles for different review mechanisms, underlining the importance of the different parts of the assemblage being able to compensate for the pressures and realities of time that arise elsewhere.

Relational distance

Relational distance is an especially challenging part of counter-terrorism review. Reflecting the academic literature on accountability,[61] many interviewees were clear that 'being at arm's length' and 'freestanding' from the body or practice under review was fundamentally important.[62] However, independence is also difficult and complicated in the counter-terrorism context. A review body may be mandated to undertake a mixture of roles, and proximity can be perceived as a means to cultivate some forms of expertise and relationships that key decision-makers, especially in government and security agencies, prioritise when determining what weight to give to the outcomes of reviews.[63]

As to the mixture of roles, there are some forms of review where the review mechanism has both a pre-authorisation and an *ex post facto* review function. The Investigatory Powers Commissioner's Office (IPCO) is an apt example. It both authorises warrants issued by the Secretary of State (the authorisation function) and produces annual reports on the use of these warrants (the review function).[64] In such cases the *ex post facto* review might be perceived as the review mechanism assessing its own earlier decision – that is, as the reviewer effectively marking its own homework.

That said, one interviewee argued that in such a situation it is not the authorising body's homework that is being marked, but rather the claims of the warrant-seeking agency,[65] although this does not account for the fact that in its later auditing IPCO also considers whether it had itself properly assessed the application for warrant in the first place. In such situations, questions clearly arise as to whether the review mechanism has sufficient relational distance to undertake that review with credibility. While that challenge is clear in this example, it is also present in other, less obvious, contexts.

A number of our interviewees indicated that proximity has its uses. For example, a reviewer's familiarity with the system they are reviewing can help to navigate its intricacies.[66] Perhaps the best example is the Independent Reviewer, who undertakes regular reviews. One former Independent Reviewer told us that while 'it was a challenge as a newcomer to try to get to grips with the right approach',[67] over time his comprehension of the processes he was required to evaluate developed significantly. Proximity may also bring other benefits: the ability to identify anomalies in practice, the opportunities to build up relationships that contextualise materials and also underpin the positive reception of review outcomes, and so on. Familiarity can, however, come with its own dangers, not least that some practices or patterns may become unremarkable the more familiar a reviewer is with the counter-terrorism milieu. The rest of the counter-terrorism review assemblage can assist here, calling out any capture that may arise from relational closeness, as was the case when one former Independent Reviewer was thought by some to be more accepting of the claims and perspectives of state agencies than might be desirable from the perspective of ensuring rigour in review.[68]

Access

The final dimension to consider here is *access*. Counter-terrorism review takes place in a context of information asymmetry. The state has the monopoly on much of the key information needed to review the counter-terrorist state in a way that enhances accountability. Counter-terrorism review is, then, partly dependent on the willingness of the state to make information and actors available to review mechanisms, and on the ability of other elements of the counter-terrorism review assemblage to challenge the accuracy, comprehensiveness and veracity of those state narratives. Numerous interviewees considered that access to intelligence and security-sensitive material is needed somewhere within the counter-terrorism review assemblage.[69] So too is the ability of review mechanisms that do not have such access to develop their own, alternative evidence bases through which official narratives can be tested or troubled.

Clearly, security clearance that allows access to sensitive material is a powerful asset for a review mechanism. As one former Independent Reviewer put it, this access is a 'really powerful weapon ... that makes people listen to what you have to say'.[70] But access must be contextualised by the fact that the state decides whether information is to be classified, putting it beyond the reach of any review mechanism other than those the state has given appropriate levels of security clearance. For a large number of our interviewees,[71] the state was far too ready to classify information and remove it from public scrutiny; 'there was always room for more information to be provided'.[72] For most of those we spoke to, the state allowing some reviewers access to that information did not resolve the difficulties of over-classification. Nevertheless, counter-terrorism review can provide some mitigation. While the Independent Reviewer cannot disclose confidential materials to which he has access, he can reach into the secret world and use what he learns in his broader considerations of counter-terrorism.[73] Through his reports and relationships with politicians, including the Home Secretary, the Independent Reviewer can also amplify and pass 'upstream' the views of those who struggle to reach opinion formers or decision makers.[74] Decision-makers, in turn, may feel assured by the Independent Reviewer's understanding of the 'reality', as they would see it, through his security clearance. They may approach his recommendations with a more open mind than if they came from other parts of the counter-terrorism review assemblage, such as civil society organisations whom key decision-makers might not consider to be 'on board' with the basic propositions of the counter-terrorist state. In this way, the Independent Reviewer's access to information both underpins the rigour of his review and provides a foundation for relationships with decision-makers that see him as trustworthy, credible and informed. Yet, the same closeness that such access implies also opens the Independent Reviewer up to the risk of regulatory capture.[75] This requires careful management and scrupulously independent conduct, to which we return later in this chapter.

Merely having access to sensitive materials may not be enough for a review mechanism to be as effective as might be desirable from an accountability perspective. This was made very clear to us by lawyers with experience of acting as and engaging with Special Advocates in closed proceedings.[76] While the effectiveness of Special Advocates is disputed, their access to security-sensitive information is, in theory, key to ensuring that closed material proceedings operate as a check on the counter-terrorist state.[77] However, real challenges exist for Special Advocates in trying to achieve this. The Special Advocate is on their own once proceedings become closed, unable to speak with the open advocate.[78] They are also isolated from the resources that lawyers usually employ to work out novel legal challenges; there are no textbooks, one cannot consult with and take advice from colleagues, and until very recently,[79] there could be real difficulties in accessing closed judgments to ascertain what if any useful precedents exist.[80] All of this calls into question the extent to which, even with access to the security-sensitive materials, Special Advocates can effectively mitigate the challenges experienced by open advocates. These challenges include not being able to see the evidence, struggling to ensure their clients understand what is going on,[81] and being required to trust in the advocacy of the Special Advocate to advance the interests of their clients.[82] As one of our interviewees put it, Special Advocates are 'better than nothing' but, while they can mitigate, they cannot 'eliminate the unfairness involved in a closed material procedure'.[83]

Of course, there are also other parts of the assemblage without access to security-sensitive information. This is the case for most parliamentary committees, for example. Indeed, only the Intelligence and Security Committee of Parliament (ISC) – which, in relation to other parliamentary committees, is established differently,[84] located separately[85] and peculiarly staffed – can see security-sensitive material. Without access to such materials, other committees' 'ability ... to build evidence can be dependent on the openness of the government department, as well as the time available to conduct their review'.[86] Openness itself will be dependent on numerous factors, including the familiarity a department has with a particular committee. However, interestingly, one former Independent Reviewer we spoke with saw part of his role to be resolving some of these information asymmetries and deficiencies for Parliament, as did an interviewee who previously worked in Parliament and saw the Independent Reviewer as 'facilitating parliamentary scrutiny and review' to the extent that he became 'kind of indispensable'.[87] A key difficulty with this, however, is that the Independent Reviewer cannot disclose the security-sensitive materials, he can only assure Parliament about the underpinning claims based on his analysis of them. Even then, the Independent Reviewer's reports are submitted to the Home Office, which subsequently publishes them in Parliament.[88] This illustrates how the differences in access to information across the counter-terrorism review assemblage have the potential to be mitigated by interactions between review mechanisms. Such interaction is, nevertheless, dependent on trusting relationships between them, so that the relatively less informed review mechanism trusts the assurances and representations of the relatively more informed mechanism and so on.

This brings us to a key question that arises when we consider the multiplicity of review mechanisms: is the counter-terrorism review assemblage capable of meeting the challenges of scale, time, relational distance and access that our interviewees perceived, and which we have outlined here? Our interviewees seemed to perceive the answer to that question as probably being dependent on whether this assemblage operates in a manner that is fragmented, or whether, in fact, there is some division of labour, even if imprecise, informal and perhaps inconsistent within the assemblage.

A division of labour in the counter-terrorism review assemblage?

The fact that multiple actors undertake review, sometimes with overlap and sometimes with cross-amplification, does not necessarily mean that the labour of counter-terrorism review – the evaluation of value or merit, engagement with reality and exercise of the capacity for action – is 'divided' between them.

A number of interviewees suggested that a division of labour can help the assemblage meet the challenges of review. For one of our interviewees, review

> has to be the responsibility of a whole interconnected network of individuals with different competencies and capacities; from our judiciary acting responsibly and being empowered to enforce domestic legal and constitutional standards through to parliamentarians having access to effective advice and support to ensure they are conducting independent and effective scrutiny, through to civil society being able to use techniques that they have, from strategic litigation through to public awareness campaigning, without being placed under undue pressure, stigma and alienation for conducting work in an area which defends individuals which the mainstream are frequently encouraged to view as reprehensible and untouchable.[89]

Some interviewees claimed that 'clear delineations of responsibility' between mechanisms were important.[90] For a former Independent Reviewer of Terrorism Legislation, such delineation allowed for full use to be made of the counter-terrorism review toolbox. A number of interviewees whose work involved them in Executive and independent review mechanisms noted how important it is to minimise overlap between review mechanisms, which they thought could be achieved through formal and informal communication between them,[91] although the assemblage is so rich in mechanisms that some of our interviewees found that they 'have to work quite hard to make connections'.[92]

Where it happens, dividing labour may be a reasonably straightforward matter of efficacy: an attempt to ensure that multiple energies are not being directed at the same issues, powers, laws or policies. However, a lack of overlap has potentially negative implications as well. Where a review mechanism is essentially comprised of one person, there was a sense among some interviewees that the review is 'only as good as the person doing it, and only as in depth and probing as the person doing it is inclined to make it'.[93] If that is so, and if overlap is minimised, then there may not be a structural mitigation should the reviewer underperform in delivering accountability through review. However, without a multiplicity of review mechanisms, the approach taken in one review in effect determines the knowledge that is produced about the law, policy or practice under review. As a result, if that review mechanism takes an approach that is exclusively statistical, or is based on terms of reference that do not mandate consideration of societal and unintended consequences, or does not engage with communities to ascertain societal perspectives on the subject matter of review, there may not be a 'corrective' review in existence that can broaden and better contextualise its findings. Furthermore, a lack of overlap between mechanisms could mean that there is little or no disagreement or tension between reviews. Indeed, one interviewee expressly mentioned that avoiding 'contradictions' between different mechanisms was an important motivation for dividing the labour,[94] even though that suggests a rather more deliberate division of labour than was indicated by other interviewees. While avoiding contradictions may appear attractive at first, the lack of disagreement or critical tension would probably have negative implications for the quality of contestation and politicisation, and undermine the accountability aspirations of counter-terrorism review.[95] Indeed, it may well exacerbate the hegemonic consensus that, as we noted in Chapter 1, is a feature of the counter-terrorist state that an accountability-optimising approach to counter-terrorism review should seek to counteract.

Some of our interviewees thought that a division of labour across the counter-terrorism review assemblage might have positive accountability impacts, so that by working together the review mechanisms could, as one put it, 'maximise our impact'.[96] There was a sense that different review mechanisms could act as 'force multiplier[s]' for others.[97] In other words, the findings or perspectives generated by one review mechanism might be picked up and amplified by another review mechanism, which might repeat, highlight or confirm them.[98] This is part of the labour of trying to exploit review's capacity for action. The success with which any review mechanism can do this will, of course, depend on who the intended audience for the amplified message is and what their relationship to the intended audience is. Numerous participants attributed such a function to the Independent Reviewer, noting the high regard in which government and politicians hold the office, and its perceived credibility.[99] However, the Independent Reviewer is not the only actor with this capacity. Sometimes a review mechanism needs to put its findings and conclusions in a way that is politically palatable, or that will not undermine or damage its relationship with government. A former Independent Reviewer of Terrorism Legislation told us that selecting the issues 'one wants to make a fuss about' is a delicate business.[100] For him, it made sense to 'select issues in such a way that at the same time as you give the Government a kicking you might also be able to give them the odd stroke'.[101] In those situations, a review mechanism might find it 'useful to record something neutrally and then get someone else to scream about it',[102] relying on civil society, the media or a politician to put in blunter terms what a review mechanism has expressed in a more constrained manner.

Although many participants noted the amplification that can arise from cooperation and cross-referencing within the counter-terrorism review assemblage, a multiplicity of review mechanisms brings competition as well as cooperation. To some extent this is quite expected: competition in multi-actor spheres is well observed in other regulatory contexts. Interestingly, however, competition emerged not only from the fact that, for example, MPs and Peers have a limited amount of time and resources to devote to a particular issue, but also from the ways in which government can distribute status or opportunities for participation across the assemblage. This occurs in various ways. Government may privilege some review mechanisms over others, clearly 'listening to' one review mechanism and giving it considerably more credence than is given to others. Indeed, one former politician indicated there is a scale of persuasive voices, with the security and intelligence services at the top, then the police, then the Independent Reviewer of Terrorism Legislation and then Select Committees.[103] The prominence of the Independent Reviewer was reflected across numerous participants, and there was a clear sense that, for government at least, the Independent Reviewer is a pivotal review mechanism,[104] while civil society is of less import.[105] Even within Parliament, it was clear from a number of interviewees that there is a sense that the Government 'forum shops', engaging with one committee rather than another, and using the fact that something is already under consideration to try to frustrate another committee's ability to engage in scrutiny.[106] Managing the flow of information to Select Committees and other review mechanisms in this way gives the impression of an implicit hierarchy between them. The Government may also effectively exclude some review mechanisms and actors, undermining their credibility and treating them as if they cannot be engaged with at all, with potentially serious impacts on some civil society actors.

Part II: Values

The second broad theme to emerge from the interview data is 'values'. This theme concerns the values that our interviewees thought counter-terrorism review did and should reflect, and, then, how those values are pursued in practice. This material helped us to identify what it was that participants considered made the counter-terrorism review assemblage function beyond the organisation and purposes of review mechanisms. As will become clear from this part of the chapter, there was a notable unity of values across the assemblage. Interviewees conceptualised counter-terrorism review as being underpinned by the values of democracy, transparency, credibility and independence. Views on how these values could be pursued through counter-terrorism review varied, often according to the attitude of the interviewee to counter-terrorism and the counter-terrorist state per se, but across the interviews we discerned the view that being independent, being experts and gathering evidence, and listening were the primary ways in which these values were enacted.

The values that drive counter-terrorism review

For many of our interviewees, counter-terrorism review was about *democracy*. As discussed in Part I, it was widely noted that the function of review is to hold the government to account for its actions,[107] and several interviewees connected this directly to democracy.[108] The key insight for many of our interviewees was that when it comes to counter-terrorism, rigorous public[109] and political[110] debate is needed,[111] and that counter-terrorism review produces the information and insight that enables that debate[112] and informs Parliament,[113] providing explanations and information to those without access to classified material.[114] For one former Home Secretary, review mechanisms and their outcomes had a democratic value because 'the public need to understand and be able to feed into an understanding of the nature and scope of what the counter-terrorist threat is, and the wide range of activities that are underway, day in, day out, rather than to have a very immediate focus on an attack or a particular threat.'[115] However, the same interviewee was of the view that the public do not always have 'the proper context ... [for] what's actually happening in the broader range of counter terror policy and operations'.[116] In their view, public understanding of counter-terrorism policy is 'not particularly high, but higher with the public strategies than it would be without'.[117] While it is likely that this was based on supposition rather than concrete evidence, it indicates that even at a high political level there is a sense that information about what is actually happening in counter-terrorism enhances democracy by enabling public knowledge and awareness. As one interviewee explained, 'it's obviously in everyone's interest that properly informed scrutiny is going on, although it can be uncomfortable for the Government'.[118] Others noted that the objective of review in particular is to 'ensure that there is a degree of impartial review of those decisions, to ensure that they are properly justified'.[119]

This chimes with our claim, in Chapter 1, that the UK is now a counter-terrorist state, and that the ordinary expectations of the state, including that actions would be justified and policy subjected to challenge and debate, should be applied to it. But to achieve this, some additional, subject-specific accountability mechanisms are required so that the challenges of confidentiality, deference and risk management that arise in the field of counter-terrorism can be negotiated. The intrusive nature of counter-terrorism is such that, for our interviewees, it cannot be left outside of the pursuit of accountability,[120] and so specialised accountability mechanisms are devised. Hence, actors such as the Independent Reviewer of Terrorism Legislation, the Investigatory Powers Tribunal and the ISC all have exceptional capacities to subject counter-terrorism to scrutiny, informing or acting as proxies for the processes of political accountability that lie at the heart of the UK constitutional system.[121] Despite this, many of our interviewees thought these mechanisms problematic. For some, the entire approach to accountability for counter-terrorism needed to be revisited, even though government was reluctant to do so.[122] For others, there was a general sense that where review is mandated as a conciliatory gesture to garner support for a desired government power, this may impact on the weight that is given to the review outcomes.[123] One example given in two interviews was that of the Newton Committee, established under the Anti-Terrorism, Crime and Security Act 2001 to reassure certain parliamentarians.[124] The report of this Committee was laid before Parliament by David Blunkett, then Home Secretary, on 18 December 2003.[125] Although he informed the House that he was 'willing to look very positively at many of the Committee's recommendations',[126] there was a sense among interviewees who referred to this process that its recommendations had largely been ignored in practice.[127]

The second value that our interviewees thought was pursued through counter-terrorism review was *transparency*. While most of our interviewees were prepared to accept some limit to transparency in counter-terrorism in order to protect operational procedures and limit security risks,[128] it was also clear that many felt the current levels of protective secrecy were excessive. For one civil society interviewee, for instance, the current approach to protecting classified material is 'too broad', frequently 'blanket' and has the effect of limiting oversight.[129] Across the spectrum of those we interviewed, there was a sense that counter-terrorism review could be a way of trying to increase transparency in counter-terrorism. As one participant put it, a function of review is to put 'more information and understanding out there as to what the Government is up to and what the risks are', which 'allows people to be better informed and hopefully to focus on ... the real problems'.[130] Clearly connected with the value of democracy, our interviewees saw transparency as key to legitimating government activity, although they were keenly aware of how difficult this was to achieve when the state controlled the question of who could access relevant information.

In this context, transparency can be enhanced in a number of different ways across different mechanisms. In some settings, how a review mechanism goes about its work is critical to whether it can enhance transparency. The Special Advocates to whom we spoke perceived of their role as being to mitigate the closedness of the procedure by trying to have information disclosed that the state argued should not be.[131] One Special Advocate we spoke to described his task as being to try to achieve 'as much disclosure as possible ... so both the individuals involved in the case, but also the public at large, are aware of what's taking place'.[132] As this indicates, achieving wider disclosure is important not only for the person in respect of whom proceedings are being taken, but also more broadly for the accountability of the judiciary and our ability to scrutinise the justification for the decision that is ultimately reached.

Counter-terrorism review may also contribute to transparency through review outputs, such as reports or recommendations, being published. This is not straightforward, however. First, not all reviews are published. 'Internal' reviews such as a Home Office internal review or a periodic performance review within a regulatory body may not be published.[133] Indeed, a number of interviewees suggested that the Home Office conducted reviews which, while they contributed to knowledge and transparency within the Home Office itself, did not enhance transparency from a public perspective.[134] We have already noted that the Government has the power to delay publication of some review outcomes, such as the reports of the Independent Reviewer. Other reviews might also not be published, or might be considerably redacted, because of the nature of the bodies or activities that are being reviewed. However, even in respect of such review outcomes, interviewees close to these processes were of the view that the 'more information you put in the public domain, the better because ... they're not doing anything they need to be ashamed of'.[135]

The final value that our interviewees thought was pursued through counter-terrorism review was *independence* and ensuring that the activities of the counter-terrorist state were subjected to independent scrutiny. This connects with transparency. Our interviewees suggested that they thought it important to maximise transparency and public engagement. This not only enhances democracy but is also 'very good for the perception that the role is serving the public and independent as opposed to just serving as a rubber stamp'.[136] The importance of independence to accountability has long been recognised,[137] but that does not mean that it is always tangible or easily identified. Our interviewees made this evident by offering a variety of views on what exactly signified independence, even across review mechanisms that contained 'independent' in their name.[138] However, what was common was that interviewees valued independence because distance between the reviewer and that which they review provides confidence in the process and in its outcomes.[139] A review mechanism that is independent '[does not] have anything to gain by going in a particular direction'.[140] Interviewees also valued independence because they perceived it as being important for the credibility of,[141] and as helping to produce trust in, review mechanisms,[142] improving the confidence of the public, civil society and the courts[143] that the counter-terrorist state is being held accountable. Interviewees were aware that this was challenging. There was a perception that trust is in short supply between the state and the counter-terrorism review assemblage. One civil society interviewee told us that 'as far as I'm aware there is no trust between civil servants working with counter-terrorism stuff and NGOs working on it'.[144] Whether that accurately reflects reality is less important than the reflection that independent counter-terrorism review mechanisms are intended to bridge that lack of trust by being a 'prism' through which 'all of the secured personnel that we meet and the material that we see' are filtered and translated into an openly available report.[145]

Realising the values that underpin counter-terrorism review

Having ascertained the main values our interviewees indicated were pursued through counter-terrorism review, the next consideration is how review mechanisms try to realise those values in practice. In other words, what attributes and approaches to their role did interviewees consider to be important from that perspective? In this respect, being independent, being experts and gathering evidence, and listening all emerged as important.

Being independent

Our interviewees thought that it was important that review mechanisms were independent in practice in order for them to pursue the values of democracy, transparency, credibility and independence. It was clear that goes beyond simply being nominally 'independent' and is fundamentally about how the review mechanism is organised and resourced, its expertise and how it conducts the review. All of these elements feed into the question of whether one can have a degree of confidence in the process, 'or as much confidence as [one] can have' given the need, as already discussed, to have some variations to the norm such as specialised procedures or the redaction of information.[146]

On the organisational front, a number of different issues arose. In some review mechanisms, such as the Independent Office for Police Conduct (IOPC), the staffing and organisation of the review mechanism can raise questions of independence and credibility. In that particular case, the Office is staffed by a mixture of those who formerly worked as police personnel and those who have never worked with or for the police.[147] For our interviewee from that office, addressing the concerns about independence that may arise from such a workforce is fundamentally about values: she made it clear that there is an institutional expectation that every person 'needs to work and demonstrate independence in every role; all the way through, all the way down, it's all of our jobs regardless of where you've come from'.[148] In that organisation this is bolstered by the articulation of a set of institutional values – 'seeking the truth, being inclusive, empowering people, being tenacious and making a difference'[149] – that are primary in the Office's activities.

Interestingly, even while valuing independence, for a number of our interviewees it was considered important that a reviewer or review mechanism was an 'insider',[150] at least to some extent. Indeed, this is reflected in the staffing of a number of review mechanisms. For example, unlike all other parliamentary committees, the ISC has a secretariat drawn from the Cabinet Office,[151] ostensibly because the Committee receives security-sensitive information, so that within Parliament it might be said to be 'a kind of a creature apart'.[152] While this may pose challenges for independence, our interviewees indicated that in situations of this kind the professional and personal insights that the people staffing a review mechanism have about the activities being reviewed can enhance their credibility in the eyes of reviewees. One interviewee, P6, told us how this can also help to foster relationships through which the recommendations for change that are made through review can successfully be actioned because of enhanced cooperation with the reviewee. This demonstrates aptly the delicate lines that need to be walked in counter-terrorism review between being independent enough to be robust and externally credible, but 'insider' enough to have the expertise and competence that underpin review,[153] and to be trusted and engaged with productively by the reviewed entity or entities.

Both the IOPC and the ISC have significant staff and resource bases, although both consider themselves under-resourced for the substantial tasks they must undertake,[154] but this is not the case for all counter-terrorism review actors. The Independent Reviewer of Terrorism Legislation, for example, runs on very slender resources, which seemed to be a matter of concern for some interviewees.[155] However, this was of less concern for the two former Independent Reviewers we interviewed. Instead there was a sense that, without a fixed substantial staff and secretariat, the Independent Reviewer could retain his independence, hire advisors, bring people on board to help out with particular reviews or issues (subject to them being vetted or having security clearance as appropriate to the task at hand), and act with a nimbleness that allowed them to commission advice or support for a particular review that was ongoing. While this may reflect the working mode to which the most recent Independent Reviewers are accustomed as barristers in their professional lives,[156] it also illustrates that there is no 'one size fits all' approach to resourcing that would best bolster independence and enhance credibility.

Finally, as regards independence, it was clear that at least some of our interviewees thought that the politics and positioning of an organisation or an individual who is appointed to key roles within the counter-terrorism review assemblage, could be important, since credibility can 'depend very much on the individual that's appointed'.[157] Speaking about a former Independent Reviewer of Terrorism Legislation, one interviewee said: 'He's an extremely robustly independent character ... [embodying] that kind of barrister quality of being ... proud to be independent ... but prepared to engage with anyone and everyone'.[158] Similarly, the chair of one Select Committee was described by another interviewee as being exceptionally independently minded, robust and committed.[159] In contrast, several interviewees referred less positively to the appointment of what one interviewee called 'a polarising figure within the Muslim community' to a leadership role in the Commission for Countering Extremism.[160] When it comes to counter-terrorism review undertaken by civil society there was a sense from some of our interviewees that some organisations are oppositional to state power and 'have a particular agenda',[161] or even a 'political agenda',[162] that influences their approach to counter-terrorism review. Some of our interviewees were rather pejorative about civil society because of their perceived opposition to core propositions of the counter-terrorist state,[163] even though this is arguably part of civil society's role within it.[164] As one civil society interviewee put it, civil society may be reluctant to offer solutions because 'the risk is you then end up endorsing in advance a new flawed counter-terrorism system'.[165]

Being experts, gathering evidence

Our interviewees indicated that expertise and gathering evidence were important in ensuring that the values of counter-terrorism review are realised in practice. Interestingly, however, there were some differences across the participants when it came to what kind of expertise mattered in this respect. Our interviewees who had experience in government considered it important that a review mechanism would understand the risks posed by terrorism, and the practical requirements of balancing security and rights. Given the political hazard that politicians appear to perceive in respect of countering terrorism, especially the sense that a security failure leading to terrorist incidents is particularly grave from a political perspective,[166] that is perhaps unsurprising. However, while non-politician interviewees were also cognisant of the high stakes involved in trying to 'strike the right balance' in counter-terrorism, they had a broader understanding of relevant expertise. For our interviewees from civil society and the civil service, this included openness to a diversity of perspectives, understanding of the wider impact of counter-terrorism and a commitment to trying to put things into the open.[167] For some other interviewees, expertise was indicated by analytical capacities, dexterity, diligence and professional experience of independently assessing evidence and information. Notwithstanding these differences, expertise of some kind was thought important across the spectrum, and in large part was connected with the ability of the reviewer to handle evidence in the process of review, reflecting the evaluative nature of counter-terrorism review.

To handle, analyse, understand and contextualise evidence, a review mechanism must have evidence in the first place. In this respect, for many interviewees, expertise and evidence gathering were connected to some extent with access to information. As we have already discussed, security clearances that allow review mechanisms to see and engage with confidential and security-sensitive information can be of great importance for review. Yet, not every review mechanism has that kind of access. Many interviewees expressed their commitment to building up an evidence base of their own, often emphasising the importance of pluralising the kind of data and evidence that is considered in the counter-terrorism review context in order to provide the kind of experiential and qualitative evidence of the impact of counter-terrorism that operational and statistical evidence may elide.[168] As one interviewee reflected, review needs to be 'informed by as objective an evidence base as is possible to obtain'.[169] In addition to considering security-sensitive information, statistics and the perspectives of official counter-terrorism actors, the Independent Reviewer has, for instance, developed a practice of speaking to communities and representative organisations to build up other kinds of evidence bases about the impact and nature of counter-terrorism in communities. The same is true of most of the civil society organisations to which we spoke. Indeed, it was notable how many of our interviewees spoke about evidence and data gathering as one of the first parts of undertaking review.

The approach to evidence gathering differs across actors. Where an organisation is required to report in a particular format on a regular basis, its focus will be on identifying and gathering the information required to fulfil that obligation. That, in turn, will be the evidence on which the regulator to which it reports bases its assessment of the operation of the counter-terrorism policies or powers in question. As we outlined in Chapter 2, for example, higher education institutions are required to make Prevent-related reports to the Office for Students, even if the institutions in question are not necessarily convinced of the efficacy or usefulness of that kind of reporting process,[170] are inclined to resist it and undertake minimal compliance,[171] or seem inclined towards over-compliance.[172] In other situations, a review mechanism might be inclined to gather evidence for a particular purpose, such as preparing litigation,[173] illustrating the transnational impacts of UK counter-terrorism,[174] or bringing to official attention the views, perceptions and experiences of communities and actors that are excluded or marginalised within official discourses,[175] or whose diversity of views may not adequately be captured within existing evidence bases.[176] For most, the processes of gathering evidence were important to ensure that review engaged with the realities of counter-terrorism beyond official narratives, and to underpin desired strategic outcomes, such as litigation. For some interviewees gathering evidence was important even if they were pessimistic about its potential to impact on review or on the trajectory and activities of the counter-terrorist state because, by gathering this evidence, they bore witness to the everyday experiences of counter-terrorism on impacted communities.[177]

Listening

Gathering evidence and trying to challenge the hegemonic consensus that underpins the counter-terrorist state in the UK requires counter-terrorism review actors to be able and willing to listen. For many of our interviewees, the ability to reach out to several communities is a distinct advantage for review mechanisms.[178] However, 'listening' in counter-terrorism review can be challenging. There is a 'cacophony of voices',[179] and even within what might be perceived as a single 'community' there will inevitably be a diversity of perspectives. As one interviewee who had experience working with Muslim communities in the UK put it, there are 'some organisations that are far more hostile and critical to government, others that are friendlier to government' but 'it's important to have all of those voices in the debate'.[180]

Government can struggle to engage with heterogeneous communities and make sense of what may appear to be internally inconsistent perspectives, meaning that some of our interviewees perceived it as tending to focus on particular 'representatives', treating their views and perspectives as reflecting those of a group of people who may in fact disagree.[181] Evidently some way of facing this challenge is needed, and counter-terrorism review may provide an answer. Numerous interviewees pointed to the range of ways in which counter-terrorism review mechanisms have actually gone about trying to engage with that wide range of perspectives and to find ways to listen, even where engaging with certain groups or challenging dominant public and political perspectives on counter-terrorism results in political hazard or public criticism.[182] Our interviewees also discussed the ways in which they feed the results of their own listening 'up' or 'across' the assemblage so that it can inform the reviews undertaken by other actors. Three civil society interviewees noted the importance of being able to provide reviewers, such as the Independent Reviewer and relevant Select Committees, with information and knowledge about community experiences of counter-terrorism.[183] This illustrates the notions of cooperation within the assemblage that we discussed above, as well as showing a keen strategic knowledge on the part of actors about how best to ensure that the evidence they gather gains traction within the broader counter-terrorism review landscape.

The two former Independent Reviewers we spoke to were themselves positive about engaging with and listening to public perspectives on counter-terrorism, and some other interviewees mentioned this as a positive aspect of how both had gone about their role. Both travelled widely during their tenure to engage with and hear perspectives from communities, and because, as one put it, 'it can be very useful in explaining things to people who don't have any kind of privileged access and may be quite suspicious about what's going on'.[184] Dialogue was 'the point of the job',[185] because unless they went out of their way to engage with communities, 'it didn't seem to me that I was demonstrably an Independent Reviewer'.[186] Independence, in this sense, 'requires being prepared to listen to the views of all'.[187] Not only did such a commitment to community engagement enable and reinforce independence, but for these reviewers it also allowed them to get a sense of regional idiosyncrasies and variations.[188]

However, a commitment to wide-ranging engagement may also have costs, including criticism in certain parts of the media if a review mechanism engages publicly with actors that are treated as politically unacceptable.[189] A further challenge is that the pressure of time and resources might curtail how much engagement can be undertaken.[190] There comes a point at which a review mechanism needs to stop engaging, but inevitably some people will be excluded as a result of that. However, interestingly, some of the smaller and less well-resourced review mechanisms seem to be the most nimble in reaching out, while larger review bodies dealing with sensitive materials and, perhaps, engaged in very formal legalistic review are less open.[191] The Independent Reviewer, for instance, uses Twitter specifically to try to engage with and reach out to people that might otherwise be hard to reach,[192] and without a media office to 'manage' the communication and 'message', it is likely to be the Independent Reviewer himself who is actually sending, receiving and reading tweets. This is a type of engagement with social media that may not be feasible for other kinds of review mechanisms.

Larger organisations can, however, undertake other kinds of listening and engagement. Our interviewee from the IOPC provided an illustrative example of how such an organisation can undertake listening and engagement in a structured and deliberate manner. In particular, she told us that the IOPC makes frequent use of community reference groups in investigations, as well as having several standing mechanisms that advise the organisation.[193] A community reference group would be convened during the investigation of a complaint, and is a 'group of representatives from the particular community that is impacted, [who] work alongside us in terms of doing things like thinking about what are the questions that the public are going to want answered [and] what should the scope of the investigation be'.[194] According to the interviewee, these groups are valuable because, first, they can provide a confidential sounding board and feed information to the IOPC during an investigation, and second, they can act as a bridge to the wider community. In these ways, they can help ensure that information on the progress of the investigation and, on its conclusion, its recommendations, filters out throughout the impacted area and communities.[195] The standing mechanisms are intended to provide similar dialogue but also to improve confidence in the IOPC of groups that may have suspicious or challenging relationships with the police, such as youth groups and local community groups. These examples illustrate how community engagement and listening might be structured formally into review mechanisms to deliver on the values that those mechanisms seek to pursue.

Part III: Impact

Understanding how to effect change through counter-terrorism review was clearly of importance to our interviewees; indeed, many mentioned enabling change among the purposes of review.[196] Trying to impact on counter-terrorism by influencing a wide range of relevant actors was critical to the activities of some of our interviewees and the organisations they work with. One interviewee we spoke to, who works with a regulatory mechanism, saw impact as involving a range of activities from responding to government consultations, making proposals for reform of law, policies and procedures, and making specific recommendations to the agencies and actors that they regulate.[197]

That this interviewee was conscious of the importance of being able to influence conversations across many different planes reflects that 'impact' is not a straightforward idea; the nature of the review in question might well determine its desired impact. To illustrate, if a body has a role in monitoring compliance with counter-terrorism duties, such as the Office for Students in respect of Prevent, its impact will largely be determined by how it influences the behaviours and compliance of its regulatees, and its activities may actually be quite compliance driven.[198] In contrast, a body with a much wider mandate such as the Independent Reviewer of Terrorism Legislation, has a less clearly defined intended outcome, so that its impact might be more diffuse and more difficult to identify. Our interviews bore that out. For some, a review is impactful if it has contributed to debates on counter-terrorism in some way, providing evidence-based assessments and information.[199] For others, such as a former Independent Reviewer, assessing the impact of the work is not so much about whether or not particular recommendations have been implemented, but about whether 'the relationship that I've built with the counter-terrorism machine has been mutually beneficial' and serves as a bedrock for influencing government either directly or by informing parliamentary and public debate.[200] In short, for most of our interviewees, the question of whether review activities led directly to change, including the revision of approaches, laws or policies that seemed not to be fit for purpose, was not determinative of whether they considered that the review had been impactful. Given the diffuse nature of impact, determining whether a counter-terrorism review mechanism has been impactful, or has realised its capacity for action, is challenging.

There were clearly factors our interviewees considered relevant to determining different review mechanisms' capacity for action. Some of these were entirely unpredictable, such as the intensification of public or media attention on a particular issue, as with the Schedule 7 example that opened this chapter, a public 'appetite for action',[201] or a political decision to revisit a law or policy after a change of government.[202] In respect of such factors, the review mechanism is not entirely irrelevant; rather, as one former Independent Reviewer expressed, 'you have to try use the wave to push things in the way that you think they ought to go'.[203] In other words, the reviewer or review mechanism needs to have a certain amount of nous in order to be able to read situations, see opportunities to influence things and then act to make the most of those opportunities.

In addition to these 'circumstantial' factors, our interviewees indicated a number of other, more stable factors that are relevant to a review mechanism's capacity for impact. The first is the standing and modes of operation of a review mechanism. For example, some parliamentary committees might be more impactful in the counter-terrorism context than others. This might be a reflection of their general standing and capacity to influence government action. As one interviewee who previously worked closely with the JCHR noted, its recommendations more or less 'always get followed by/adopted by the Government or implemented by the Government or the changes that they suggest to SIs [statutory instruments] or legislation get adopted'.[204] This was not specific to the JCHR's work on counter-terrorism, but rather reflective of a general trend. However, as we noted above, the Government may try to manage the flow of information and issues across committees, potentially undermining the opportunities a committee with this kind of potential might have to make an impact. Where a committee is largely technical – such as a pre-legislative committee – it can also have a very high rate of uptake on recommendations, as their work is, in effect, 'mainly done at official level'.[205] In a similar vein, there may sometimes be value in focusing on the Lords rather than the Commons when trying to gain attention 'for the less exciting points' during legislative scrutiny,[206] not least because, as a number of our interviewees noted,[207] Peers are not subject to the same political and constituency pressures as MPs, and can engage in different ways with contentious, technical or unpopular arguments.[208]

As already noted above, the hierarchy of review mechanisms that we discussed earlier in this chapter also has some potential to shape whether and how a review mechanism can have an impact.

Second, some of our interviewees thought that the form of review was relevant. A number mentioned that a decision from a court is a particularly strong form of review output since it must be complied with and, even where it relates only to a specific case, may influence government activity or approaches in subsequent cases.[209] This may explain why, for some of the civil society actors we interviewed, undertaking litigation is a key part of their approach to counter-terrorism review and accountability.[210] However, the form and the nature of the review was relevant beyond litigation. In particular, some interviewees considered whether a review is mandated in legislation or not to be a relevant consideration. One of our interviewees was of the view that sunset clauses can lead to a debate-based review that avoids the challenges posed to government receptiveness to change by the 'mood of particular committees and chairs and so forth'.[211] However, when pressed on whether previous sunset clauses had in fact led to rigorous debates of the kind he was describing, the interviewee was more sceptical.[212] He postulated that there may be ways to make sunset clauses more effective, perhaps by requiring that the debates they mandate are preceded by some kind of independent review which could provide the underpinning for parliamentary consideration of whether to renew the powers in question.[213] We have already seen (in Chapter 2) that some reviews were mandated in legislation in order to secure the law's passage. In other words, they were provided as conciliatory gestures by government. Where that is the case, some interviewees considered that these reviews were less likely to be impactful, not least because they were only committed to for instrumental purposes and '[the Government's] minds were already made up' about the measures under review.[214] The example of the Newton Committee, which we discussed above, is germane here. Finally, in this respect, where government can set the terms of reference of a review that it mandates, it has the capacity to empower only a very narrow review and, accordingly, to circumscribe the kinds of findings that might be made and the potential for the review to have a broader impact.[215] Hence, while there were some indications that being legally mandated might be relevant to a review mechanism's capacity to be impactful, it is not at all clear that this is necessarily the case.

The third factor mentioned by our interviewees is time. As previously discussed, time and timeliness are relevant to review, sometimes in complex ways. We have already seen that, for some of our interviewees, the passage of time between the subject of review and the review was helpful. This is because the review could take place with information about the actual operation of the law, which would have had time to bed down, and be completed and received in a less febrile and politically challenging context than the immediate aftermath of an attack, when the law or policy in question may have been introduced. In a similar vein, where review involves a particular case, the passage of time and the aversion of a risk or threat thought to be imminent at the time the actions under review were taken, can in fact be helpful. As one Special Advocate explained, it can help someone to succeed either because the accusations put are insufficiently 'imminent' to justify the measures employed or because it is easier to look at things dispassionately from a distance.[216] However, some contemporaneity can be useful. For instance, if there has been a significant incident or security failure, a review mechanism being able to review and come to conclusions about what happened may bolster public confidence.[217] It may also provide recommendations for action that can be implemented promptly, although some failures only come to light as the result of a later court case. However, the passage of time can also result in some elements of counter-terrorism becoming so embedded that the practical challenges of revising or changing it seem almost insurmountable.[218]

The fourth factor that emerged from the interviews might best be described as 'pitch', that is, the way in which the conclusions of a review are framed or recommendations put. This is a delicate and challenging point: on the one hand, a review that is especially forthright about failures, implications for rights, societal impact and so on may be perceived as challenging a key policy or approach in counter-terrorism in an unhelpful or oppositional way, and not well received by government. On the other hand, a review that elides these challenges where they exist, even if this is done for pragmatic reasons and in the hope of affecting positive change, might fail adequately to challenge the counter-terrorist state. Reviewers must make judgements about how to 'pitch' their reviews, and about what issues to press and which they might not focus on. To some extent, some interviewees seemed to perceive this as a matter of political and strategic sense. As one interviewee working within Parliament said 'there has to be a bit of targeting as to what's sensible',[219] both in terms of topic selection and in terms of how a recommendation or review finding is put. In the context of pre-legislative scrutiny and consultation, which as noted can be a forum where review outcomes are applied to try to learn from the past, she noted – and others agreed – that 'if people can be persuaded that [the recommendation is] in everyone's interests, that it's done properly [and] … that there's an alternative way forward, that doesn't impact the relevant authorities too negatively in their ability to do their job',[220] then proposed changes are likely to be agreed to. Similarly, a former Independent Reviewer noted the importance of making strategic decisions both about what to focus on and about how to express findings, especially ones that would be perceived as critical. In some ways, this was about making review findings 'palatable', but this was important in order to maintain the relationships that underpin the Independent Reviewer's capacity to influence government policy and, through that influence, enact change. A recommendation might therefore be gently put in a review report, but other parts of the assemblage, including in some cases the media,[221] might amplify it so that the power of the finding is enforced, without the critical relationship between reviewer and government being undermined to the ultimate detriment of accountability optimisation through review. In such situations, and as discussed above, the diversity of actors within the assemblage may be useful.

The final factor on impact that emerged from the interviews was about to whom key decision-makers were likely to listen. We have already outlined above the perception, borne out by interviews with former high-level politicians, that some review mechanisms are given more weight than others, especially by government. Our interviewees showed an acute awareness of this and of the implications it had for how they could ensure their review was impactful. Clearly, this raises questions of how to ensure that decision-makers might listen to and be open to a greater diversity of voices and review mechanisms, but it also raises questions of how the actors within the counter-terrorism review assemblage negotiate this challenge through their own actions. We have already discussed how, for some review mechanisms, outreach and engagement are key to hearing a diversity of perspectives by pluralising their evidence base and trying to produce review outcomes that are as well informed as possible. We have also seen that different actors within the review assemblage take deliberate steps to feed into and inform the reviews of mechanisms that are recognised as being more influential with government than they are themselves.

The counter-terrorism review assemblage: conclusions from the interviews

What we have presented here is, of course, not a comprehensive account of the rich data that we acquired through our interviews. However, the thematic approach to analysis that we adopted allowed us to draw from those interviews the elements that illustrate the ways in which counter-terrorism review as currently practiced in the UK is evaluative, that is, considers the merits of the subject of review, engages with reality, is capable of action and is practiced in a way that aligns with our intuition that counter-terrorism review is concerned with accountability. That is evident in particular from the purposes of review, the values that drive review, and the ways in which those purposes are pursued and values put into action within the practice of the people we spoke to for this research.

However, our interviews also identified real challenges with trying to understand and analyse counter-terrorism review in the UK. As we have already indicated, what is in operation here is best understood as an assemblage: there are multiple actors, multiple different mechanisms, and multiple reviews and desired outcomes ongoing at any given time. Importantly, while these are all distinct, they are not unrelated. There is not, as our interviews attested, a formal and structurally stable division of labour between the different review mechanisms, but there is an acute sense among our interviewees of the different roles, levels of access and levels of influence across the assemblage. This awareness is at times translated into action, for example in the form of a highly influential review mechanism, such as the Independent Reviewer, taking the initiative to engage widely to try to amplify marginalised voices and perspectives. It may also take the form of a civil society actor making concerted efforts to engage with and influence as many parts of the counter-terrorist state and counter-terrorism review assemblage as possible through broad engagement in formal and informal consultation. The review mechanisms influence one another in sometimes intangible ways; as with any other network, informal engagements, sidebar conversations and relationships can be as influential as formal participation in a review mechanism's programme of work. Information, understanding and awareness flow throughout the assemblage, sometimes in ways that can try to counteract official government exclusions of groups and perspectives thought to be unpalatable and unacceptable. In this way the counter-terrorism review assemblage is neither a system nor a mess, but something more akin to a pluralistic jumble; without fixed design or an overreaching 'conductor', it has its own rhythms and practices.

However, that in itself poses challenges of which the actors are aware. For one thing, the lack of some kind of overarching review mechanism that takes stock of every element of counter-terrorism and sees the counter-terrorist state in the round was widely acknowledged by our interviewees to be problematic. It may well be that there are areas where counter-terrorism review coverage is poor, such as with immigration, citizenship and passport-related powers. Interviewees themselves accepted that. For example, even though the Independent Reviewer can self-initiate reviews, one former Independent Reviewer told us that the subject matter of those reviews must already be within the scope of his remit, that is, it must be included within the legislation subject to statutory review. As he put it: 'I don't think I could just say, right, I'm doing a review on immigration detention.'[222] Furthermore, even where he can undertake reviews on his own initiative, the realities of workload and resource constraints are such that many areas of counter-terrorism remain largely un- or under-reviewed. At the same time, other areas of counter-terrorism may be subject to multiple reviews, but it might well be the case that it is that multiplicity of review that generates sufficient evidence to finally influence change, even if doing so might also be reliant on the news cycle, political developments or a particular high-profile incident. The sheer scale and diversity of the counter-terrorist state is also such that, at least for some of our interviewees, it was hard to imagine a single entity being able to review it.[223]

A question that remains unanswered from this interview data is whether counter-terrorism review, as it currently operates, actually challenges the hegemonic consensus that, as we note in Chapter 1, is a feature of the contemporary counter-terrorist state. The dominance of the current counter-terrorism paradigm – where it is widely accepted that counter-terrorism is necessary, that a 'balance' between rights and security is both possible and desirable, and that some secrecy or confidentiality is required – seems largely undisturbed within the counter-terrorism review assemblage. For a small number of interviewees, even some more controversial propositions – for example that countering extremism through preventive intervention was a matter of safeguarding, and unquestionably an appropriate role for educational institutions to be engaged with – were accepted without question.[224] Explaining this is complex. Certainly, the pragmatic realities of trying to make change happen can play a role; the importance that the politicians we interviewed placed on reviewers understanding the nature of the risk and the challenge of protecting the populace, even while protecting rights, indicated very clearly that any review mechanism that rejected this starting proposition was unlikely to have influence over government policy. Review actors we interviewed seemed aware of this, almost always accepting that counter-terrorism of some form is necessary. Nevertheless, there is resistance within the assemblage. Some interviewees told us how they worked to challenge precisely this paradigm, focusing on identifying problems and not on proposing solutions that might simply reinforce counter-terrorist state power,[225] or designing processes to ensure minimal compliance where counter-terrorism obligations were felt to be overly intrusive on rights.[226] But in the main, the interviews seemed to illustrate the bind that counter-terrorism review actors find themselves in: if they push back at the fundamentals, they will be seen as less credible by decision-makers and therefore lose their capacity to influence change, but, if they do not, then the basic propositions upon which the counter-terrorist state rests may go unchallenged.

Perhaps reflecting this, there was a clear awareness among some of our interviewees that the enhancement of accountability through counter-terrorism review could not be assumed. Counter-terrorism review is susceptible to cynical deployment by government, with terms of reference, mandates, and reviews being framed, established, accepted, ignored, published (or not) and acted upon (or not) largely only if and when the Government thought it desirable to do so. Reviews established in order to assure parliamentarians that counter-terrorism powers were going to be subject to effective oversight were sometimes later ignored; reports, even of the Independent Reviewer, were sometimes held back for significant periods of time by government; wide-ranging policies were sometimes not subjected to official review at all, even when multiple actors across the assemblage reiterated the need for it. Mechanisms of review that were 'better than nothing' were still, in some ways, acknowledged to be propping up the counter-terrorist state.[227] So, for example, Special Advocates might be better than nothing, but if closed material proceedings, which are themselves only rights compliant in part because of the involvement of Special Advocates, did not exist, then the material now going into closed would have to be made available in open.[228] This raises the real question, persistent right from the Introduction to this book, of whether – even while enhancing accountability – counter-terrorism review is also making the counter-terrorist state possible.

The outstanding questions then are whether, and, if so, how, the status quo could be improved in order further to optimise accountability through counter-terrorism review. Building on the insights gained from these interviews and our analysis of counter-terrorism review 'on paper', we turn now to address these vital issues.

Notes

1. Figures based on Home Office, 'Operation of Police Powers under the Terrorism Act 2000 Statistics' (GOV.UK, 7 March 2019), Available from: https://www.gov.uk/government/collections/operation-of-police-powers-under-the-terrorism-act-2000 [Accessed 19 March 2019]. No official statistics are available on the use of the power to stop, search, and question at the UK's entry and exit points between the commencement of the Act in February 2001 and 2009. Terrorism Act 2000, Schedule 7, 2(1).

2. Schedule 7 provides the power to stop, search and hold individuals at ports, airports and international rail stations.

3. Lord Carlile, *Report on the Operation in 2007 of the Terrorism Act 2000 and of Part I of the Terrorism Act 2006* (2008) para 134. Responding to that annual report the Government accepted that 'intuitive stops' needed to be based on better intelligence

but no further actions to minimise their use were outlined: Home Office, *The Government Reply to the Report by Lord Carlile of Berriew Q.C.* (Cm 7249, 2008) 9.

4   For example, the work of the Federation of Student Islamic Societies (FOSIS) has been highlighted. See Tufyal Choudhury, 'Campaigning on Campus: Student Islamic Societies and Counterterrorism,' (2007) 40(12) Studies in Conflict & Terrorism 1004, 1014–17; P9.

5   Tufyal Choudhury and Helen Fenwick, 'The Impact of Counter-terrorism Measures on Muslim Communities' (Research Report 72, Equality and Human Rights Commission 2011).

6   Joint Committee on Human Rights, *Legislative Scrutiny: Anti-social Behaviour, Crime and Policing Bill* (2013–14, HL 56, HC 713); Joint Committee on Human Rights, *Legislative Scrutiny: Anti-social Behaviour, Crime and Policing Bill (second Report)* (2013–14, HL 108, HC 951).

7   Home Office, 'Review of the Operation of Schedule 7: A Public Consultation' (GOV.UK, September 2012), Available from: https://assets.publishing.service. gov.uk/government/uploads/system/uploads/attachment_data/file/157896/ consultation-document.pdf [Accessed 19 March 2019].

8   David Anderson, *The Terrorism Acts in 2011* (Stationery Office 2012) 100; David Anderson, *The Terrorism Acts in 2013* (Stationery Office 2014).

9   Quote from P2.

10   *David Miranda v Secretary of State for the Home Department* [2016] EWCA Civ 6.

11   P2.

12   We outline the methodological approach taken in the Introduction to this book.

13   P24.

14   P11.

15   P3.

16   P12.

17   P1; P7; P10.

18   P1; P2; P5; P7; P10; P11.

19   P7; P11; P13; P14.

20   P2; P6; P9.

21   P1; P2; P5; P7.

22   P8; P9; P11; P12; P13.

23   P1; P2; P3; P4; P5; P7; P10; P11; P12; P13.

24   P1; P2; P4; P6; P11.

25   P2; P4; P5; P9; P13; P21.

26   P1; P11; P12; P13; P15; P18

27   P14.

28   P5.

29   P2; P13; P15; P22.

30   P16.

31   P1; P2; P5; P7; P10; P11.

32   P2; P3; P4; P7; P9; P12; P13; P14.

33   P1; P8; P9; P11; P12; P13.

34   P2; P6; P12; P15; P20; P24.

35   Concerns about students came from P16.

36   For example, review mechanisms that evaluate and take into account the possibility that UK practices might be used as a template for best practice internationally, may be able to inhibit the development of 'copycat legislation' in jurisdictions that might lack the same accountability culture as the UK: P12.

[37] P13.

[38] P13.

[39] P10; P21.

[40] P6.

[41] P10.

[42] P1; P7; P9; P10; P20; P21.

[43] Martin Chamberlain 'Special Advocates and Amici Curiae in National Security Proceedings in the United Kingdom' (2018) 68(3) University of Toronto Law Journal 496, 496–510; Tamara Tulich 'Adversarial Intelligence? Control Orders, TPIMs and Secret Evidence in Australia and the United Kingdom' (2012) 12(2) Oxford University Commonwealth Law Journal 341, 341–69; John Ip 'The Rise and Spread of the Special Advocate' [2008] Public Law 717, 717–41.

[44] P2; P4; P7; P13.

[45] P2; P5; P7; P13.

[46] David Anderson, *Report of The Bulk Powers Review* (Cm 9326, 2016).

[47] P6.

[48] On retrospectivity and review see Introduction.

[49] P1.

[50] P11.

[51] P5.

[52] P11; P12.

[53] P5.

[54] P3.

[55] P10. P23 also noted that consultation with relevant stakeholders may not take place prior to legislation and that review could allow for that to happen as part of the evaluation process.

[56] P10.

[57] P2; P5.

[58] P2; P6; P15.

[59] P13; P19; P24. Yet this will not always be the case; inquests and inquiries that take place long after an event in which there is particular public interest or in respect of which there is especially heightened concern (for example the Saville Inquiry into Bloody Sunday; Lord Saville of Newdigate et al *Report of the Bloody Sunday Inquiry Vols I–X* (2010 HC 29-I-X)) are likely still to be of interest, but are also usually of a much greater scale than an 'ordinary' counter-terrorism review.

[60] P2; P13.

[61] Dawn Oliver, 'Accountability and the Foundations of British Democracy – the Public Interest and Public Service Principles' in Nicholas Bamforth and Peter Leyland (eds), *Accountability in the Contemporary Constitution* (Oxford University Press 2013) 289; Julia Black, 'Constructing and Contesting Legitimacy and Accountability in Polycentric Regulatory Regimes' (2008) 2(2) Regulation and Governance 137; Donald Black, *The Behaviour of Law* (Academic Press 1976); Julia Black, *Rules and Regulators* (Oxford University Press 1997); Christopher Hood et al, *Regulation Inside Government* (Oxford University Press 2000); Peter Grabosky and John Braithwaite, *Of Manners Gentle* (Oxford University Press 1986).

[62] P15.

[63] P1; P5; P6; P7; P11.

[64] Investigatory Powers Act 2016, ss 229–36.

[65] P19.

[66] P12.

67 P15.
68 P12; P13; P22 and (implicitly) P2.
69 P1; P2; P3; P4; P5; P6; P10; P11; P13; P14; P15; P18; P19; P22; P24.
70 P2.
71 P1; P2; P4; P8; P9; P12; P13; P15; P18; P19; P20; P23.
72 P22.
73 P2.
74 P2.
75 George Stigler, 'The Theory of Economic Regulation' (1971) 2(1) Bell Journal of Economics and Management Science 3; Richard A. Posner, 'The Concept of Regulatory Capture: A Short, Inglorious History' in Daniel Carpenter and David Moss (eds) *Preventing Regulatory Capture: Special Interest Influence and How to Limit It* (Cambridge University Press 2013); Rebecca Slayton and Aaron Clark-Ginsberg 'Beyond regulatory capture: Coproducing expertise for critical infrastructure protection' (2018) 12 Regulation & Governance 115, 115–30; Jessie Blackbourn 'Evaluating the Independent Reviewer of Terrorism Legislation' (2014) 67(4) Parliamentary Affairs 955, 955–68; P6; P7; P9.
76 P3; P4; P13; P14; P19.
77 P2; P3; P4; P13; P14.
78 P3.
79 Lord Burnett of Maldon and Sir Ernest Ryder, *Practice Direction: Closed Judgments* (14 January 2019), Available from: https://www.judiciary.uk/announcements/practice-direction-closed-judgments/ [Accessed 19 March 2019], following *Guardian News & Media Ltd v R & Incedal* [2016] EWCA Crim 11.
80 P3.
81 P14.
82 P14.
83 P4.
84 See a history in Mark Phythian, 'The British Experience with Intelligence Accountability' (2007) 22(1) Intelligence and National Security 75; Andrew Defty 'Coming in from the cold: bringing the Intelligence and Security Committee into Parliament' (2019) 34(1) Intelligence and National Security 22, 22–37.
85 P22; Defty claims that the ISC is located 'at secure premises in Victoria rather than on the Parliamentary Estate' Defty (ibid) 29. In response to a query, the ISC confirmed that it meets in premises that form part of the Cabinet Office estate (email on file with authors).
86 P10.
87 P22.
88 See, for example: Terrorism Act 2006, ss 36(2) and (5).
89 P9.
90 P6.
91 P6; P15; P24.
92 P24.
93 P19.
94 P8; P15
95 P2; P3; P6; P8; P9; P10; P12; P14; P24.
96 P24.
97 P2.
98 P2; P9; P12.
99 P1; P4; P5; P6; P10; P12; P13; P19; P20; P22; P24.

[100] P2.

[101] P2.

[102] P2.

[103] P11.

[104] P2; P3; P7; P18.

[105] P1.

[106] P1; P9; P10; P12; P13; P18; P19; P22.

[107] P1; P3; P4; P6; P11; P14; P15; P16; P17; P18; P19; P20; P21; P22; P23; P24.

[108] P5; P6; P24.

[109] One interviewee considered that public engagement with the outcomes of reviews was more minimal than might be expected, and that politicians, lawyers, advisors, journalists and researchers were the primary audience for review: P19.

[110] P7.

[111] P3; P8; P10; P12; P14.

[112] P9.

[113] P2; P4; P5; P13; P22.

[114] P2; P6; P7; P12; P15.

[115] P11.

[116] P11.

[117] P11.

[118] P22.

[119] P14.

[120] P2; P6; P11; P13; P18.

[121] Defty (n 84); Tom Hickman 'The Investigatory Powers Tribunal: a law unto itself?' [2018] Public Law 584, 584–94.

[122] P8; P9; P12; P13.

[123] P2; P5; P7; P13.

[124] Anti-Terrorism, Crime and Security Act 2001, s 122.

[125] HC Deb 18 December 2003, vol 415, cols 145–7WS.

[126] Ibid col 146WS.

[127] P5; P7.

[128] P14.

[129] P12.

[130] P10.

[131] P3; P4.

[132] P3; P4; P14.

[133] P21 describing their institution as 'keeping our approach as part of a sort of effective regulatory practice under review'.

[134] P8; P10; P12; P20.

[135] P6.

[136] P12.

[137] Independence appears in several forms. In general, see Colin Scott, 'Independent Regulators' in Mark Bovens et al (eds) *The Oxford Handbook of Public Accountability* (Oxford University Press 2014). On the role of impartiality in judicial oversight, see: Carol Harlow 'Accountability and Constitutional Law' in Bovens et al (ibid); and on arms-length oversight, see: Christopher Hood et al, 'Regulation of Government: Has it Increased, is it Increasing, Should it be Diminished?' (2000) 78(2) Public Administration 283. Independence also underpins the need to protect against regulatory capture: Posner (n 75).

[138] P2; P4; P7; P8; P9; P10; P12; P13; P14; P18; P21; P22; P23; P24.

139 P4; P6; P7; P8; P10; P14; P24.

140 P15.

141 P12; P13.

142 P2; P6; P7; P9; P22; P24.

143 P13.

144 P12.

145 P15.

146 P14.

147 Although s 9(3) Police Reform Act 2002 requires only that the Director-General may not have worked for the police, he can determine other posts that are to be treated as being in that category. P24 stressed the importance of a good mix of former police and non-police personnel for public confidence in the Office.

148 P24.

149 P24.

150 P1; P2; P6; P13.

151 P22; Defty (n 84) 22; Justice and Security Act 2013, sch 1, 3.

152 P22. An opinion confirmed in the academic literature: Defty (n 84) 13, 16.

153 P24.

154 Defty (n 84); P18; P24. It is also worth noting that both these mechanisms provide accountability over and above counter-terrorism related review.

155 P2; P6; P10; P15; P18; P22; P24.

156 Lord Alex Carlile QC, David Anderson QC (now Lord Anderson), Max Hill QC and Jonathan Hall QC.

157 P9.

158 P22.

159 P18.

160 P9.

161 P1; P11.

162 P12.

163 P6; P11; P16; P18.

164 P10; P12.

165 P12.

166 P1; P11; P18.

167 P3; P4; P7; P9; P10; P12; P22; P24.

168 P2; P6; P7; P12; P15; P22.

169 P22.

170 P17.

171 P8.

172 P16.

173 P12.

174 P12; P13.

175 P9; P12; P13; P20; P22.

176 For example, the Muslim Council of Britain is undertaking a National Listening Exercise on the views of Muslims in Britain on counter-terrorism, Available from: https://mcb.org.uk/project/nle/ [Accessed 29 March 2019].

177 P20.

178 P9; P20.

179 P10.

180 P9.

181 P9; P20.

182 P11; P13.
183 P9; P20; P23.
184 P2.
185 P2.
186 P15.
187 P15.
188 P2; P15; P20; P24.
189 P2; P15; P23.
190 P23.
191 P2; P15 contra P6; P18.
192 P22 expressly noted the Reviewer being 'adventurous with communications' by using Twitter.
193 Independent Office for Police Conduct, *Strategic Plan 2018–2022* (Nov 2018) 18, Available from: https://policeconduct.gov.uk/sites/default/files/Documents/Who-we-are/accountability-performance/IOPC_Strategic_plan_2018.pdf [Accessed 19 March 2019]; Independent Police Complaints Commission, *Stakeholder engagement strategy 2016–2018* (Oct 16) 20, Available from: https://www.policeconduct.gov.uk/sites/default/files/Documents/Who-we-are/who_we_are_IPCC_Stakeholder_engagement_strategy_2016-18.pdf [Accessed 19 March 2019].
194 P24.
195 P24.
196 P1; P10; P11; P12; P13; P18; P21.
197 P24.
198 P21.
199 P2; P4; P5; P7; P9; P12; P13.
200 P15.
201 P11.
202 P8; P13.
203 P2.
204 P22.
205 P22.
206 P10.
207 P5; P7; P18; P22; P23.
208 This reflects findings in previous research. See for example Aileen Kavanagh, 'The Joint Committee on Human Rights: A Hybrid Breed of Constitutional Watchdog' in Murray Hunt, Hayley Hooper and Paul Yowell (eds) *Parliaments and Human Rights: Redressing the Democratic Deficit* (Hart Publishing 2014).
209 P3; P4; P10; P13; P14; P19; P22.
210 P12; P13.
211 P9.
212 P9.
213 P9.
214 P7.
215 This was the case with the review of bulk powers, commissioned by the Government. The reviewer was given a highly circumscribed remit to review the operational case for the powers. The inevitable finding that bulk powers had 'a clear operational basis' was then used to justify placing them on a statutory footing. Anderson (n 46).
216 P14.

217 A number of participants made this point at our stakeholder workshop.
218 P3.
219 P10.
220 P10.
221 P2; P12; P13; P15.
222 P2.
223 For example, as P24 said, 'you couldn't possibly have one thing, I don't think it's a solution to have one thing that did everything because (a) it would be enormous and (b) you know, the specialisms it would have to cover are just so diverse'.
224 P16; P17; P21.
225 P8; P9; P12; P13; P20; P23.
226 P3; P4; P12; P13; P14; P22.
227 P4.
228 P14.

4

Problematising
Counter-Terrorism Review

In some ways, counter-terrorism review operates well. The 'pluralistic jumble' that is the counter-terrorism review assemblage has significant strengths. It is often able to ensure that counter-terrorism is subjected to real evaluation: that merit is assessed, that reality is engaged with and that there is a capacity for action as a result of review. In important ways, the assemblage operates as a 'web of accountability' in the counter-terrorist state, subjecting its activities to scrutiny against a range of legal, societal and operational standards. However, challenges to realising the accountability potential of counter-terrorism review persist. In large part, those challenges reflect the persistence of exceptionalist thinking within the counter-terrorist state. In this chapter, we zoom out from the detailed accounts given in Chapters 2 and 3 to problematise counter-terrorism review from the perspective of accountability. We dwell on four persistent challenges that emerged from our research: the secret state, the abundance of executive control, the limitations of Parliament and the absence of trust. These challenges have a serious impact on counter-terrorism review but, to a large extent, their resolution may be beyond the reach of the assemblage itself.

Part I: The secret state endures

In spite of the Government's avowed commitment to accountability and transparency in counter-terrorism,[1] and of the near-universal agreement across our interviewees that reducing secrecy and increasing transparency was at the heart of counter-terrorism review,[2] the counter-terrorist state is a secret state. Often enabled and legitimised by accountability mechanisms such as courts,[3] this secrecy poses significant challenges to the optimisation of accountability through counter-terrorism review. To explain this, we adopt Morgan's tripartite characterisation of the secret state as engaging in esoteric, operational and efficient secrecy.[4] We argue all three elements can be observed within the counter-terrorist state in ways that undermine, and in some cases seem to be structured into, the counter-terrorism review assemblage. Seen in this way, state secrecy not only poses obstacles for accountability in the counter-terrorist state, but also exacerbates the hierarchy, competition and marginalisation that, as we discussed in Chapter 3, are apparent in the counter-terrorism review assemblage. It also creates remarkable levels of opacity around counter-terrorism review, which are observed throughout the assemblage's working.

Esoteric secrecy restricts access to information and decision-making to certain categories of individual.[5] It controls information in such a way to restrict it to a privileged group, the insiders in 'the secret state'.[6] Admission to that privileged group is a marker of both perceived expertise and a kind of insider-ness. By implication, this marks those not in the privileged group as outsiders, and marginalises actors in the zone of activity to which esoteric secrecy is applied. Here, the insider group is a privileged class, an elite. However, insider-ness and elitism are not necessarily determined by many of the usual markers of elitism in British political culture.[7] For example, not all parliamentarians exist within this privileged insider group. Only those who have security clearance, such as members of the Intelligence and Security Committee (ISC) or the Privy Council, are admitted. Others are excluded, to the detriment of their ability to challenge the logics, information, decision-making and classification that takes place within the zone of activity to which the insider group has access.[8]

Esoteric secrecy can be observed in numerous activities of the counter-terrorist state. For instance, evidence and related information that underpin perceived threat levels, and ground the policy- and law-making initiatives intended to address those threats, is often privileged. Where this is the case, only those with appropriate security clearance can access this information. Only those review mechanisms with the same level of security clearance can assess its scale, quality and application in state decision-making about how to pursue counter-terrorism.[9] One former Secretary of State we spoke to suggested that understanding the threat and the challenges of 'balancing' rights and security, in order to assess the adequacy and effectiveness of the law, is the essence of counter-terrorism review.[10] If this is so, then access both reflects assumptions about requisite expertise, and underpins the perceived credibility of the reviewer in question. In part, the general agreement among our interviewees on the power and importance of access to such information partly explains the dominance of the Independent Reviewer of Terrorism Legislation across our interview data and, by implication, within the counter-terrorism review assemblage.[11]

Having security clearance, the Independent Reviewer can request classified information, making him a member of the security elite. As a former Independent Reviewer told us, 'unlimited access to classified information ... is the really powerful weapon you have, that's what makes people listen to what you have to say, and that's what is the basis for any influence that you might have'.[12] Given how important government seems to think a reviewer 'understanding' the nature of the threat that the state seeks to avert is,[13] it seems likely that access to such information is one of the things that contributes to the Independent Reviewer's perceived credibility. It means a Secretary of State 'take[s] ... very seriously' what the Independent Reviewer says.[14] However, that insider-ness also threatens to undermine their independence. As we saw in Chapter 3, independence is vital to ensuring that the Independent Reviewer is seen as credible, that their efforts at community engagement and outreach are meaningfully received, and that the evidence they receive is qualitative, experiential, grounded in and reflective of societal experience. The ability to assess the societal impact of counter-terrorism legislation is, in the view of another former Independent Reviewer we spoke to, core to the role.[15]

In providing the Independent Reviewer with insider status, the state manages to bolster its claims to secrecy by allowing 'external' scrutiny within the zone of secrecy. In doing so, it presents secrecy as legitimate because it does not preclude independent review. However, the state also contributes to the extent to which that mechanism is on a 'tightrope'.[16] It requires the office holder delicately to balance relationships inside and outside of the privileged group to try to maintain access to the information and insight they need to undertake evaluation. It also requires them to retain the independence they need to ensure this evaluation is seen as credible by both the counter-terrorist state and the other actors within the counter-terrorism review assemblage.[17] This illustrates the ways in which secrets can empower those who hold them: they empower the state to decide who has admission to the privileged group, and the admitted actor to be treated as credible within that group. These decisions also reinforce the state's control over who gets to be perceived as credible and impactful, and who is listened to by the counter-terrorist state. As we showed in Chapter 3, the counter-terrorism review assemblage is characterised in part by competition and hierarchy. Different actors will have different views of what constitutes credibility, but it is clear that by marginalising certain actors, government, in particular, can determine which voices are heard, or at least heard by those most able to make change.

It seems this may operate to create a subtle but powerful disincentive to 'resist' the counter-terrorist state within review processes.[18] One effect is that to exercise any influence through counter-terrorism review may require an actor to concede to the logics of the counter-terrorist state in order to be heard, at least officially. Furthermore, being perceived to have an 'agenda' for resistance might lead an entity to be side-lined by other review mechanisms, conscious of possible implications of resistance for perceived credibility.[19] As one civil society interviewee told us, even when an actor seems out of favour with the government officially, quiet or unofficial discourse may be happening behind the scenes, sometimes with one government department but not others.[20] Marginalisation of this kind may be performative or partial, but in all cases seems to empower the state and disempower the excluded actor. This is likely to be exacerbated for actors within the counter-terrorism review assemblage that are already marginalised, suggesting that some actors may have more capacity to resist than others. As one interviewee working in a Russell Group university explained, they perceived that they could take a light touch approach to Prevent and resist some of the problematic assumptions underpinning it without much risk of negative consequences, because the sanctions for non-compliance are 'not something that applies to us and never would do ... this is for [name of post-1992 university] not us'.[21] Such an approach is certainly not uniform across universities,[22] but arguably higher education institutions with a weaker influence and less 'status' might struggle to adopt such a position.

These examples show the importance of insider/outsider and marginalised status for counter-terrorism review actors. By deploying esoteric secrecy to create hierarchies and stratifications within the counter-terrorism review assemblage, the state can generate competition as well as the kind of informal division of labour through which some of these constraints are at least somewhat ameliorated. However, amelioration can lead to outsiders relying on insiders to receive and amplify their review outcomes and perspectives, while those insiders must occasionally act pragmatically to retain the enhanced capacity to influence the counter-terrorist state that comes with admission to the privileged space of esoteric secrecy.

Operational secrecy protects access to information about techniques, procedures and investigations in order to maintain their functional efficacy.[23] The intelligence and security agencies, their operation and some police activities are the most common locus for operational secrecy in the UK as elsewhere.[24] The underpinning assumption of operational secrecy is that the institutions, operations and techniques could not function effectively if certain information about them were not kept secret.[25] The purpose is not to keep this information from citizens, but rather from the actors the agencies are operating against: the suspected terrorists, the terrorist organisers, the persons kept under surveillance and so on.[26] The agencies' work is as much about keeping information about *how* they work from those they may be investigating, as it is about keeping information about particular investigations themselves secret, although the former may require the latter. Indeed, sometimes the law prohibits oversight bodies from disclosing agencies' operational methods.[27]

Nowadays, some oversight mechanisms that effectively operate as review mechanisms exist within the space of operational secrecy.[28] In the UK, the ISC is an apposite example. As we have already noted, this Committee has full security clearance, but it is also treated somewhat differently to other parliamentary committees: it is resourced by the Cabinet Office and undertakes its meetings in a separate secure location within the Cabinet Office estate.[29] Although it can now take some public evidence, the ISC mostly meets in private,[30] its members are appointed by Parliament but nominated by the Prime Minister,[31] and while it reports to Parliament, its reports must first be sent to the Prime Minister who has a substantial redaction power,[32] and even since its reform in 2013 publication of the Committee's reports has sometimes been delayed.[33] In other words, even when operating to undertake counter-terrorism review, the Committee is integrated into the zone of secrecy within which its reviewed operations have taken place, and its members report feeling significantly constrained by government in important ways.[34] There are mixed views on how well the Committee has undertaken this work. Morgan argues that the quality of its work is variable and that sometimes it has only 'offered the bare minimum penetration into the working procedures of the security and intelligence agencies',[35] whereas others consider that it has 'exceeded expectations in terms of access to information and ... sought to establish itself as a serious critic of the agencies',[36] especially since its reform through the Justice and Security Act 2013. Some argue, along with some of our interviewees, that this success relies on the determination and skill of the Committee's members,[37] and on the commitment and personality of its chair.[38] The secrecy under which the ISC operates is presented as the inevitable cost of operational integrity,[39] as it is contended to be the only way to undertake accountability and review processes in the zone of operational sensitivity. Even as international standards requiring enhanced transparency as part of the oversight of intelligence and security standards proliferate,[40] the technology of secrecy continues to operate and, as a result, the accountability-optimising potential of counter-terrorism review seems undermined.

This is exacerbated when we consider that the logic and nature of operational secrecy is such that safeguards, introduced through law to try to limit and control over-reach or the misapplication of repressive powers, such as authorisation and warrant requirements, also operate within the zone of operational secrecy.[41] In some cases, that means that a body already established with the necessary security clearances ends up acting as both an authorising and a review or oversight body. For example, warrants issued for bulk interception and acquisition of data or equipment interference are issued by the Secretary of State and then authorised by the Investigatory Powers Commissioners Office (IPCO),[42] a process known as the 'double lock'. IPCO is also responsible for the review and oversight of interception, acquisition and equipment interference through its audit, inspection and investigation powers, which includes the process of authorising the warrants.[43] In such systems secrecy operates on multiple scales: authorisations for investigatory powers are automatically *ex parte* because they are not court issued in the same way as most warrants, but issued by the Secretary of State and then approved by the Commissioners. Not only is the information underpinning requests for authority classified and monopolised by the state agencies seeking the authorisation,[44] but it is an offence for an organisation or person to whom a warrant is issued to reveal its existence.[45] The ISC is informed of all investigatory powers warrants approved every three months.[46] All stages of review are impacted by secrecy. This is exacerbated by the fact that all relevant actors – the Secretary of State, the authorising Judicial Commissioner, and the ISC – are likely to be risk averse (if not deferential) to the claims of state agencies, both when assessing applications for warrants and when undertaking the subsequent review. The extent of redaction at all stages makes determining the level of deference almost impossible.

The challenges of undertaking counter-terrorism review within a zone of operational secrecy became clear when we spoke to Special Advocates who told us how the professional isolation that closed proceedings impose on them undermines their ability to achieve what some perceived to be their primary purpose of challenging the claims of operational secrecy by trying to secure disclosure orders for as much evidence as possible to be placed into the open.[47] The difficulties they face in achieving this reinforce the view of one parliamentarian that 'safeguards' such as Special Advocates resulted in a set of terrorism-related judicial and *quasi*-judicial processes best described as 'Kafka played by the rules of cricket';[48] the behaviour may seem genteel, but the result remains repressive.

The logics of operational security pose at least three severe challenges to counter-terrorism review's capacity to optimise accountability in the counter-terrorist state. First, the claims of necessity that underpin arguments of operational secrecy cannot easily be challenged because they are based on classified information. Second, the risks of miscalculation are potentially severe because the welfare of state agents or the integrity of whole operations may be put at risk. Finally, the institutions designed to provide oversight and review in respect of them seem themselves to be constructed within, rather than to challenge, the structures and technologies of operational secrecy.

Efficient secrecy refers to 'the pragmatic sense in which secret conditions allow faster decision-making and the conceptual limits of transparency in a modern complex state'.[49] Of this there is plenty to observe within the counter-terrorist state, with significant implications for counter-terrorism review. Efficient secrecy is premised on the idea that while full disclosure might be desirable in a modern liberal democracy, it is implausible. Not all information can be made public, and even if it could, that would not be desirable because it would slow down decision-making, introduce inefficiencies in governance, and potentially undermine people's willingness to engage in good faith with government and to change their minds because some secrecy can aid deliberation. It might even facilitate accountability to some extent. One former Secretary of State we spoke to noted that 'the confidentiality of the [ISC] proceedings' enabled it 'to get the operational levers of the security services to talk reasonably frankly about what was happening, which they would never do in an open environment'.[50]

As a general matter, we do not expect full transparency about everything the Government does and every discussion that it has; for example, deliberations in Cabinet are generally confidential. Instead, the practice is such that Parliament largely accedes to the proposition that some secrecy of this kind is not only inevitable but necessary for good government. However, that accession comes with its limitations: there is a general assumption that such secrecy will not last forever.[51] For example, Freedom of Information legislation allows for claims of secrecy to be challenged, although that too has its limits.[52] While some politicians and public servants consider the Freedom of Information Act 2000 unduly burdensome,[53] such laws and practices were intended to ensure that the claims of efficient secrecy could not be deployed excessively and that the state must still justify its activities and act in a transparent manner.[54] However, in the counter-terrorist state, the mechanisms attempting to limit efficient secrecy are constrained by the nature of the security claim itself, reflected in the numerous legislative exemptions from Freedom of Information.[55] It is not only that information cannot be disclosed for purposes of efficiency, but also that disclosure would have operational implications. This is well illustrated in the debates on the Freedom of Information Act 2000. Take this extract from the speech of Richard Shepherd MP for example:

> There will be, and there are, matters that cause every one of us, on a prima facie reading of the information, to think that that information may touch upon the security of the state, which is one of the blanket exemptions. As a consequence, all information on MI5 and MI6 is exempt for the purposes of the Bill – and I see hon. Members nodding in absolute agreement that those bodies should be beyond an inquiry.[56]

Efficient and operational secrecy overlap in ways that allow for the opacity of much executive review, in particular, to be maintained. We mentioned earlier that a former Secretary of State to whom we spoke noted that the confidentiality of ISC proceedings meant that security agencies would speak openly in that forum. However, the implication of this is that operational actors accounted to the Committee because it was closed (efficient secrecy) but that if no such closed forum were available, they would not have given account of their activities to any external forum in the ordinary course of events (operational secrecy).

When it comes to executive review there is in many cases a high level of political control of whether, when and with what mandate it takes place – a point we return to in Part II of this chapter. However, there is also opacity as to its basic existence and operation. Take, for example, the Prevent Oversight Board, which we discussed in Chapter 2. In January 2017, the junior minister for Countering Terrorism described the Board as playing an 'essential and ongoing role in driving delivery and scrutinising the Prevent programme to ensure it continues to effectively safeguard people vulnerable to radicalisation'.[57] However, apart from a few brief mentions of the membership of the Board in an early iteration of the Prevent Strategy and in recent Guidance,[58] little information about this Board exists. We know that the Secretary of State chairs the board, and that its membership includes the 'Secretaries of State responsible for the relevant sectors within which Prevent operates including Education, Health, Local Communities and Justice' as well as 'a number of independent members'.[59] We do not know who those independent members are, although Lord Carlile recently mentioned that he was on it.[60] We do not know how often it meets, but again according to Lord Carlile it 'has not been meeting as often as it should'.[61] We do not know what kinds of questions it asks. We do not know what kind of evidence base it applies. Furthermore, when we sought to find these basic things out – things that did not relate to any particular decision or review undertaken by the Board – we were told that it was exempt from Freedom of Information law either under a qualified exemption after the application of a harm-based public interest test under national security,[62] or under an absolute exemption under the formulation of public policy.[63]

State secrecy has significant implications for counter-terrorism review. For most of the counter-terrorism review assemblage it means that vital information is beyond its reach. While, as we saw in Chapter 3, counter-terrorism review actors can and do develop their own evidence bases, they seem likely always to be disadvantaged in respect of influencing and making change when seen alongside the 'insider' review mechanisms. Even those mechanisms that do have access to secret and classified information must compromise as a result, it seems. Their credibility is seen as a product of their insider-ness, but that same insider status raises questions of pragmatism that may risk their legitimating rather than providing accountability-based challenge to the counter-terrorist state.

Part II: The abundance of executive control

We have already seen that the Executive can, and does, make decisions about access and secrecy that create and (re)enforce insider/outsider distinctions within the counter-terrorism review assemblage. This illustrates the extent to which the Executive controls the conditions, contexts, reception and impact of counter-terrorism review. Given the long-standing practice of deference to the Executive in matters of national security,[64] the political culture of secrecy,[65] and the existence of a hegemonic consensus on counter-terrorism,[66] the Executive's ability substantially to control counter-terrorism review is both unsurprising and troubling. This manifests in numerous ways, but we focus here on executive control over whether review takes place, the conditions of review, the publication of review outputs and the implementation of review recommendations.

As illustrated in Chapter 2, state-mandated counter-terrorism review can take place because of a statutory provision mandating it, because litigation was commenced, on the initiative of a review mechanism, or following ad hoc establishment of a review mechanism to evaluate a certain issue or incident. However, across these realms, the review mechanisms that appear to be most likely to influence counter-terrorism are those undertaken and/or amplified by mechanisms that are considered to be particularly credible in the eyes of the Executive, or those forms that cannot be resisted by the Executive, namely, court orders arising from litigation. As discussed in Chapter 3, this subtle but powerful executive control has serious implications for how the 'pluralistic jumble' of the counter-terrorism review assemblage operates. As with the Executive's control over access to 'secrets', it imposes and reinforces hierarchies and competition between review mechanisms, marking some as 'insider' and some as 'outsider'. Even when it comes to the particularly influential review mechanisms such as Parliament or the Independent Reviewer, a surprising amount of counter-terrorism review is dependent on an antecedent political decision by the Executive before it can be triggered. We already noted this in Chapter 2, but it is worth dwelling here on the frequency and also the impact of this form of executive control, that is control over whether a review – including a review apparently mandated by legislation – takes place or not.

In large part these are reviews that kick in when particular counter-terrorist powers are exercised on individuals, as well as when a decision is made to seek the renewal or continuation in force of 'temporary' legislation. As outlined in Chapter 2, reviews relating to individual cases can themselves constitute evaluative review of a power or law, albeit likely somewhat narrow in scope, or feed into broader evaluative reviews. They are critically important safeguards for individuals subjected to the power of the counter-terrorist state as well as being important sources of information and evidence about the 'reality' of counter-terrorism for use in subsequent review processes and by other review mechanisms. Terrorism Prevention and Investigation Measures (TPIMs), as discussed in Chapter 2, provide a particularly good example of this. Except in an urgent situation, the Secretary of State must apply to a Court before she can impose a TPIM on an individual.[67] The Court's role is to determine whether the decision of the Secretary of State to impose a TPIM is obviously flawed.[68] If it is not, then the TPIM can be issued. The issuing of a TPIM sets in train a number of additional review mechanisms that apply to the individual subject to it. This includes, first and foremost, a review hearing to take place in Court. The Court reviews the Secretary of State's decision that statutory conditions required for a TPIM to be imposed have been, and continue to be, met.[69] This review is no paper tiger; the Court can quash a TPIM.[70] Further, the TPIM Review Group and the TPIM Strategy Meeting both meet quarterly, the former to review every individual TPIM in effect, and the latter to discuss strategic issues concerning the operation and future of individual TPIMs.[71] None of these reviews would take place in the absence of the Secretary of State's decision to impose a TPIM against an individual.

Even where review takes place without an antecedent executive decision that triggers it, the Executive often has a significant amount of control over the conditions of review, including the mandate and selection of reviewers. In some cases, the Executive will have control over the appointment of reviewers. Where an ad hoc review is established it is entirely at the discretion of the Executive to appoint someone to undertake it. Not uncommonly, this person has had previous experience in undertaking counter-terrorism review. For example, David Anderson QC was asked to carry out a number of additional reviews both during his time as Independent Reviewer of Terrorism Legislation and since, including a review of citizenship revocation powers and of deportation with assurances,[72] and reviews of investigatory powers and bulk powers undertaken to inform the parliamentary debate on the Investigatory Powers Bill 2016.[73] Anderson was also invited to conduct an independent assessment of internal reviews by MI5 and the police in the aftermath of the 2017 terrorist attacks.[74]

By asking a current or former Independent Reviewer to undertake such reviews, the Government gets to deal with a known entity, as do other parts of the counter-terrorism review assemblage. In those exercises of counter-terrorism review, the Independent Reviewer's perceived credibility and expertise will probably set some expectations about the nature and rigour of the review that has been commissioned, and may attract criticism when those expectations seem not to be met.[75] While the Government cannot predict the outcome of the review from the start, it is likely to have a reasonable expectation of a certain approach to review, and perhaps of a certain kind of disposition towards the counter-terrorist state. Indeed, our interview data reflected this, with a number of interviewees noting that a government would be unlikely to initiate a review unless it could predict at least to some extent what the outcome would be,[76] whether that was to reinforce the claims that underpin the measure or policy under review,[77] or to set the conditions for a change in approach or provisions, especially following a change in government.[78]

Until relatively recently even the Independent Reviewer of Terrorism Legislation – who, as was clear from the analysis in Chapters 2 and 3, has a particularly high status within the counter-terrorism review assemblage – was appointed through a 'tap on the shoulder'. There was no advertisement, and no way of knowing how a candidate came to the attention of the Secretary of State and ended up being invited to accept the role. David Anderson QC described the method of his appointment thus:

> I was offered the part-time post of Independent Reviewer by three strangers. They gained access to my Chambers by subterfuge, having told my clerks that their employer, the Home Office, sought my legal advice. Once in the conference room, they revealed their identities and conveyed the wish of the Home Secretary – to whom I had no connection or political affiliation – that I should accept the job.[79]

Although Anderson's appointment was made using the criteria laid out for public appointments,[80] there was no public advertisement of the role, and the Office of the Commissioner for Public Appointments had no regulatory role.[81] Indeed, Max Hill QC was the first Independent Reviewer to be appointed through a public appointments process: the role was advertised, a panel constituted under the Code of Practice for Public Appointments proposed a shortlist of candidates, and following an interview procedure, Ministers selected an appointee from that list. The same was true for Jonathan Hall QC, appointed in May 2019, more than six months after Hill vacated the role to become the Director of Public Prosecutions. Even the ISC, which we consider more later, has an adjusted process compared to other committees: its members are appointed by Parliament, but on the nomination of the Prime Minister.[82]

As well as effectively appointing reviewers, sometimes without any external control or oversight, the Executive can exert control over the conditions of review by determining the terms of reference or mandate for the review. Continuing with the example of the Independent Reviewer, there is, effectively, no clear mandate. Although legislation specifies what provisions the Independent Reviewer must review, the Independent Reviewer also undertakes ad hoc reviews when asked to do so by government and can undertake review on his own initiative. However, *how* these reviews are to be carried out and, specifically, what questions the Independent Reviewer should ask are largely unspecified, at least as far as the statutory reviews are concerned. It is, instead, for the Independent Reviewer to determine how to go about that, which makes the question of appointment perhaps an even more pressing one.

For as long as an Independent Reviewer has been in place, the tendency has very much been to review the legislation from a primarily operational perspective, with one Independent Reviewer going so far as to review control orders by, in his words, 'replicat[ing] exactly the position of the Home Secretary at the initiation of a control order ... call[ing] for and [being] given access to the same files as were placed in front of the Secretary of State when [he or she] was asked to determine whether a control order should be made'.[83] In these reviews, Lord Carlile effectively asked whether the Secretary of State had made a decision that was 'obviously flawed' about whether a control order should be made in a specific case,[84] and on that basis drew conclusions about the merits of control orders. That is evidently a narrow approach to review, and, in common with many other reviews,[85] does not seem to reflect a commitment to assessing counter-terrorism against a variety of standards. However, such an approach was enabled by the fact that the Independent Reviewer had no statutory mandate or terms of reference. Instead, the instructions they received in their letters of appointment noted that they should review the 'operation' of the relevant laws.[86] These vague instructions meant that each Independent Reviewer could use his own judgement on how to approach review and, by implication, on what role his review played. Was it to supplement existing judicial review by asking different, less legalistic, questions? Or was it to focus simply on the application of the power in question? For Lord Carlile, it seems, it was the latter. As he wrote himself, his reports were largely 'concerned with the working and fitness for purpose of the Acts of Parliament in question, rather than with broader conceptual issues';[87] they were not 'academic treatise[s]'.[88]

Giving definition or direction to the role is in large part a matter for the Independent Reviewer himself, and the approach taken to that question reveals much about the role of review and about the importance of personality and personal interpretation by the office holder. Both of the former Independent Reviewers we spoke to told us that in their view they could and should ask questions about the impact of counter-terrorism legislation beyond the 'strictly legal'.[89] What this reveals is that *if* the government controls appointment, and *if* the mandate is subject to a large amount of personal interpretation *then* the office holder, his personality and his approach to the role matters to the extent to which it can and does contribute to the achievement of accountability through counter-terrorism review. Even now that the role is publicly advertised, the Executive retains much control.

Importantly, the Executive largely controls what happens to the outcome of a review. In some cases, this means that whether a review is published or not, and the extent to which it is redacted, is a matter of executive control. Even when a review is not published at all, a review actor may try to find a way to ensure its main findings enter the public domain. For example, in 2014, the then Independent Reviewer, David Anderson QC, was asked to conduct an urgent review of TPIMs in order to inform the introduction of legislative changes to the regime. The report of that review was classified secret and was not then, and has not since, been made public. Anderson published the summary conclusions of the review on the Independent Reviewer website in November 2014.[90]

As we discussed in Chapter 3, whether a review actually has any impact on the formation of law or policy is largely a matter for executive determination, especially where, as is usually the case, the Executive can depend on its majority to determine the outcome of parliamentary business. Our interviewees repeatedly referred to the impact of executive entrenchment on the likelihood of a review resulting in any change. This ranged from interviewees noting that government was unlikely to accede to any recommendations that had serious operational implications[91] – and most non-civil society reviews tend to focus on operational questions to a very significant extent – to interviewees surmising that changes in tack are most likely in the wake of a change in government because the political costs of changing approach may well otherwise be considered too high.[92] In some cases, nothing but a judicial finding of incompatibility with the European Convention on Human Rights will suffice to force a change of direction, even where parliamentary committees have already identified similar rights-based flaws.[93]

Even if, as one interviewee said, counter-terrorism review can provide 'cover' for a change in approach by government,[94] the impact of hegemonic consensus may be such that a change in approach is heavily criticised. Take, for example, the decision of the Conservative-led government to abandon control orders and use TPIMs instead, which we considered in Chapter 2. In the debates on the Terrorism Prevention and Investigation Measures Act 2011, some Opposition members complained bitterly that this change in approach – underpinned as it was by a review process claimed to be oriented towards 'balancing' security and freedom – was inappropriately 'soft' on terrorism.[95] When, a few years later, TPIMs were revised to allow for the imposition through them of greater restrictions on suspected terrorists, the reaction from the Opposition was to emphasise how this proved that they had been right to resist the introduction of less repressive measures.[96] While the Executive has a large amount of control over what happens with the outcome of reviews, the realities of parliamentary politics and the hegemonic consensus that underpins the counter-terrorist state are such that there may be pressures to exert that control to repressive rather than liberating ends, even on the seemingly rare occasions when government impulse is to the contrary.

Part III: The limitations of Parliament

These examples illustrate the implications for the effectiveness of counter-terrorism review as an accountability mechanism of the ultimate reliance on Parliament. Throughout our interviews, Parliament was viewed as a key – if not the key – actor when it came to counter-terrorism review.[97] This is quite in line with the constitutional structure of the UK,[98] and in that respect will suffer from the same limitations of executive dominance, under-representativeness, partisanship and so on that always impact on the politics of change in our parliamentary system.[99] However, when it comes to counter-terrorism review and to making the most of review's capacity for action, reliance on Parliament raises sharp questions, which in many ways track the well-established concerns about whether Parliament does provide particularly strong scrutiny as a general matter.[100]

We have already seen that the ordinary politics of the Official Opposition, on which the constitutional structure relies for the purposes of ensuring justification and accountability of government,[101] are strained when it comes to counter-terrorism. Deference, the moral hazards of misjudgement and the hegemonic consensus that we observed in Chapter 1 have clear implications for the extent to which Parliament can, and does, challenge government approaches to countering terrorism. In spite of this, there is a persistent and strong inclination within the counter-terrorism review assemblage that Parliament is where counter-terrorism review can have its greatest, systemic impact.[102] The Independent Reviewer talks about informing Parliament as their primary role;[103] civil society actors reflect on how they try to get their evidence and perspective into parliamentarians' hands in order to try to influence policy;[104] regulators speak of engaging with parliamentary consultations and parliamentary actors in the attempt to bring their perspectives to the relevant arena;[105] and so on. However, when we look at what actually happens within that arena, questions arise about the adequacy of Parliament as an accountability mechanism, both as a counter-terrorism review actor itself and as a conduit for the application of the fruits of counter-terrorism review labour undertaken across the assemblage.

We have already seen that when it comes to secret material Parliament cannot assess the primary materials itself, even though actors such as the Independent Reviewer consider that, through informing Parliament – by speaking to parliamentarians and by engaging with parliamentary committees – they can address some of the information asymmetries that pose such a challenge to accountability in the counter-terrorist state.[106] Instead, Parliament must trust the information provided by the Independent Reviewer and other contributors, such as agency witnesses to parliamentary committees, when they appear.[107] While this is in some ways not unlike how Parliament informs itself in other areas of policy, one of the key points here is that – as we mentioned earlier – Independent Reviewers have considerable flexibility in terms of how they interpret their role, how they undertake assessment and what standards of review they apply. Where an Independent Reviewer takes a predominantly operational perspective, they will bring that perspective to Parliament. But where they take a broader perspective, for example by thinking about societal impact, as well as operational matters, the perspective they bring will be somewhat different. Ultimately, the Independent Reviewer determines how to undertake review, how to inform Parliament and how to ask the questions through which they undertake the evaluative elements of review we discussed earlier: assessing merit, engaging with reality and proposing action. Other witnesses to parliamentary committees, making representations to MPs and Peers and so on may be able to fill in some of the gaps about the societal impact of counter-terrorism. However, whether these other witnesses will represent a diversity of views,[108] whether there is time in the parliamentary calendar to invite them, whether inquiries and consultations will be framed in a way to capture broad qualitative questions,[109] and whether committee reports and recommendations will impact on parliamentary business sufficiently to challenge the government approach or the prevailing law and policy seems as much a matter of happenstance and the commitments and decisions of committee chairs and staff as of institutional design.

Parliament is a strange institution; it 'speaks with many voices' and has many different kinds of business to undertake.[110] Counter-terrorism is only one part of Parliament's agenda, and counter-terrorism review – where it takes place in or through Parliament – must take place within the time allocated and available for counter-terrorism matters.[111] Parliamentary time and political attention are finite resources, and their allocation is not always a matter of design. Crisis, politics and partisanship can intervene to determine what receives parliamentary attention. Statutory provisions such as sunset clauses can force counter-terrorism onto the agenda, but, as we saw in Chapter 2, the timing of the debates is still largely a matter for government via business motions, and time for debate can be greatly constrained.[112]

It is also now clear that, even though demands for review mechanisms such as sunset clauses seems to be a standard part of counter-terrorism 'opposition',[113] those mechanisms do little actually to apply rigorous scrutiny to counter-terrorism law. Rather, they 'offer at best only a modest contribution to advancing or improving democratic deliberation'.[114] The debates they mandate are often poorly attended with few people speaking, and legislation is routinely renewed. In other cases, the 'safeguard' is a requirement that the Secretary of State 'consult' with counter-terrorism review mechanisms such as the Independent Reviewer before proposing any renewal of powers. However, in such cases, all the Secretary of State is required to do is confirm to Parliament that she has consulted.[115] The content of the recommendation is not disclosed. Parliament is expected to take on trust that this constitutes a meaningful consultation, approached by the Secretary of State with an open mind, and underpins a recommendation for renewal that can be considered review-based.

It is worth remembering that, in many cases, these statutory provisions seemingly mandating review were, themselves, concessions made to anxious parliamentarians. They served to assure them that the power in question would be reviewed and that its continuation in force would be dependent on a review that affirmed its proportionality, legality, effectiveness, or adherence to another stipulated standard. Parliament continues to insist on – and to be satisfied by – such provisions as meaningful checks on the counter-terrorist state, even though practice suggests that, if their purpose is to ensure accountability through evaluative, evidence-based, action-oriented review, they generally fall considerably short.

Part IV: The absence of trust

As 'trust involves placing faith in a person or institution where something serious is at stake',[116] trust clearly matters in the counter-terrorist state. Here, not only security and well-being are at stake, but also the legitimacy, liberty, rights protection and constitutional commitments to accountability and the rule of law that underpin the liberal democratic polity itself. However, trust is complex. It is not only about A trusting B to do X, but also about checking that B actually is doing X.[117] That is, trusting C – a body or entity tasked with undertaking that checking function – to make sure of that, and having in place appropriate mechanisms to make good on that trust. Without structural mechanisms and principled recognition that give effect to the principle that trust must be earned rather than 'simply' demanded and given, liberal democracy may slide into autocratic and paternalistic statehood.[118] However, what makes one group of people or actors trust B or C will be different to what generates trust for others. That is always the case, and no less so in respect of the counter-terrorist state and the operation of counter-terrorism review.

To understand how trust operates in the counter-terrorist state and why that matters for counter-terrorism review, we must first recognise the importance of relationships.[119] As indicated in Chapter 3, in important ways, the counter-terrorism review assemblage is reliant on relationships of trust: between reviewees and review mechanisms, between review mechanisms themselves, and between review actors and the counter-terrorist state. Within these relationships, counter-terrorism review actors elicit the evidence that allows them to understand and document the 'reality' of counter-terrorism, to assess its merits, and to have any chance of impacting on the counter-terrorist state with its insights and outcomes. They are also the relationships within which the informal division of labour within the counter-terrorism review assemblage operates.[120]

As ever, within this matrix of relationships, there will be different markers of trustworthiness for different actors. Legal obligations to secrecy may underpin security agencies' trust in a review body. Security clearance and a perceived appreciation of the ethical, operational and political challenges of 'balancing' rights and security may ground government's trust in a review body. Confidence in professional efficiency and ethics may lead to trust between open advocates and Special Advocates in closed material proceedings. Trust in the good faith of a review mechanism may be required for communities and marginalised persons to disclose their lived experiences of counter-terrorism, and enable the generation of a qualitative evidence base on the measure's or policy's impact, and so on. The interaction of these different markers makes trust in counter-terrorism review mutable. Different actors need different things from different review mechanisms in order to secure the trust that is needed for counter-terrorism review to be able to undertake the kind of evaluative processes we envisage throughout this book. Furthermore, some review mechanisms may act to try to generate trust on behalf of other actors. For example, one interviewee noted that the Independent Reviewer can facilitate trust between the Executive and Parliament in its role as a scrutinising entity.[121] As another interviewee put it: 'if you have a reviewer who is trusted ... you have somebody who is a credible voice who can speak both to government and to civil society'.[122]

In all democratic polities, the 'reservoir of political trust ... helps preserve fundamental democratic achievements in times of economic, social and political crises',[123] and, by implication, in the new normalcy of the counter-terrorist state. Even the intelligence and security agencies appreciate and recognise this. As Jonathan Evans, former Director General of the Security Service, said:

> Public trust is becoming an increasingly important issue for many organisations ... and we need to ensure that our work is sufficiently understood. Although our operations must remain secret for them to be successful, we have a responsibility to keep the public informed about the threats they face and what we are doing to counter them.[124]

Trust, in this respect, is an antecedent condition for the legitimacy of the counter-terrorist state. It is also widely recognised as necessary for counter-terrorist policing and the gathering of community intelligence.[125] However, trust also matters if counter-terrorism review is to operate effectively.[126] Although critical, for some of our interviewees it is in short supply.[127] One civil society actor to whom we spoke put this bluntly. In their view, there is 'no trust between civil servants working with counter-terrorism stuff and NGOs working on it'.[128] Other interviewees, while somewhat more nuanced in their views, also noted an absence of trust. One noted that 'partly through the difficulty of engaging with those people, sometimes their unwillingness to engage, [or a] lack of trust on their part' can frustrate the process of review.[129] Accordingly, it was not only the difficulty of challenging denials of access to information that caused this lack of trust, but also the wider impact of the measures themselves.[130] But what causes this absence of trust, and what are its implications for accountability through counter-terrorism review?

First, the way in which the UK counter-terrorist state has emerged and how it operates have had serious implications for trust among primarily impacted communities. We know from a wide range of empirical and sociological research that policy innovations have frayed the already delicate connections of trust within the counter-terrorist state.[131] They have been interpreted as co-opting community groups, securitising communities, constructing community leaders and family members as counter-radicalisation and counter-terrorist actors,[132] introducing wide discretionary powers, and seeming not to listen when communities attempt to demonstrate the negative impacts of these laws and policies on social cohesion and belonging.[133] For some, this failure to listen reflects a latent Islamophobia within the contemporary counter-terrorist state;[134] this is a view exacerbated by the perceived neglect of right-wing and white supremacist radicalisation and terrorist activities when compared to so-called Islamist terrorism. When we see this against the scale, pervasiveness and impulse towards increased responsiblisation in the counter-terrorist state, which we considered in Chapter 1, the societal factors that underpin a general lack of trust in the counter-terrorist state for at least some communities begin to become clear. This has important implications for review, as in many cases these are the communities of knowledge on which review mechanisms rely to generate the qualitative evidence needed properly to understand the unintended consequences of counter-terrorism. Given this, it is perhaps unsurprising that some NGOs and civil society actors may appear to show an 'unwillingness to engage, [a] lack of trust' in the state and in the review mechanisms,[135] especially bearing in mind the possibility – considered in Chapter 1 – that review may be an instrument for the legitimation, rather than accountability, of the counter-terrorist state.

These challenges are not always ameliorated by how the counter-terrorist state appears to think about trust and its own need for legitimacy. Rather than recognising that trust is based on a relationship and must be earned,[136] and that a commitment to accountability is a way of giving effect to that relationship, there seems to be a tendency to treat trust as something to be demanded rather than earned by the counter-terrorist state. The continuing reliance on esoteric secrecy, the persistence of executive control over counter-terrorism and, to a large degree, counter-terrorism review, and the implications of hegemonic consensus for Parliament's ability to provide robust opposition combine to create an expectation that by asking the polity to 'trust us, we mean well',[137] the state is doing enough to ensure that trust. We conclude this notwithstanding the insight from Jonathan Evans about the need to inform the public about how security services are working to counter the threat from terrorism. As a number of our interviewees recognised, the way the state goes about some of its counter-terrorist work in fact undermines trust. For instance, it introduced and designed a Prevent duty without consultation or sufficient familiarity with the dynamics of the sectors in which it would operate.[138] It placed the burden of 'proving' objections to counter-terrorism laws and policies on the polity, rather than recognising a duty to justify state intrusions into liberty.[139] The limitations of the counter-terrorism review assemblage – including the hierarchies, competition and marginalisation constructed by government engagement with it – seem to prevent it effectively from addressing those effects.

Trust is also fragile in the counter-terrorism review assemblage. As we saw in Chapter 3, the values of the assemblage – democracy, transparency and independence – pursued through strategies of being independent, being experts and gathering evidence, and listening, are intended to enhance the credibility of review mechanisms. They aim to build this trust within the assemblage as well as with the state. Where a review mechanism operates in a way that seems to undermine those values – or is perceived to – that frays these relationships either temporarily or permanently. The opposite is also true. A 'robustly independent' chair of the ISC enhances the perceived credibility of that Committee,[140] as does the independence of one Independent Reviewer, who was said to have 'embraced' independence,[141] and 'live[d] the role'.[142] This in contrast to a predecessor who one interviewee said was 'co-opted, and everything he was going to say was going to be pro further legislation, pro whichever option the agencies were asking for, and with very little criticism aimed at either government in the operation of the legislation that he was expected to scrutinise'.[143]

Conclusion

In this chapter we have focused on the patterns of state and political behaviour, and on the dynamics of trust and mistrust in respect of counter-terrorism, that have implications for counter-terrorism review.

We identified these from the analysis presented in both Chapters 2 and 3, as well as the assessment of what we have ascertained about counter-terrorism review from the research that underpins this book when it is considered against the approach to review as accountability that we outlined in the Introduction. Our desk-research, interviews and analytical approach indicate that, if counter-terrorism review is meaningfully to contribute to making the counter-terrorist state more accountable, we need not only practical and institutional reform of counter-terrorism review, but also a dispositional shift towards security and counter-terrorism throughout the apparatus of the counter-terrorist state. In the conclusion, we articulate a vision for accountability building on the insights from the work we have so far presented in this book.

Notes

[1] HM Government, *CONTEST: The United Kingdom's Strategy for Countering Terrorism* (Cm 9608, 2018).

[2] See analysis in Chapter 3, Part II.

[3] Stéphane Lefebvre, 'What do judges say on the protection of intelligence secrets?' (2019) 34(1) Intelligence and National Security 62.

[4] Lydia Morgan, '(Re)conceptualizing State Secrecy' (2018) 69(1) Northern Ireland Legal Quarterly 59; more extensive discussion in Lydia Morgan, 'Reading Secrets: Do State Secrets Challenge the Idea of the UK as Liberal?' (PhD thesis, University of Bristol 2015).

[5] Morgan, '(Re)conceptualizing State Secrecy' (n 4) 76–7.

[6] David Vincent, *The Culture of Secrecy: Britain, 1832–1998* (Oxford University Press 1998); Christopher Moran, *Classified: Secrecy and the State in Modern Britain* (Cambridge University Press 2013); Edward Palmer Thompson, 'The Secret State' (1979) 20(3) Race and Class 219.

[7] For a critical overview see for example Catherine Durose et al, '"Acceptable Difference": Diversity, Representation and Pathways to UK Politics' (2013) 66(2) Parliamentary Affairs 246.

[8] We acknowledge that there are serious debates about the desirability of parliamentarians generally having access to classified materials, not least the concern that parliamentarians might consider themselves to be restrained from challenging proposed actions using the information, knowledge or understanding gleaned because of their security clearance. See Aidan Wills et al, *Study: Parliamentary Oversight of Security and Intelligence Agencies in the European Union* (European Parliament 2011) 117–18.

[9] There are three levels of classification (OFFICIAL, SECRET and TOP SECRET) and three formal respective levels of clearance (Counter-Terrorist Check, Security Check, Developed Vetting) although all three require Baseline Personnel Security Standard, see Cabinet Office, *Government Security Classifications* (May 2018), Available from: https://assets.publishing.service.gov.uk/government/uploads/system/uploads/attachment_data/file/715778/May-2018_Government-Security-Classifications-2.pdf [Accessed 25 March 2019]; Houses of Parliament, *National Security Vetting Your Questions Answered* (January 2017), Available from: https://www.parliament.uk/documents/PSD-Security-Vetting-booklet.pdf [Accessed

20 March 2019]. See further information from the UK Security and Vetting service: https://www.gov.uk/guidance/security-vetting-and-clearance [Accessed 20 March 2019].

10 P1.

11 P1; P2; P3; P4; P5; P6; P10; P11; P13; P14; P15; P18; P19; P22; P24.

12 P2. P15 also noted the importance of the access.

13 P1; P11.

14 P1.

15 P15.

16 P2.

17 Importantly, P2 did not think he was put under undue pressure by Government: 'Often the assumption is there is a lot of pressure on you from government, to which my answer would be, surprisingly, no. No one in government, or in the intelligence agencies, really sought to apply any pressure to me. Did they seek to influence my views, well, yes, but they responded to my queries in a generally very correct civil service manner … Where I think there is pressure on someone like me, who is at the Bar and exists in a generally fairly liberal milieu, is actually from the other side, it was from some of the NGOs, some of the prominent human rights activists, who, I think, wanted my support, and could therefore apply pressure in a way that it was very painful to resist, but I did have to learn to resist.'

18 Only P8 and P12 clearly stated that resistance, understood as complete rejection, was a function of counter-terrorism review, several others suggested it: P9; P13; P20.

19 P10, also suggested by P12.

20 P20.

21 P8.

22 P16; P17; P21.

23 Morgan, '(Re)conceptualizing State Secrecy' (n 4) 77–80.

24 See generally Ian Leigh and Wegge Njord, 'Intelligence and Oversight at the outside of the 21st Century' in Ian Leigh and Wegge Njord (eds), *Intelligence Oversight in the Twenty-First Century: Accountability in a Changing World* (Routledge 2018) 7; Peter Gill, *Policing Politics: Security Intelligence and the Liberal Democratic State* (Routledge 2012).

25 *Attorney General v Blake* [2001] 1 AC 268.

26 See: *R v Home Secretary ex parte Hosenball* [1977] 3 All ER 452, *per* Lord Denning, [460]; *Home Office v Tariq* [2011] UKSC 35 *per* Lord Kerr at [128].

27 Such a restriction is imposed on the Investigatory Powers Tribunal, for example: Rule 6, The Investigatory Powers Tribunal Rules 2000, SI 2000/2665 as interpreted in *Belhadj & Ors v Security Service & Ors* [2015] UKIPTrib 12_132-H (determination).

28 See generally Ian Leigh, 'Intelligence and the Law in the United Kingdom' in Lock K. Johnson (ed), *Oxford Handbook of National Security Intelligence* (Oxford University Press 2010) 642; Tom Hickman 'The Investigatory Powers Tribunal: A Law unto Itself?' [2018] Public Law 584. For an insider's take, see Martin Chamberlain 'Special Advocates and Amici Curiae in National Security Proceedings in the United Kingdom' (2018) 68(3) University of Toronto Law Journal 496, 496–510.

29 See for example Cabinet Office, Annual Report and Accounts 2017–18 (2018) HC 1293.

30 Justice and Security Act 2013, pt 2. The Committee has recently increased its open evidence sessions and so on: See the account of the Committee's reform in Andrew Defty, 'The Intelligence and Security Committee: A Committee in Decline?', PSA Parliaments Groups Blog, 10 January 2018. Available from: https://parliamentsandlegislatures.wordpress.com/2018/01/10/intelligence-security-committee/ [Accessed 22 March 2019], and Andrew Defty, 'Coming in From the Cold: Bringing the Intelligence and Security Committee into Parliament' (2019) 34(1) Intelligence & National Security 22.

31 Justice and Security Act 2013, s 1.

32 Ibid s 3, s 3(3), s 3(4).

33 Upon becoming Chair of the Committee in 2017, Dominic Grieve MP prioritised the publication of outstanding reports and annual reporting now seems somewhat timelier than was previously the case: Intelligence and Security Committee of Parliament, 'Press Release' (23 November 2017).

34 See the interview data reported in Defty (n 30).

35 Morgan, '(Re)conceptualizing State Secrecy' (n 4) 79.

36 Hugh Bochel, Andrew Defty and Jane Kirkpatrick, *Watching the Watchers: Parliament and the Intelligence Services* (Palgrave 2014) 75.

37 P13; P18; P19; P22. See also Mark Phythian, 'A Very British Institution: The Intelligence and Security Committee and Intelligence Accountability in the United Kingdom' in Johnson (n 28) 699–718, 715.

38 P3; P18; P22. One interviewee noted the chairmanship of Dominic Grieve specifically: 'there is progress … the ISC under Dominic Grieve for example has massively strengthened that aspect of the review system'. P22. Another was more circumspect: 'I have a huge amount of regard for Dominic Grieve, but I don't think one individual, or even a few individuals, would be able to properly wade through what I suspect is a fair amount of material, given … the amount of material that has been disclosed into the public, the amount of cases that have been talked about in public, for them to be able to properly review themselves.' P3.

39 See for example the Marquess of Lothian's contributions to the House of Lords debates on the Justice and Security Bill. HL Deb 19 June 2012, vol 737, cols 1685–7. At the time, the Marquess of Lothian was also a member of the Committee.

40 As well as general international human rights law being applicable to states' duties to design oversight, specific soft norms include the compilation of principles of good practice on the legal and institutional frameworks for intelligence agencies and their oversight prepared by the UN Special Rapporteur on the Protection and Promotion of Human Rights while Countering Terrorism (17 May 2010, A/HRC/14/46).

41 Investigatory Powers Act 2016, ss 3, 11, 23–5, 53–9, 75, 77, 88–93, 108–14, 140, 146, 159, 165, 179, 187, 208.

42 Ibid ss 140, 146–7, 159, 165–6; ss 179–80, 187–8.

43 Ibid ss 229–37.

44 Intelligence Services Act 1994; Security Services Act 1989 and 1996; Official Secrets Act 1911–89.

45 Investigatory Powers Act 2016, ss 82, 134, 174.

46 Ibid ss 142(8), 161(8), 183(9) 212(9).

47 P3; P4; P14.

48 P5.

49 Morgan, '(Re)conceptualizing State Secrecy' (n 4) 60.

50 P1.

51 Hence, for example, most Cabinet papers are released into public records after 30 years: Public Records Act 1958 *as amended by* Public Records Act 1967. Particularly 'sensitive' Cabinet records can be withheld.

52 Documents 'relating to' the formation of government policy, which can include Cabinet documents, are exempted (Freedom of Information Act 2000, s 35(1)(a)) and this is widely interpreted: *Department for Education and Skills v Information Commissioner and Evening Standard* (EA/2006/0006) (19 January 2007) [53]; *Office of Government Commerce v Information Commission and HM Attorney General on behalf of the Speaker of the House of Commons* [2008] EWHC 737 (Admin) [79].

53 For example Tony Blair, *A Journey* (Random House 2010) 516–17; Roland Watson, Rachel Sylvester and Alice Thomson, 'Keep Cabinet Secret: says Civil Service Chief', *The Times*, 17 December 2011.

54 See generally Patrick Birkinshaw, *Freedom of Information: The Law, the Practice, and the Ideal* (4th edn, Cambridge University Press 2010).

55 Freedom of Information Act 2000, ss 23–4.

56 HC Deb 12 July 1999, vol 340, col 770.

57 Baroness Williams of Trafford, *Prevent Oversight Board: Written Question – HL 4388* (2017–19 HL 4388).

58 HM Government, *Prevent Strategy* (Cm 8092, 2011) 96; HM Government, *Revised Prevent Duty Guidance for England and Wales* (2015) 5.

59 Ibid

60 HC Deb 17 December 2018, vol 794, col 1638. As a Peer, we do not know if Lord Carlile sits on the Board as an 'independent' member, or in some other capacity.

61 Ibid.

62 Freedom of Information Act 2000, s 24(1).

63 Freedom of Information Act 2000, s 35. For more detail on our challenge see: https://counterterrorismreview.com/2018/07/16/home-office-refuses-foi-request-on-the-prevent-oversight-board/ [Accessed 25 Mar 2019].

64 Andrew W. Neal, *Security as Politics: Beyond the State of Exception* (Edinburgh University Press 2019).

65 David Vincent, *The Culture of Secrecy: Britain 1832–1998* (Oxford University Press 1998).

66 Chapter 1.

67 Terrorism Prevention and Investigation Measures Act 2011, s 3(5).

68 Ibid s 6(3).

69 Ibid s 9(1).

70 Ibid ss 9(5)(a).

71 See Chapter 2.

72 David Anderson, *Citizenship Removal Resulting in Statelessness* (2016); David Anderson, *Deportation with Assurances* (Cm 9462, 2017).

73 David Anderson, *A Question of Trust: Report of the Investigatory Powers Review* (2015); David Anderson, *Report of the Bulk Powers Review* (Cm 9326, 2016).

74 David Anderson, *Attacks in London and Manchester March–June 2017* (2017).

75 Liberty, for example, criticised Anderson for 'not assess[ing] the necessity or proportionality of the bulk powers, but rather the "utility" according to the security and intelligence agencies' terms'. Liberty, *Briefing on Report of the Bulk Powers Review* (2016) 3.

76 P11.

77 P11.

78 P1; P12; P13.
79 David Anderson, 'The Independent Review of UK Terrorism Law' (2014) 5(4) New Journal of European Criminal Law 432, 434.
80 Cabinet Office, *Making and Managing Public Appointments: A Guide for Departments* (4th edn, Cabinet Office 2006)
81 UK, FOI Request 26205 (28 February 2013) cited in Jessie Blackbourn, 'Independent Reviewers as an Alternative: An Empirical Study from Australia and the United Kingdom' in Fergal F Davis and Fiona de Londras (eds), *Critical Debates on Counter-Terrorism Judicial Review* (Cambridge University Press 2014) 173–4.
82 Justice and Security Act 2013, s 1.
83 Lord Carlile, *First Report of the Independent Reviewer Pursuant to Section 14(3) of the Prevention of Terrorism Act 2005* (Stationery Office 2006) 11; Lord Carlile, *Second Report of the Independent Reviewer Pursuant to Section 14(3) of the Prevention of Terrorism Act 2005* (Stationery Office 2007) 12; Lord Carlile, *Third Report of the Independent Reviewer Pursuant to Section 14(3) of the Prevention of Terrorism Act 2005* (Stationery Office 2008) 12; Lord Carlile, *Fourth Report of the Independent Reviewer Pursuant to Section 14(3) of the Prevention of Terrorism Act 2005* (Stationery Office 2009) 12; Lord Carlile, *Fifth Report of the Independent Reviewer Pursuant to Section 14(3) of the Prevention of Terrorism Act 2005* (Stationery Office 2010) 39; Lord Carlile, *Sixth Report of the Independent Reviewer Pursuant to Section 14(3) of the Prevention of Terrorism Act 2005* (Stationery Office 2011) 39–40.
84 Lord Carlile, *First Report of the Independent Reviewer* (n 83) 12; Lord Carlile, *Second Report of the Independent Reviewer* (n 83) 13; Lord Carlile, *Third Report of the Independent Reviewer* (n 83) 13; Lord Carlile, *Fourth Report of the Independent Reviewer* (n 83) 13; Lord Carlile, *Fifth Report of the Independent Reviewer* (n 83) 40; Lord Carlile, *Sixth Report of the Independent Reviewer* (n 83) 40.
85 See the analysis of standards of review in Chapter 2.
86 In his first report on the Terrorism Act 2000, Lord Carlile noted: 'the terms of reference may be found in the letters of appointment to my predecessors and myself. They are to be found too in the Official Report of the House of Lords debate of the 8th March 1984'. Lord Carlile, *Report on the Operation in 2001 of the Terrorism Act 2000* (2002) 5. In 1984, Lord Elton outlined the terms of reference that would apply to the person appointed to conduct the newly established review of the Prevention of Terrorism (Temporary Provisions) Act 1984: 'It would be his task to look at the use made of the powers under the Act. To consider, for example, whether he saw emerging any change in the pattern of their use which required to be drawn to the attention of Parliament'. HL Deb 8 March 1984 vol 449, cols 405–6.
87 Lord Carlile, *The Definition of Terrorism* (Cm 7052, 2007) 1.
88 Ibid, 2.
89 P2; P15.
90 David Anderson, 'Relocation, Relocation, Relocation' (25 November 2014). Available from: https://webarchive.nationalarchives.gov.uk/20170301155827/https://terrorismlegislationreviewer.independent.gov.uk/relocation-relocation-relocation/ [Accessed 29 March 2019].
91 P10.
92 P8; P13.
93 This was the case with detention powers under the Anti-Terrorism, Crime and Security Act 2001, which were not addressed until after the House of Lords decision in *A v Secretary of State for the Home Department* [2004] UKHL 56, notwithstanding

earlier JCHR reports. See the analysis in Janet Hiebert, 'Parliamentary Review of Terrorism Measures' (2005) 68(4) Modern Law Review 676.

[94] P13.

[95] See for example Shabana Mahmood MP claiming that, as originally proposed, the Government's 'TPIMs regime ... will decrease and weaken the powers available to the police and the Home Secretary to control the behaviour of terror suspects ... Control order powers are either needed or they are not ... the Government should have been honest and admitted that sometimes, stringent control order measures such as relocation and 16-hour curfews are necessary'. HC Deb 5 September 2011, vol 532, col 104.

[96] See for example Yvette Cooper MP objecting to the removal of relocation powers on the introduction of TPIMs: HC Deb 5 September 2011, vol 532, col 104.

[97] P2; P5; P7; P10; P13; P15; P18; P19; P22.

[98] See generally Michael Gordon, *Parliamentary Sovereignty in the UK Constitution: Process, Politics and Democracy* (Hart Publishing 2015); David Judge, *The Parliamentary State* (Sage 1993).

[99] For a critical assessment of the strengths and limitations of Parliament see, for example, Philip Norton, 'Reforming Parliament in the United Kingdom: The Report of the Commission to Strengthen Parliament' (2000) 6(3) The Journal of Legislative Studies 1; Alexandra Kelso, 'Parliament' in Flinders et al, *The Oxford Handbook of British Politics* (Oxford University Press 2009).

[100] On which see, David Judge, *Representation: Theory and Practice in Britain* (Routledge 1999); Lucinda Maer and Mark Sandford, 'Select Committees under Scrutiny' (The Constitution Unit 2004); Felicity Matthews and Matthew Flinders, 'Patterns of Democracy: Coalition Governance and Majoritarian Modification in the United Kingdom 2010–2015' (2017) 12(2) British Politics 157; Aileen McHarg, 'Reforming the United Kingdom Constitution: Law, Convention, Soft Law' (2008) 71(6) Modern Law Review 853.

[101] See generally Grégoire Webber, 'Loyal Opposition and the Political Constitution' (2017) 37(2) Oxford Journal of Legal Systems 357.

[102] P1; P2; P5; P6; P7; P9, P10; P11; P12; P13; P15; P18; P19; P20; P22; P24. A similar point was made and generally agreed to at our workshop in Oxford.

[103] According to the website of the Independent Reviewer of Terrorism Legislation: 'The Independent Reviewer's role is to inform the public and political debate on anti-terrorism law in the United Kingdom. I do this in the regular reports that are prepared for the Home Secretary or Treasury and then laid before Parliament, in evidence to parliamentary committees, in articles and speeches, in media interviews and debates, in posts on this website and via twitter (@terrorwatchdog)', Available from: https://terrorismlegislationreviewer.independent.gov.uk/about-me/ [Accessed 29 March 2019]. Also P2.

[104] P9; P12; P13; P23.

[105] P6; P24.

[106] Chapter 3.

[107] P10; P18

[108] A lack of diversity among witnesses to parliamentary committees is recognised and being addressed: House of Commons Liaison Committee, 'Witness Gender Diversity' (2018) HC 1033.

[109] As shown in Chapter 2, counter-terrorism review by non-civil society actors has tended to focus largely on operational questions.

[110] Julia Black, 'Constructing and Contesting Legitimacy and Accountability in Polycentric Regulatory Regimes' (2008) 2(2) Regulation and Governance 137

[111] A number of attendees at the stakeholder workshop for this project who have experience of working in Parliament especially noted the challenge that this can present.

[112] See the analysis in Chapter 2.

[113] While the Government included an annual renewal sunset clause in the Anti-Terrorism Crime and Security Bill 2001 as proposed, two further sunset clauses were incorporated into the legislation during its parliamentary passage. Section 29(7) set a termination date for the Part 4 indefinite detention provisions. It was proposed by the House of Commons Select Committee on Home Affairs and inserted by the House of Lords. See: (House of Commons Select Committee on Home Affairs, *The Anti-Terrorism, Crime and Security Bill 2001* (2001–2, HC 351) paras 36–43). The provision requiring review by a committee of members of the Privy Council was proposed and incorporated during the committee stage in the House of Lords (HL Deb 29 November 2001, vol 629, col 460). The Commons and Lords wrangled over a sunset clause in the passage of the Prevention of Terrorism Act 2005. The Lords repeatedly inserted a sunset clause into the Bill and the Commons repeatedly rejected it. Ultimately, the House of Lords settled for an annual renewal sunset clause (See Lord Lloyd of Berwick's description of the enactment process on the sunset clause: HL Deb 15 February 2006, vol 678, col 1221).

[114] John E. Finn, 'Sunset Clauses and Democratic Deliberation: Assessing the Significance of Sunset Provisions in Antiterrorism Legislation' (2010) 48 Columbia Journal of Transnational Law 442, 497.

[115] As discussed in Chapter 2, the Secretary of State was required to consult the Independent Reviewer of Terrorism Legislation, the Investigatory Powers Commissioner, and the Director General of the Security Service before she could lay an order before Parliament to renew the Terrorism Prevention and Investigation Measures Act 2011. The confirmation came in the form of a statement to Parliament during debate on the renewal order. Third Delegated Legislation Committee (Draft Terrorism Prevention and Investigation Measures Act 2011 (Continuation) Order 2016). HC Deb 26 October 2016, col 5.

[116] David Nelkin, *The Futures of Criminology* (Sage 1994) 4.

[117] Russell Hardin, *Trust and Trustworthiness* (Russell Sage Foundation 2002) 9.

[118] John Dunn, 'Trust and Political Agency' in Diego Gambetta (ed), *Trust: Making and Breaking Cooperative Relations* (Basil Blackwell 1990) 73.

[119] As P15 put it: 'it's all about the relationship that you have month on month and the ways in which you can bring at least a soft influence to bear, which you hope is trusted by the wider public'.

[120] Chapter 3.

[121] P22.

[122] P13.

[123] Sonja Zmerli and Tom W.G. van der Meer 'The Deeply Rooted Concern with Political Trust' in Sonja Zmerli and Tom W.G. van der Meer (eds), *Handbook on Political Trust* (Edward Elgar 2017) 1.

[124] Jonathan Evans, 'Intelligence, Counter-Terrorism, and Trust'. Speech to the Society of Editors' 'A Matter of Trust' Conference, Radisson Edwardian Hotel, Manchester, 5 November 2007, Available from: www.mi5.gov.uk/fa/node/404#sthash.US217jv8.dpuf [Accessed 23 March 2019].

[125] Basia Spalek, 'Community Policing, Trust, and Muslim Communities in Relation to "New Terrorism"' (2010) 38(4) Politics and Policy 789.

[126] P2; P6; P7; P9; P22; P24; P15.

[127] P9; P12; P13; P15; P18; P19.

[128] P2.

[129] P19.

[130] P19.

[131] Leda Blackwood, Nick Hopkins and Steve Reicher, 'I Know Who I Am, But Who Do They Think I Am? Muslim Perspectives on Encounters with Airport Authorities' (2013) 36(6) Ethnic and Racial Studies 1090; Aziz Huq, Tom R. Tyler and Stephen Schulhofer, 'Mechanisms for Eliciting Cooperation in Counterterrorism Policing: Evidence from the United Kingdom' (2011) 8(4) Journal of Empirical Legal Studies 728; Lee Jarvis and Michael Lister 'What Would You Do? Everyday Conceptions and Constructions of Counter-terrorism' (2016) 36(3) Politics 277; Madeline-Sophie Abbas, 'Producing "Internal Suspect Bodies": Divisive Effects of UK Counter-terrorism Measures on Muslim Communities in Leeds and Bradford' (2019) 70(1) The British Journal of Sociology 261; Tufyal Choudhury and Helen Fenwick, 'The Impact of Counter terrorism Measures on Muslim Communities' (Research Report 72, Equality and Human Rights Commission 2011).

[132] Abbas (n 131); Choudhury and Fenwick (n 131).

[133] Gabe Mythen '"No One Speaks for Us": Security Policy, Suspected Communities and the Problem of Voice' (2012) 5(3) Critical Studies on Terrorism 409; Mary J. Hickman et al, 'Social Cohesion and the Notion of "Suspect Communities": A Study of the Experiences and Impacts of Being "Suspect" for Irish Communities and Muslim Communities in Britain' (2012) 5(1) Critical Studies on Terrorism 89; Therese O'Toole et al, 'Governing through Prevent? Regulation and Contested Practice in State–Muslim Engagement' (2016) 50(1) Sociology 160.

[134] One interviewee noted in their work with communities that 'they felt that Islamophobia for example wasn't taken seriously': P20. See also Baroness Sayeeda Warsi, *The Enemy Within: A Tale of Muslim Britain* (Penguin 2018) chp 3.

[135] P19.

[136] Philip Pettit, 'Liberty and Leviathan' (2005) 4(1) Politics, Philosophy & Economics, 131; Conor Gearty, *Liberty and Security* (Polity 2013).

[137] P18.

[138] P1 considered that part of the reason why Prevent seemed to lack public confidence was that it was designed in the Home Office, which had limited knowledge of sectors, like education, where it was to be applied.

[139] HC Deb 22 Jan 2019, vol 653, col 173.

[140] P22.

[141] P22.

[142] P13.

[143] P13.

Conclusion:
Accountability and Review in
the Counter-Terrorist State

Our aspiration in this book has been to develop an empirically grounded understanding of counter-terrorism review in the UK. When does it take place? How does it work? Who is involved? What kinds of impacts does it have? These questions were motivated not only by the potential insights that might flow from considering as an assemblage a variety of activities and actors more commonly considered separately,[1] but also by our curiosity about whether counter-terrorism review contributes to making the counter-terrorist state accountable in a meaningful way. We were thus engaged not only in an act of description but also of re-description, articulating an understanding of counter-terrorism and counter-terrorism review in the UK that attempts to shift it out of the zone of exceptionality and to assess it against the constitutional value of accountability.

Our belief in the necessity of that exercise reflects not only our long-standing concerns with evaluation,[2] review[3] and secrecy[4] in relation to counter-terrorism, but also constitutionalist anxieties about the counter-terrorist state. In particular, if counter-terrorism is now part of the everyday business of the state, as we argue it is,[5] and if counter-terrorism review is presented by that state as a means of ensuring oversight and accountability, as it is,[6] then does the review assemblage deliver accountability and, if not, can the counter-terrorist state make any claims to liberal democratic legitimacy?

As has become clear throughout this book, the answers to these questions are mixed. To some extent counter-terrorism review *does* involve entities in undertaking the kind of evaluative review that we argue can constitute accountability-enhancing activities. Reviewers do assess the merits of counter-terrorism laws, policies and measures against, at least, standards of legality and operational effectiveness. They do engage with reality by gathering data, including in some cases generating their own qualitative and experiential evidence bases. They also have capacity for action inasmuch as they are often forward looking and engaged in making proposals for change. However, counter-terrorism review also has serious shortcomings. For some review mechanisms, establishing and enacting independence in a way that makes them credible across multiple constituencies and stakeholders poses a real challenge. For others, the difficulty may be in making themselves heard within the counter-terrorism review assemblage, especially if they have been marginalised or have lower 'status' in the eyes of key stakeholders (such as the Executive) than other actors. Where government has the power to decide whether and when a report or other review outcome is published, ensuring publicity for their findings may be difficult. And for most counter-terrorism review actors, realising their capacity for action – or making change happen – is truly challenging.

Unless political and state actors are meaningfully committed to accountability and the values that it serves (transparency, rights-protection, effectiveness, legitimacy and open-mindedness), then counter-terrorism review will face real difficulties in acting as an accountability mechanism. Without such commitment, access to information, access to key actors and access to influence may be unattainable for reviewers. As one might expect within the UK constitutional system, it is the Executive and Parliament that need to demonstrate commitment to these values if accountability is to be secured in the counter-terrorist state. As the analysis presented in this book shows, in significant ways both tend to fall short.

If this is so, what can be done to make counter-terrorism review a more effective mechanism for the optimisation of accountability in the counter-terrorist state? Undoubtedly, there are some ways in which the current assemblage could be stabilised and its capacity shored up. Long-awaited reforms to the Intelligence and Security Committee that would bolster its independence could be implemented, for example, so that its secretariat is drawn from the parliamentary staff rather than the Cabinet Office.[7] Similarly, there should always be an Independent Reviewer of Terrorism Legislation in office, and that office could be more effectively resourced.[8] Perhaps even a single, comprehensive and evaluative review of counter-terrorism that considers qualitative as well as quantitative evidence and evaluates counter-terrorism against a range of standards – including societal – could be commissioned.[9] Government could commit to more systematic engagement with civil society, *including* those who resist or challenge the underpinning rationalities and premises of the counter-terrorist state and its programmes and laws, recognising that a diversity of views and of evidence types is needed if truly evaluative review is to be undertaken. This would require the state to acknowledge that opposition to some of the counter-terrorist state's activities is not synonymous with extremism or support for terrorism, or grounds for 'blacklisting'.[10] Rather, contestation is at the heart of an accountable state. That is as much the case in the counter-terrorist state as otherwise.

However, while institutional reforms of this kind would probably assist in pursuing the values of counter-terrorism review – that is, in being independent, being experts and gathering evidence, and listening to a range of actors across and beyond the assemblage – what has become clear from this research is that the primary challenges to optimising accountability in the counter-terrorist state are dispositional rather than structural.

As we showed in Chapter 1, successive governments have pursued counter-terrorism in a way that has mainstreamed, normalised and spread its logics across the state. In doing so, they have reflected and enabled the entrenchment of a hegemonic consensus on terrorism and counter-terrorism. This consensus suggests that terrorism is a different kind of threat; that preventive approaches including counter-extremism pursued through law are necessary and appropriate to counter that threat; that 'politics' bears a particular moral burden of protecting 'us' from terrorists; that secrecy is necessary if not desirable; and that the state should be trusted to 'strike the right balance' even if it fails to demonstrate trustworthiness through a meaningful commitment to transparency, accountability and rights-respectfulness. In other words, the counter-terrorist state instantiates a paradox: counter-terrorism is *ordinary* inasmuch as it is the daily responsibility of us all and embedded in permanent legislative and policy frameworks, but *extraordinary* inasmuch as it justifies variations in our 'normal' constitutional expectations of the state and in how we give effect to them.

This suggests that optimising accountability in the counter-terrorist state requires more than the stabilisation, or in some cases reform, of counter-terrorism review mechanisms. It requires a fundamental shift in how we think about counter-terrorism in the contemporary state.

The state must be willing to revisit core propositions about counter-terrorism and be pushed to do that through a politics of opposition and challenge. For that to be achieved, review actors must be mandated to ask fundamental questions about counter-terrorism and, where they do ask them, their conclusions must be listened to, even if reform is ultimately not pursued. The value of pluralism within the counter-terrorism review assemblage must be recognised. Government must be willing to hear more voices and more perspectives, to recognise the importance of qualitative evidence to understanding the impact and potential effectiveness of counter-terrorism, and to acknowledge the expertise of civil society actors whose evidence base emanates from engagement in the everyday cultural and social life of counter-terrorism in our communities. For this to be possible, the politics of counter-terrorism must also change. The hegemonic consensus that underpins the counter-terrorist state must be disrupted so that the political costs of long-term thinking in counter-terrorism, of changing tack and of demonstrating reflexivity are reduced.

It would be wrong to say that the shortcomings of counter-terrorism review when considered as an accountability mechanism are 'merely' political. They also reflect deep-seated logics of security, secrecy and authority that predate and underpin the counter-terrorist state,[11] highlighting the need for the state not only to profess transparency, but to practice it; not only to demand trust, but to earn it.

We accept that some secrecy may not only be inevitable but also necessary; indeed, as we conceded in Chapter 4, efficient secrecy is part of statehood and facilitates proficient government.[12] However, the state must make a shift from over-claiming secrecy to justifying an absence of transparency, and put in place mechanisms to mitigate the lack of transparency when it arises. Organisational transparency should be the minimum expectation of the counter-terrorist state when it comes to review. Information about when review is taking place, who is undertaking it, what its terms of reference are, what methodology it applies, how someone can submit to or participate in it, and what standards it will be asked to undertake its review against should be available as a matter of course. There should be a presumption that outcomes will be published, with redaction being appropriately justified and subject to challenge. Furthermore, Government should be open, at least in some cases, to co-designing review with other actors from across the counter-terrorism review assemblage, whether that is in articulating principles of inclusion and participation for the conduct of the review, designing terms of reference or establishing advisory boards, for example.[13] There cannot be a 'one size fits all' approach; instead, counter-terrorism reviews need to be designed against their stated objectives. One of those objectives should be meaningful accountability in the counter-terrorist state.

Commitment to *meaningful* accountability means a commitment to more than bare information provision, performative transparency or 'mere' legality. It means a commitment to evaluation, to the diversification of evidence, to hearing and recognising the importance of communities' experiences of the unintended social and security impacts of counter-terrorism, and to the possibility of change. This is perhaps the greatest dispositional shift required if the counter-terrorist state is ever to be able to ground its claim to liberal democratic legitimacy, and if it is to avoid the neo-democracy of which Gearty warns.[14]

Such a shift would require the state to recognise that counter-terrorism is now an ordinary state of affairs and that, as a result, the state can no longer appeal to 'the exception' in the attempt to exempt itself from our ordinary constitutional expectations when taking steps to combat terrorism. Instead, it must inculcate a culture of justification in counter-terrorism that is based not only on bare claims of necessity, but on arguments of legitimacy, legality, long- and short-term effectiveness, rights-respectfulness and openness to challenge.[15]

Rather than challenging 'those critics of [counter-terrorism], who often use distortions and spin, to produce solid evidence of their allegations',[16] such a dispositional shift would recognise the role of counter-terrorism review in evaluating those claims in the pursuit of a rigorous, plural and usable evidence base that can not only ground reform, where needed, but also contribute positively to sustainable security in the UK. Without that, counter-terrorism review may well be co-opted into the counter-terrorist state, serving as an instrument of cynical legitimation, rather than democratic legitimacy.

Notes

[1] Jessie Blackbourn, 'Evaluating the Independent Reviewer of Terrorism Legislation' (2014) 67(4) Parliamentary Affairs 955; Jessie Blackbourn, 'Secret Material and Anti-Terrorism Review in Australia and Canada' in Greg Martin, Rebecca Scott Bray and Miiko Kumar (eds), *Secrecy, Law and Society* (Routledge 2015); Hugh Bochel, Andrew Defty and Jane Kirkpatrick, *Watching the Watchers: Parliament and the Intelligence Services* (Palgrave Macmillan 2014); Stuart Farson and Mark Phythian (eds), *Commissions of Inquiry and National Security: Comparative Approaches* (Praeger 2010); Andrew Lynch 'The Impact of Post-Enactment Review on Anti-Terrorism Laws: Four Jurisdictions Compared' (2012) 18(1) The Journal of Legislative Studies 63.

[2] For example, Fiona de Londras, 'Evaluation and Effectiveness of Counter-Terrorism' in J. Peter Burgess et al (eds), *Socially Responsible Innovation in Security: Critical Reflections* (Routledge 2018).

[3] Jessie Blackbourn, 'Independent Reviewers as an Alternative: An Empirical Study from Australia and the United Kingdom' in Fergal F. Davis and Fiona de Londras (eds), *Critical Debates on Counter-Terrorism Judicial Review* (Cambridge University Press 2014).

[4] Lydia Morgan, *State Secrecy in the UK: Understanding the Role of Secrecy in a Modern Liberal Democracy* (Forthcoming, Routledge 2020)

[5] See Chapter 1.

[6] HM Government, *CONTEST: The United Kingdom's Strategy for Countering Terrorism* (Cm 9608, 2018), para 333.

[7] See generally Andrew Defty 'Coming in From the Cold: Bringing the Intelligence and Security Committee into Parliament' (2019) 34(1) Intelligence and National Security 22.

[8] Interestingly, while some interviewees considered that the Independent Reviewer needed more resources, the former Independent Reviewers we spoke to were more

ambivalent about this, seeing the 'smallness' of the office as enabling adaptability, imagination and nimbleness: P2; P15.

9   While a number of interviewees thought a 'stocktake' review of this kind was needed (P1; P7; P8; P9; P10; P12; P13; P20; P21; P24), there was a general recognition – including at our workshop – that this posed significant logistical difficulties.

10 Concern has been expressed that the Government's commitment not to 'provide funding or support which inadvertently gives extremists a platform or sense of legitimacy' (HM Government, *Counter-Extremism Strategy* (Cm 9148, 2015), para 96) leads to NGOs being effectively 'blacklisted' so that Government ceases to engage with them, at least on an official basis.

11 For a critical perspective, see, for example, Mark Neocleous, *A Critique of Security* (Edinburgh University Press 2008)

12 Lydia Morgan, '(Re)conceptualizing State Secrecy' (2018) 69(1) Northern Ireland Legal Quarterly 59.

13 See for example Rights Watch UK's proposals for the design and execution of the Independent Review of Prevent, announced in 2019: 'Briefing Note: Independent Review of Prevent' (14 March 2019) (on file with authors).

14 Conor Gearty, *Liberty and Security* (Polity 2013)

15 Drawing on Dyzenhaus, for example: David Dyzenhaus, 'What is a Democratic Culture of Justification?' in Murray Hunt, Hayley Hooper and Paul Yowell (eds), *Parliaments and Human Rights* (Hart Publishing 2015) and Kant: Immanuel Kant, 'On the Common Saying: "This may be True in Theory but It does not Apply in Practice"' in H.S. Reiss (ed), *Kant: Political Writings* (2nd edn, Cambridge University Press 1991).

16 This was how Minister Ben Wallace MP constructed the Independent Review of Prevent, which he announced in January 2019: Home Office News Team, 'Government announces independent review of Prevent', 22 January 2009, available from: https://homeofficemedia.blog.gov.uk/2019/01/22/government-announces-independent-review-of-prevent/ [Accessed 26 March 2019].

Appendix

Interview Questions

Basic Participant Information [background only]
1. Participant Name
2. Participant Job Title
3. How long have you been in this role?
4. What is your professional background?

Participant view of counter-terrorism review
5. What do you think counter-terrorism review is?
6. What do you think is the purpose of counter-terrorism review?

Participant role in relation to counter-terrorism review
7. What role do you have in relation to counter-terrorism review?
8. How do you view this role as relating to other forms of counter-terrorism review?

Desired change or role constraints
9. Is there anything you think you should have the power to review that you do not currently have the power to review?
10. Is there anything you do have the power to review that you think you do not really need to review?

Process
11. Can you tell me how you go about doing [reference to described counter-terrorism review role]?

Access to information
12. What information do you need to undertake your counter-terrorism review role?

Constraints, frustrations, strengths of counter-terrorism review currently

13. What are the main challenges/frustrations that you face in the context of your counter-terrorism review work?

14. What would change/meet those challenges?

15. What changes would you like to see to the current approach to counter-terrorism review?

16. What, in your view, are the strengths of the current approach to counter-terrorism review?

Impact

17. What happens on the basis of your recommendations/findings/reports?

18. What affects whether a review will bring about change or not?

Audience

19. When writing your recommendations/findings/reports who do you expect will read it? For whom are you writing?

20. When you read the reports arising from other mechanisms (government, Independent Reviewer of Terrorism Legislation, Select Committees, Courts etc.) who do you think the target audience is?

Mandate questions

21. How would you change your counter-terrorism review process if you had the opportunity?

22. If you could design a system of counter-terrorism review, how would you approach it? What would you include? How would you improve it?

Bibliography

Abbas, Madeline-Sophie. 'Producing "Internal Suspect Bodies": Divisive Effects of UK Counter-terrorism Measures on Muslim Communities in Leeds and Bradford' (2019) 70(1) The British Journal of Sociology 261

Amicelle, Anthony. 'Towards a "New" Political Anatomy of Financial Surveillance' (2011) 4(2) Security Dialogue 161

Aradau, Claudia. 'Security and the Democratic Scene: Desecuritization and Emancipation' (2004) 7(4) Journal of International Relations and Development 388

Ashworth, Andrew and Zedner, Lucia. *Preventive Justice* (Oxford University Press 2014)

Bamforth, Nicholas and Leyland, Peter (eds). *Accountability in the Contemporary Constitution* (Oxford University Press 2013)

Bannink, Duco and Ossewaarde, Ringo. 'Decentralization: New Modes of Governance and Administrative Responsibility' (2012) 44 Administration & Society 595

Barry, Andrew, Osborne, Thomas and Rose, Nikolas. *Foucault and Political Reason: Liberalism, Neo-liberalism and Rationalities of Government* (University of Chicago Press 1996)

Bates, Crispin (ed). *Mutiny at the Margins: New Perspectives on the Indian Uprising of 1857* (Sage Publishing 2003–17)

Behn, Robert D. *Rethinking Democratic Accountability* (Brookings Institution Press 2001)

Bennett, Huw *Fighting the Mau Mau: The British Army and Counter-Insurgency in the Kenya Emergency* (Cambridge University Press 2013)

Bentham, Jeremy. *The Collected Works of Jeremy Bentham: Writings on the Poor Laws*, vol. 1, ed. Michael Quinn (Oxford University Press 2001)

Birkinshaw, Patrick. *Freedom of Information: The Law, the Practice, and the Ideal* (4th edn, Cambridge University Press 2010)

Birks, Melanie and Mills, Jane. *Grounded Theory: A Practical Guide* (2nd edn, Sage 2015)

Black, Donald. *The Behaviour of Law* (Academic Press 1976)

Black, Julia. *Rules and Regulators* (Oxford University Press 1997)

Black, Julia. 'Constructing and Contesting Legitimacy and Accountability in Polycentric Regulatory Regimes' (2008) 2(2) Regulation and Governance 137

Blackbourn Jessie. 'Evaluating the Independent Reviewer of Terrorism Legislation' (2014) 67(4) Parliamentary Affairs 955

Blackbourn Jessie. *Anti-Terrorism Law and Normalising Northern Ireland* (Routledge 2015)

Blackbourn Jessie. 'Independent Reviewers as an Alternative: An Empirical Study from Australia and the United Kingdom' in Davis Fergal F. and de Londras Fiona (eds), *Critical Debates on Counter-Terrorism Judicial Review* (Cambridge University Press 2014)

Blackbourn Jessie. 'Secret Material and Anti-Terrorism Review in Australia and Canada' in, Greg Martin, Rebecca Scott Bray and Miiko Kumar (eds), *Secrecy, Law and Society* (Routledge 2015)

Blackbourn, Jessie, Kayis, Deniz and McGarrity, Nicola. *Anti-Terrorism Law and Foreign Terrorist Fighters* (Routledge 2018)

Blackwood, Leda, Hopkins, Nick and Reicher, Steve. 'I Know Who I Am, But Who Do They Think I Am? Muslim Perspectives on Encounters with Airport Authorities' (2013) 36(6) Ethnic and Racial Studies 1090

Blair, Tony. *A Journey* (Random House 2010)

Bochel, Hugh, Defty, Andrew and Kirkpatrick, Jane. *Watching the Watchers: Parliament and the Intelligence Services* (Palgrave Macmillan 2014)

Born, Hans, Johnson, Loch K. and Leigh, Ian. *Who's Watching the Spies: Establishing Intelligence Service Accountability* (Potomac Books 2005)

Bovens, Mark. *The Quest for Responsibility: Accountability and Citizenship in Complex Organisations* (Cambridge University Press 1998)

Bovens, Mark. (2010) 33 West European Politics 946

Bovens, Mark. 'Analysing and Assessing Accountability: A Conceptual Framework' (2007) 13(4) European Law Journal 447

Bovens, Mark, and Schillemans, Thomas 'Meaningful Accountability' in Mark Bovens, Robert E. Goodin and Thomas Schillemans (eds), *The Oxford Handbook of Public Accountability* (Oxford University Press 2014)

Brinkmann, Svend, 'Unstructured and Semi-Structured Interviewing' in Patricia Leavy (ed), *The Oxford Handbook of Qualitative Research* (Oxford University Press 2014)

Brinkmann, Svend, Jacobsen, Muchael Hviid and Kristiansen, Søren. 'Historical Overview of Qualitative Research in the Social Sciences' in Patricia Leavy (ed), *The Oxford Handbook of Qualitative Research* (Oxford University Press 2014)

Busher, Joel, Choudhury, Tufyal, Thomas, Paul and Harris, Gareth. *What the Prevent Duty Means for Schools and Colleges in England: An Analysis of Educationalists' Experiences* (Aziz Foundation 2017)

Cairney, Paul. *The Politics of Evidence-Based Policy Making* (Springer 2016)

Campbell, Colm. *Emergency Law in Ireland, 1918–1925* (Clarendon Press 1994)

Carpenter, Daniel and Moss, David (eds). *Preventing Regulatory Capture: Special Interest Influence and How to Limit It* (Cambridge University Press, 2013)

Chamberlain, Martin. 'Special Advocates and Amici Curiae in National Security Proceedings in the United Kingdom' (2018) 68(3) University of Toronto Law Journal 496

Chandler, J.A. (ed). *The Citizen's Charter* (Dartmouth Publishing 1997)

Charmaz, Kathy. *Constructing Grounded Theory: A Practical Guide Through Qualitative Analysis* (2nd edn, Sage 2014)

Charmaz, Kathy. 'The Lens of Constructivist Grounded Theory' in Frederick J. Wertz, Charmaz, Kathy, McMullen, Linda M., Josselson, Ruthellen, Anderson, Rosemarie and McSpadden, Emalinda. *Five Ways of Doing Qualitative Analysis: Phenomenological Psychology, Grounded Theory, Discourse Analysis, Narrative Research, and Intuitive Inquiry* (Guilford 2011)

Choudhury, Tufyal. 'Campaigning on Campus: Student Islamic Societies and Counterterrorism' (2007) 40(12) Studies in Conflict & Terrorism 1004

Choudhury, Tufyal and Fenwick Helen, 'The Impact of Counter-terrorism Measures on Muslim Communities' (Research Report 72, Equality and Human Rights Commission 2011)

Clarke, John. *Changing Welfare, Changing States: New Directions in Social Policy* (Sage Publishing 2004)

Cohen, Joshua. 'Procedure and Substance in Deliberative Democracy' in Thomas Christiano (ed), *Philosophy and Democracy: An Anthology* (Oxford University Press 2003)

Cook, Thomas D. and Shadish Jr., William R. 'Program Evaluation: The Worldly Science' (1986) 37(1) Annual Review of Psychology 193

Cooper, Sarah. 'Holding the Police to Account: A Critical Analysis of the Structures of Police Accountability and the Introduction and Operation of Police and Crime Commissioners' (PhD thesis, University of Essex 2018)

Cotterrell, Roger. 'Why Must Legal Ideas Be Interpreted Sociologically?' (1998) 25(2) Journal of Law and Society 171

Crenshaw, Martha. *Explaining Terrorism: Causes, Processes, and Consequences* (Routledge 2011)

Curtin, Deirdre and Senden, Linda. 'Public Accountability of Transnational Private Regulation: Chimera or Reality?' (2011) 38(1) Journal of Law and Society 163

Dahl, Robert A. *Polyarchy: Participation and Opposition* (Yale University Press 1971)

Davis Fergal F and de Londras, Fiona 'Counter-Terrorism Judicial Review: Beyond Dichotomies' in Davis Fergal F. and de Londras Fiona (eds), *Critical Debates on Counter-Terrorism Judicial Review* (Cambridge University Press 2014)

de Goede, Marieke. 'The Chain of Security' (2018) 44(1) Review of International Studies 24

de Graaf, Beatrice. *Evaluating Counterterrorism Performance: A Comparative Study* (Routledge 2011)

de Londras, Fiona. *Detention in the 'War on Terror': Can Human Rights Fight Back?* (Cambridge University Press 2011)

de Londras, Fiona. 'Accounting for Rights in EU Counter-Terrorism: Towards Effective Review' (2016) 22(2) Columbia Journal of European Law 237

de Londras, Fiona. 'Evaluation and Effectiveness of Counter-Terrorism' in J. Burgess, Peter, Reniers, Genserik, Ponnet, Koen, Hardyns, Wim and Smit Wim (eds). *Socially Responsible Innovation in Security: Critical Reflections* (Routledge 2018)

de Londras, Fiona and Davis, Fergal F. 'Controlling the Executive in Times of Terrorism: Competing Perspectives on Effective Oversight Mechanisms' (2010) 30(1) Oxford Journal of Legal Studies 19

Defty, Andrew. 'Coming in from the Cold: Bringing the Intelligence and Security Committee into Parliament' (2019) 34(1) Intelligence and National Security 22

Dixon, Paul. *Northern Ireland: The Politics of War and Peace* (2nd edn, Palgrave 2008)

Donohue, Laura K. 'Regulating Northern Ireland: The Special Powers Acts, 1922–1972' (1998) 41(4) The Historical Journal 1089

Donohue, Laura K. *Counter-Terrorist Law and Emergency Powers in the UK 1922–2000* (Irish Academic Press 2007)

Donohue, Laura K. *The Cost of Counterterrorism: Power, Politics and Liberty* (Cambridge University Press 2008)

Drohan, Brian. *Brutality in an Age of Human Rights: Activism and Counterinsurgency at the End of the British Empire* (Cornell University Press 2017)

Duffy, Deirdre Niamh. *Evaluation and Governing in the 21st Century: Disciplinary Measures, Transformative Possibilities*

Dunn, John 'Trust and Political Agency' in Gambetta, Diego (ed). *Trust: Making and Breaking Cooperative Relations* (Basil Blackwell 1990)

Durose, Catherine et al. '"Acceptable Difference": Diversity, Representation and Pathways to UK Politics" (2013) 66(2) Parliamentary Affairs 246

Duyvesteyn, Isabelle and Schuurman, Bart. 'Popular Support and (Counter) Terrorism' in Andrew Silke (ed), *Routledge Handbook of Terrorism and Counter-Terrorism* (Routledge 2019)

Dyzenhaus, David 'What is a Democratic Culture of Justification?' in Murray Hunt, Hayley Hooper and Paul Yowell (eds), *Parliaments and Human Rights: Redressing the Democratic Deficit* (Hart Publishing 2014)

Elliot, Mark 'Ombudsmen, Tribunals, Inquiries: Re-fashioning Accountability beyond the Courts' in Nicholas Bamforth and Peter Leyland (eds), *Accountability in the Contemporary Constitution* (Oxford University Press 2013)

Ellison, Graham and Smyth, Jim. *The Crowned Harp: Policing Northern Ireland* (Pluto Press 2000)

Farson, Stuart and Phythian, Mark (eds). *Commissions of Inquiry and National Security: Comparative Approaches* (Praegar 2010)

Fenwick, Helen. 'Terrorism and the Control Orders/TPIMs Saga: A Vindication of the Human Rights Act or a Manifestation of "Defensive Democracy"?' [2017] Public Law 609

Fenwick, Helen. 'The Anti-Terrorism, Crime and Security Act 2001: A Proportionate Response to 11 September?' (2002) 65(5) Modern Law Review 724

Ferejohn, John. 'Incumbent Performance and Electoral Control' (1986) 50(1) Public Choice 5

Finn, John E. 'Sunset Clauses and Democratic Deliberation: Assessing the Significance of Sunset Provisions in Antiterrorism Legislation' (2010) 48 Columbia Journal of Transnational Law 442

Fioramonti, Lorenzo. *How Numbers Rule the World: The Use and Abuse of Statistics in Global Politics* (Zed Books 2014)

Flinders, Matthew. *The Politics of Accountability in the Modern State* (Routledge 2001)

Friedrich, Carl J. 'Nature and Function of Secrecy and Propaganda' in Susan Maret and Jan Goldman (eds), *Government Secrecy: Classic and Contemporary Readings* (Libraries Unlimited 2009)

Fox, Justin and Shotts, Kenneth W. 'Delegates or Trustees? A Theory of Political Accountability' (2009) 71(4) The Journal of Politics 1225

Freedland, Mark and Sciarra, Silvanna (eds). *Public services and Citizenship in European Law: Public and Labour Law Perspectives* (Clarendon Press 1998)

Gearty, Conor. *Liberty and Security* (Polity 2013)

Giddings, Philip (ed). *Parliamentary Accountability: A Study of Parliament and Executive Agencies* (Palgrave Macmillan UK 1995)

Gill, Peter. *Policing Politics: Security Intelligence and the Liberal Democratic State* (Routledge 2012)

Goold, Benjamin and Lazarus, Liora, 'Security and Human Rights: The Search for a Language of Reconciliation' in Benjamin Goold and Liora Lazarus (eds), *Security and Human Rights* (Hart Publishing 2007)

Gordon, Michael. *Parliamentary Sovereignty in the UK Constitution: Process, Politics and Democracy* (Hart Publishing 2015)

Grabosky, Peter and Braithwaite, John. *Of Manners Gentle* (Oxford University Press 1986)

Greene, Alan. 'The Quest for a Satisfactory Definition of Terrorism: *R v Gul*' (2017) 77(5) Modern Law Review 780

Greene, Alan. *Permanent States of Emergency and the Rule of Law: Constitutions in an Age of Crisis* (Hart Publishing 2018)

Gross, Oren. '"Once More unto the Breach": The Systematic Failure of Applying the European Convention on Human Rights to Entrenched Emergencies' (1998) 23 Yale Journal of International Law 437

Gutmann, Amy and Thompson, Dennis. *Democracy and Disagreement* (Belknap Press 1996)

Habermas, Jürgen. *The Theory of Communicative Action*, vol. 2: *A Critique of Functionalist Reason* (T. McCarthy, trans.) (Polity Press 1987)

Habermas, Jürgen. *Between Facts and* Norm: *Contributions to a Discourse Theory of Law and Democracy* (Polity Press 1996)

Hack, Karl. 'The Malayan Emergency as Counter-Insurgency Paradigm' (2009) 32(3) Journal of Strategic Studies 383

Hallsworth, Simon and Lea, John. 'Reconstructing Leviathan: Emerging Contours of the Security State' (2011) 15(2) Theoretical Criminology 141

Hardin, Russell. *Trust and Trustworthiness* (Russell Sage Foundation 2002)

Heath-Kelly, Charlotte and Strausz, Erzsébet 'Counter-Terrorism in the NHS: Evaluating Prevent Duty Safeguarding in the NHS' (University of Warwick 2018)

Heath-Kelly, Charlotte and Strausz, Erzsébet. 'The Banality of Counterterrorism "After, After 9/11"? Perspectives on the Prevent Duty from the UK Health Care Sector' (2019) 12(1) Critical Studies on Terrorism 89

Hewitt, Steve. 'Great Britain: Terrorism and Counter-terrorism since 1968' in Silke, Andrew (ed). *Routledge Handbook of Terrorism and Counter-Terrorism* (Routledge 2019)

Hickman Mary J., Thomas, Lyn, Silvestri, Sara and Nickels, Henri. '"Suspect Communities"? Counter-Terrorism Policy the Press, and the Impact on Irish and Muslim Communities in Britain' (London Metropolitan University 2011)

Hickman Mary J., Thomas, Lyn, Nickels, Henri C. and Silvestri, Sara. 'Social Cohesion and the Notion of "Suspect Communities": A Study of the Experiences and Impacts of Being "Suspect" for Irish Communities and Muslim Communities in Britain' (2012) 5(1) Critical Studies on Terrorism 89

Hickman, Tom. 'The Investigatory Powers Tribunal: A Law unto Itself?' [2018] Public Law 584

Hiebert, Janet. 'Parliamentary Review of Terrorism Measures' (2005) 68(4) Modern Law Review 676

Hillyard, Paddy. *Suspect Community: People's Experience of the Prevention of Terrorism Acts in Britain* (Pluto Press 1993)

Hood, Christopher. 'A Public Management for all Seasons' (1991) 69(1) Public Administration 3

Hood, Christopher. 'Transparency' in Paul Barry Clarke and Joe Foweraker (eds). *Encyclopedia of Democratic Thought* (Routledge 2001)

Hood, Christopher. 'Transparency in Historical Perspective' in Christopher Hood and David Heald (eds). *Transparency: The Key to Better Governance? (Proceedings of the British Academy)* (Oxford University Press 2006)

Hood, Christopher. *The Blame Game: Spin, Bureaucracy, and Self-Preservation in Government* (Princeton University Press 2010)

Hood, Christopher, James, Oliver, Peters, B. Guy and Scott, Colin (eds), *Controlling Modern Government: Variety, Commonality and Change* (Edward Elgar 2004)

Hunt, Adrian. 'From Control Orders to TPIMs: Variations on a Number of Themes in British Legal Responses to Terrorism' (2014) 62(3) Crime, Law and Social Change 289

Hunt, Gaillard (ed). *The Writing of James Madison, 1819–1836*, vol. 9 (G.P. Putnam's Sons 1910)

Huq Aziz, Tyler Tom, and Schulhofer Stephen. 'Mechanisms for Eliciting Cooperation in Counterterrorism Policing: Evidence from the United Kingdom' (2011) 8(4) Journal of Empirical Legal Studies 728

Huysmans, Jef. *Security Unbound: Enacting Democratic Limits* (Routledge 2014)

Innes, Martin, Roberts, Colin and Innes Helen, with Lowe, Trudy and Lakhani, Suraj. *Assessing the Effects of Prevent Policing: A Report to the Association of Chief Police Officers* (Cardiff University 2011)

Ip, John. 'The Rise and Spread of the Special Advocate' [2008] Public Law 717

Jarvis, Lee and Lister, Michael. 'What Would You Do? Everyday Conceptions and Constructions of Counter-terrorism' (2016) 36(3) Politics 277

Jenkins, Laura. 'The Difference Genealogy Makes: Strategies for Politicisation or How to Extend Capacities for Autonomy' (2011) 59(1) Political Studies 156

Judge, David. *The Parliamentary State* (Sage 1993)

Judge, David. *Representation: Theory and Practice in Britain* (Routledge 1999).

Kahn, Robert and Cannell, Charles. *The Dynamics of Interviewing: Theory, Technique and Cases* (Wiley 1957)

Kavanagh, Aileen, 'The Joint Committee on Human Rights: A Hybrid Breed of Constitutional Watchdog' in Murray Hunt, Hayley Hooper and Paul Yowell (eds), *Parliaments and Human Rights: Redressing the Democratic Deficit* (Hart Publishing 2014)

Kelso, Alexandra. *Parliamentary Reform at Westminster* (Manchester University Press 2009)

Kelso, Alexandra. "Parliament" in Flinders, Matthew, Gamble, Andrew, Hay, Colin and Kenny, Michael (eds). *The Oxford Handbook of British Politics* (Oxford University Press 2009)

Kennedy-Pipe, Caroline. *The Origins of the Present Troubles in Northern Ireland* (Routledge 1997)

Kitson, Frank. *Low Intensity Operations: Subversion, Insurgency, Peacekeeping* (Faber and Faber 1970)

Kundnani, Arun. *Spooked! How Not to Prevent Violent Extremism* (Institute of Race Relations 2009)

Kvale, Setinar and Brinkmann, Svend. *InterViews: Learning the Craft of Qualitative Research Interviewing* (2nd edn, Sage 2008)

Lægreid, Per 'Accountability and New Public Management' in Bovens, Mark, Goodin, Robert E. and Schillemans, Thomas (eds). *The Oxford Handbook of Public Accountability* (Oxford University Press 2014)

le Seur, Andrew 'Developing Mechanisms for Judicial Accountability in the UK' (2004) 24(1–2) Legal Studies 73

Lefebvre, Stéphane. 'What Do Judges Say on the Protection of Intelligence Secrets?' (2019) 34(1) Intelligence and National Security 62

Leigh, Ian 'Intelligence and the Law in the United Kingdom' in Loch K. Johnson (ed). *Oxford Handbook of National Security Intelligence* (Oxford University Press 2010)

Leigh, Ian and Njord, Wegge 'Intelligence and Oversight at the Outside of the 21st Century' in Ian Leigh and Wegge Njord (eds). *Intelligence Oversight in the Twenty-First Century: Accountability in a Changing World* (Routledge 2018)

Levi, Michael. 'Combating the Financing of Terrorism: A History and Assessment of the Control of "Threat Finance"' (2010) 50(4) British Journal of Criminology 650

Lim, Preston Jordan. *The Evolution of British Counter-Insurgency during the Cyprus Revolt 1955–1959* (Palgrave Pivot 2018)

Lincoln, Yvonna S. and Guba, Egon G. 'The Distinction between Merit and Worth in Evaluation' (1980) 2(4) Educational Evaluation and Policy Analysis 6

Lister, Stuart and Rowe, Michael (eds). *Accountability of Policing* (Routledge 2015)

Loader, Ian and Walker, Neil. *Civilising Security* (Cambridge University Press 2007)

Lowndes, Vivien and Roberts, Mark. *Why Institutions Matter: The New Institutionalism in Political Science* (Palgrave 2013)

Luban, David 'The Publicity Principle' in Robert E. Goodin (ed). *The Theory of Institutional Design* (Cambridge University Press 1996)

Lynch, Andrew. 'The Impact of Post-Enactment Review on Anti-Terrorism Laws: Four Jurisdictions Compared' (2012) 18(1) The Journal of Legislative Studies 63

McDonald, Michael D. and Budge, Ian. *Elections, Parties, Democracy: Conferring the Median Mandate* (Oxford University Press 2005)

Mac Ginty, Roger, Muldoon, Orla and Ferguson, Neil. 'No War, No Peace: Northern Ireland after the Agreement' (2007) 28(1) Political Psychology 1

McHarg, Aileen. 'Reforming the United Kingdom Constitution: Law, Convention, Soft Law' (2008) 71(6) *Modern Law Review* 853

McKittrick, David and McVea, David. *Making Sense of the Troubles, A History of the Northern Ireland Conflict* (Penguin 2012)

McKittrick, David, Kelters, Seamus, Feeney, Brian, Thornton, Chris and McVea, David. *Lost Lives: The Stories of the Men, Women and Children who Died as a Result of the Northern Ireland Troubles* (Mainstream Publishing 2007)

Maer, Lucinda and Sandford, Mark. 'Select Committees under Scrutiny' (The Constitution Unit 2004)

Majone, Giandomenico 'From the Positive to the Regulatory State: Causes and Consequences of Changes in the Mode of Governance' (1997) 17(2) Journal of Public Policy 139

Malik, Nikita. *Radicalising Our Children: An Analysis of Family Court Cases of British Children at Risk of Radicalisation, 2013–2018* (HJS Centre on Radicalisation and Terrorism February 2019)

Marks, Susan. 'Naming Global Administrative Law' (2004) 4(4) New York University Journal of International Law and Politics 995

Matthews, Felicity and Flinders, Matthew. 'Patterns of Democracy: Coalition Governance and Majoritarian Modification in the United Kingdom 2010–2015' (2017) 12(2) *British* Politics 157

Mawby, Spencer. *British Policy in Aden and the Protectorates 1955–67: Last Outpost of a Middle East Empire* (Routledge 2005)

Middleton, Ben. 'Rebalancing, Reviewing or Rebranding the Treatment of Terrorist Suspects: The Counter-Terrorism Review 2011' (2011) 75(3) Journal of Criminal Law 225

Mishler, Elliot. *Research Interviewing: Context and Narrative* (Harvard University Press 1986)

Moran, Christopher. *Classified: Secrecy and the State in Modern Britain* (Cambridge University Press 2013)

Moran, Michael. 'The Rise of the Regulatory State in Britain' 54(1) Parliamentary Affairs 19

Morgan, Lydia. 'Reading Secrets: Do State Secrets Challenge the Idea of the UK as Liberal?' (PhD Thesis, University of Bristol, 2015)

Morgan, Lydia. '(Re)conceptualizing State Secrecy' (2018) 69(1) Northern Ireland Legal Quarterly 59

Morgan, Lydia. *State Secrecy in the UK: Understanding the Role of Secrecy in a Modern Liberal Democracy* (Forthcoming, Routledge 2020)

Morgan, Lydia and de Londras, Fiona. 'Is there a Conservative Counter-Terrorism?' (2018) 29(2) King's Law Journal 187

Mouffe, Chantal. 'Which Public Sphere for a Democratic Society' (2002) 49(99) Theoria: A Journal of Social and Political Theory 55

Moyes, William, Wood, Julian and Clemence, Michael. *Nothing to Do with Me? Modernising Ministerial Accountability for Decentralised Public Services* (Institute for Government 2011)

Mythen Gabe. '"No One Speaks for Us": Security Policy, Suspected Communities and the Problem of Voice' (2012) 5(3) Critical Studies on Terrorism 409

Neal, Andrew W. 'Parliamentary Security Politics as Politicisation by Volume' (2018) 5(3) European Review of International Studies 70

Neal, Andrew W. *Security as Politics: Beyond the State of Exception* (Edinburgh University Press 2019)

Nelkin, David. *The Futures of Criminology* (Sage 1994)

Neocleous, Mark. *A Critique of Security* (Edinburgh University Press 2008)

Normanton, E. Leslie, 'Public Accountability and Audit: A Reconnaissance' in Bruce L.R. Smith and Douglas Hague (eds), *The Dilemma of Accountability in Modern Government: Independence Versus Control* (Macmillan 1971)

Norton, Philip. 'Reforming Parliament in the United Kingdom: The Report of the Commission to Strengthen Parliament' (2000) 6(3) *The Journal of Legislative Studies* 1

Ó Dochartaigh, Niall. *From Civil Rights to Armalites: Derry and the Birth of the Irish Troubles* (2nd edn, Palgrave Macmillan 2005)

Oliver, Dawn 'Accountability and the Foundations of British Democracy – the Public Interest and Public Service Principles' in Nicholas Bamforth, and Peter Leyland (eds), *Accountability in the Contemporary Constitution* (Oxford University Press 2013)

O'Toole, Therese, Meer, Nasar, DeHanas, Daniel Nilsson, Jones, Stephen H. and Modood, Tariq. 'Governing through Prevent? Regulation and Contested Practice in State–Muslim Engagement' (2016) 50(1) Sociology 160

Pantazis, Christina and Pemberton, Simon. 'From the "Old" to the "New" Suspect Community: Examining the Impacts of Recent UK Counter-Terrorist Legislation' (2009) 49(5) British Journal of Criminology 646

Pettit, Philip. 'Liberty and Leviathan' (2005) 4(1) Politics, Philosophy & Economics 131

Phillips, John. 'Agencement/Assemblage' (2006) 23(2–3) Theory, Culture & Society 108

Phythian, Mark. 'The British Experience with Intelligence Accountability' (2007) 22(1) Intelligence and National Security 75

Pollitt, Christopher 'Forty Years of Public Management Reform in UK Central Government: Promises, Promises...' in Sarah Ayres (ed), *Rethinking Policy and Politics: Reflections on Contemporary Debates in Policy Studies* (Policy Press 2017)

Prince, Simon. *Northern Ireland's '68: Civil Rights, Global Revolt and the Origins of the Troubles* (Irish Academic Press 2007)

Prosser, Tony. *Law and the Regulators* (Clarendon Press 1997)

Radin, Beryl. *Challenging the Performance Movement: Accountability, Complexity and Democratic Values* (Georgetown University Press 2006)

Rawls, John. *Political Liberalism – Expanded Edition* (Columbia University Press 2005)

Reichertz, Jo 'Induction, Deduction, Abduction' in Flick, Uwe (ed), *The SAGE Handbook of Qualitative Data Analysis* (Sage 2014)

Reiss, H.S. (ed) *Kant: Political Writings* (2nd edn, Cambridge University Press 1991)

Rhodes, R.A.W. 'The Hollowing Out of the State: The Changing Nature of the Public Service in Britain' (1994) 65(2) Political Quarterly 138

Sampson, Helen. 'Navigating the Waves: The Usefulness of a Pilot in Qualitative Research' (2004) 4(3) Qualitative Research 383

Schedler, Andreas 'Conceptualising Accountability' in Andreas Schedler, Diamond, Larry and Plattner, Marc F. (eds), *The Self Restraining State: Power and Accountability in New Democracies* (Lynne Rienner Publishers 1999)

Scott, Colin. 'Accountability in the Regulatory State' (2000) 27(1) Journal of Law and Society 38

Shapiro, Ian. *The Moral Foundations of Politics* (Yale University Press 2012)

Shirlow, Peter and Coulter, Colin. 'Northern Ireland: 20 Years after the Cease-Fires' (2014) 37 Studies in Conflict and Terrorism 713

Singh, Amrit. *Eroding Trust: The UK's PREVENT Counter-Extremism Strategy in Health and Education* (Open Society Justice Initiative 2016)

Slayton, Rebecca and Clark-Ginsberg, Aaron. 'Beyond Regulatory Capture: Coproducing Expertise for Critical Infrastructure Protection' (2018) 12 Regulation & Governance 115

Stevens, Alex. 'Telling Policy Stories: An Ethnographic Study of the Use of Evidence in Policy-making in the UK' (2011) 40(2) Journal of Social Policy 237

Stigler, George. 'The Theory of Economic Regulation' (1971) 2 (1) Bell Journal of Economics and Management Science 3

Stone, Bruce. 'Administrative Accountability in the "Westminster" Democracies: Towards a New Conceptual Framework' (1995) 8(4) Governance: An International Journal of Policy and Administration 505

Sunstein, Cass R. *After the Rights Revolution: Reconceiving the Regulatory State* (Harvard University Press 1990)

Sutton, Rupert. *Myths and Misunderstandings: Understanding Opposition to The Prevent Strategy* (Centre for the Response to Radicalisation and Terrorism Policy Paper No. 7 2016)

Taylor, Charles. *The Ethics of Authenticity* (Harvard University Press 1991)

Taylor, David and Balloch, Susan (eds). *The Politics of Evaluation: Participation and Policy Implementation* (Policy Press 2015)

Taylor, Rachel. 'Religion as Harm? Radicalisation, Extremism and Child Protection' (2018) 30(1) Child and Family Law Quarterly 41

Thompson, Edward Palmer. 'The Secret State' (1979) 20(3) Race and Class 219

Tomkins, Adam. 'The Guardianship of the Public Interest: a British Tale of Contestable Administrative Law' (2016) 24(2) George Mason Law Review 417

Tonge, Jonathan. *Northern Ireland: Conflict and Change* (2nd edn, Pearson Publishing 2002)

Torrance, Harry. 'Building Confidence in Qualitative Research: Engaging the Demands of Policy' (2008) 14(4) Quantitative Inquiry 507

Travers, Max. *Understanding Law and Society* (Routledge 2010)

Tulich, Tamara. 'Adversarial Intelligence? Control Orders, TPIMs and Secret Evidence in Australia and the United Kingdom' (2012) 12(2) Oxford University Commonwealth Law Journal 341

Uwe Flick (ed). *The SAGE Handbook of Qualitative Data Analysis* (Sage 2014)

Vile, M.J.C. *Constitutionalism and the Separation of Powers* (Oxford University Press 1967)

Vincent, David. *The Culture of Secrecy: Britain 1832–1998* (Oxford University Press 1998)

Wæver, Ole. 'Politics, Security, Theory' (2011) 42(4–5) Security Dialogue 465

Walker, Clive. *The Prevention of Terrorism in British Law* (Manchester University Press 1992)

Walker, Clive. 'The Bombs in Omagh and their Aftermath: The Criminal Justice (Terrorism and Conspiracy) Act 1998' (1999) 62(6) Modern Law Review 879

Walker, Clive. *Blackstone's Guide to the Anti-Terrorism Legislation* (3rd edn, Oxford University Press 2014)

Walker, Clive. 'Counter-terrorism and Counter-extremism: The UK Policy Spirals' [2018] Public Law 725

Warsi, Baroness Sayeeda. *The Enemy Within: A Tale of Muslim Britain* (Penguin, 2018)

Webb, Emma. *For Our Children: An Examination of Prevent in the Curriculum* (HJS Centre for the Response to Radicalisation and Terrorism Policy Paper No. 10 2017)

Webber, Grégoire 'Loyal Opposition and the Political Constitution' (2017) 37(2) Oxford Journal of Legal Studies 357

Weiss, Carol H. *Evaluation Research: Methods for Assessing Program Effectiveness* (Prentice Hall International 1972)

Weller, Patrick and Haddon, Catherine. 'Westminster Traditions: Continuity and Change' (2016) 29(4) Governance: An International Journal of Policy, Administration, and Institutions 483

Weller, Patrick. 'Cabinet Government' in Brian Galligan and Scott Brenton (eds), *Constitutional Conventions in Westminster Systems: Controversies, Changes and Challenges* (Cambridge University Press 2015)

Wertz, Frederick J., Charmaz, Kathy, McMullen, Linda, M., Josselson, Ruthellen, Anderson, Rosemarie and McSpadde, Emalinda. *Five Ways of Doing Qualitative Analysis: Phenomenological Psychology, Grounded Theory, Discourse Analysis, Narrative Research, and Intuitive Inquiry* (Guilford 2011)

Wills, Aidan, Vermeulen, Mathias, Born, Hans, Scheinen, Martin, Wiebusch, Micha, and Thornton, Ashley. *Study: Parliamentary Oversight of Security and Intelligence Agencies in the European Union* (European Parliament 2011)

Windelband, Wilhelm. *A History of Philosophy* [1893] (Macmillan 1979)

Wood, Matthew. 'Politicisation, Depoliticisation and Anti-Politics: Towards a Multilevel Research Agenda' (2016) 14(4) Political Studies Review 521

Woodhouse, Diana. 'The Constitutional Reform Act 2005 – Defending Judicial Independence the English Way' (2007) 5(1) International Journal of Constitutional Law 153

Young, Iris Marion. 'The Logic of Masculinist Protection: Reflections on the Current Security State' (2003) 29(1) Journal of Women in Culture and Society 1

Zmerli, Sonja and van de Meer, Tom W.G., 'The Deeply Rooted Concern with Political Trust' in Sonja Zmerli and Tom W.G. van de Meer (eds), *Handbook on Political Trust* (Edward Elgar 2017)

Zuckerman, Ian. 'One Law for War and Peace? Judicial Review and Emergency Powers between the Norm and the Exception' (2006) 13(4) Constellations 522

Index